C000269715

The Philosophical Salon

Speculations, Reflections, Interventions

Critical Climate Change

Series Editors: Tom Cohen and Claire Colebrook

The era of climate change involves the mutation of systems beyond 20th century anthropomorphic models and has stood, until recently, outside representation or address. Understood in a broad and critical sense, climate change concerns material agencies that impact on biomass and energy, erased borders and microbial invention, geological and nanographic time, and extinction events. The possibility of extinction has always been a latent figure in textual production and archives; but the current sense of depletion, decay, mutation and exhaustion calls for new modes of address, new styles of publishing and authoring, and new formats and speeds of distribution. As the pressures and re-alignments of this re-arrangement occur, so must the critical languages and conceptual templates, political premises and definitions of 'life.' There is a particular need to publish in timely fashion experimental monographs that redefine the boundaries of disciplinary fields, rhetorical invasions, the interface of conceptual and scientific languages, and geomorphic and geopolitical interventions. Critical Climate Change is oriented, in this general manner, toward the epistemo-political mutations that correspond to the temporalities of terrestrial mutation.

The Philosophical Salon

Speculations, Reflections, Interventions

Edited by Michael Marder and Patrícia Vieira

( )

OPEN HUMANITIES PRESS

London 2017

First edition published by OPEN HUMANITIES PRESS 2017

Copyright © 2017 Michael Marder and Patrícia Vieira and respective authors

Freely available online at:
http://openhumanitiespress.org/books/titles/the-philosophical-salon

This is an open access book, licensed under Creative Commons By Attribution Share Alike license. Under this license, no permission is required from the authors or the publisher for anyone to download, reuse, reprint, modify, distribute, and/or copy their work so long as the authors and source are cited and resulting derivative works are licensed under the same license. Statutory fair use and other rights are in no way affected by the above. Read more about the license at http://www.creativecommons.org/licenses/by-sa/4.0

Cover Art, figures, and other media included with this book may be under different copyright restrictions. Please see the *Permissions* section at the back of this book for more information.

PRINT ISBN 978-1-78542-038-2

PDF ISBN 978-1-78542-039-9

OPEN HUMANITIES PRESS

OPEN HUMANITIES PRESS is an international, scholar-led open access publishing collective whose mission is to make leading works of contemporary critical thought freely available worldwide. More at http://openhumanitiespress.org

Contents

Part II

A. *The End of Civilization*

B. *Rights and Wrongs*

For Eli Frederico

Welcome to The Philosophical Salon

Michael Marder and Patrícia Vieira

Since their emergence in the early part of the sixteenth century, salons have been places where the boundaries between the private and the public are blurred and where strict class and even gender hierarchies are often tipped. One might say that they are the spatial symbols for the exercise of a reasoned debate cultivated in European modernity. Reaching their apogee during the French Enlightenment, salons have been places hospitable to a discussion of philosophical ideas, of political developments and of the latest literary and artistic trends. Responding to, though not limited by current events, conversation conducted in this most public area of the private dwelling was a semi-formal endeavor: neither a mere casual chat amongst family members nor bound by the strictures of political debate. A social and intellectual laboratory propitious to experimental modes of reasoning, the classical salons injected fresh ideas into the forming body of Enlightenment thought.

The Philosophical Salon, published online first as part of *The European Magazine* and later as a channel of the *LA Review of Books,* is a digital-age avatar of the Enlightenment gatherings that has adopted many of its predecessors' traits. Though vetted by the two editors, a contemporary version of the *salonnières* of old, the texts published in the salon touch upon a wide variety of topics and express multiple, often contradictory, points of view. Similar to its Enlightenment counterparts, the salon did not impose an editorial line or preconceived notion of what its collaborators should discuss. Rather, it strove to be a place that nurtured a free exchange of ideas. It encouraged in-depth consideration of and comment upon contemporary socio-political and artistic events, interpreted in the context of philosophical and political thought and steeped in cutting-edge literary and art criticism.

But there are also some significant differences that distinguish the online from the flesh-and-blood salons. While the Enlightenment assemblies took place in a physically delimited space, digital-age salons are no longer tied to a tangible residence. Part of the immaterial web of the Internet, the new salon can be accessed from the most secluded of spaces—a living room, a bedroom, in your gym clothes or pajamas—while, at the same time, being available to anyone. An incorporeal room populated by bodiless visitors, the contemporary salon is a-topic, a-synchronous and, as a result, a-phonic, seeing that in-presence discussions, real-time opinions and retorts have been replaced by written texts and comments sometimes penned many hours or even days after publication. This necessarily changes the kind of society forged around new salon debates. On the one hand, it generates an asymmetry between the writers of the main articles and the readers, the response of the latter reduced to a footnote at the bottom of the page. On the other hand, it creates a more inclusive community, since everyone is welcomed into the salon, with participation no longer determined by social status. The evolution of this informal institution from a determined gathering place for concrete bodies to a communion of bodiless minds is symptomatic of our age, when, despite increasing population concentration in large metropoles, social interactions are more and more relegated to the intangible, "safer" and free-access space of the Internet.

The inclusiveness of the new salon is worth pondering further in light of the lines of privilege redrawn in the digital age. While discussions of philosophical, aesthetic, and political affairs in the Enlightenment were a prerogative of the aristocracy and of the upper bourgeoisie, today a separate "intellectual" class has appropriated such activities. Participation in the digital salon is, no doubt, more democratic, but it remains confined to individuals with enough leisure time, the luxury of Internet access, and accustomed to a certain way of presenting an argument. Granted: the portion of the online public sphere we have endeavored to open may help create communities of interest among people who would not have otherwise had a chance for a face-to-face encounter, whether due to the physical distance between them or due to their belonging to different social circles. Yet, this expansion still leaves whole swathes of the world and social strata outside its scope: those without digital tools, those outside the originally European tradition of discussion and debate carried on by the contemporary salon, those with pressing immediate economic concerns taking up all of their attention…

No single project is in a position to lift these unfortunate limitations, but the transformation of the online salon into a book, which you are witnessing, may go some way toward addressing the oft-imperceptible global injustices. It is not by chance that the edited volume you are about to peruse has been published by Open Humanities Press that is precisely *open*, much like the digital forum upon which it is based. The free PDF of the manuscript can be downloaded, printed out, and distributed among those outside the fold of the Internet. In and of itself, the book version of the salon will provide a mediation between the classical gatherings and the digital forum bearing this name: it will be material like the former and portable or re-contextualizable like the latter. We hope that its easy availability and relevance to our actuality will appeal to readers who are not usually attracted to conventional academic works, encouraging what Gayatri Spivak calls in her contribution *a critical "teaching reading."* If it succeeds in this task, it will propose not so much a predigested interpretation of reality but a possible method (or clues to a method) for approaching the timely and timeless problems facing humanity today.

The other limitation, against which the salon had to struggle, is in fact a de-limitation, diametrically opposed to the issue of the unequal access and distribution of knowledge and criticism. When any Internet user can publish an opinion and double as a critic, for instance ranking books on amazon.com or goodreads.com, what is the meaning of public intellectual engagement? That is one of the questions Daniel Innerarity raises in his essay, where he contemplates the "algorithms of taste" that set the parameters for our "likes" and "dislikes" in a world increasingly under the influence of social media. After all, total openness where "everything goes" spells out a complete closure of thinking, which, to paraphrase Hannah Arendt, first needs its banisters before it risks advancing without them. In the midst of instantaneous reactions demanded of us everywhere, it is necessary to gain the time and space for reflectiveness, for weighing, measuring, and judging without objectively pre-given scales or standards, but with those scales and standards that harken back to the "inner measure" of the Ancients and derive from the weighed and judged matters themselves.

The immediacy of many online exchanges, whereby anyone can express a spontaneous retort to ongoing events through a tweet or Facebook post goes back to the salons of old, where all members could share their unfiltered thoughts with the group, a situation now extended to the wider community of Internet users. Shying away from this model of thought as simple riposte, our digital salon cherished the time of and for contemplation. Even though the editors encouraged submissions on current topics—global warming, the refugee crisis in Europe, the 2016 US election—the articles published were not mere reactions but speculations, interventions, and reflections, as the title of this collection suggests. The very format of the platform, in which there was a lag between the writing of a text, the time when it was posted, the moment it was read and the crafting of a comment creates room for thought that was absent both from Enlightenment salons and from most social media platforms. The book version of the salon continues to foster this reflective attitude in that the various posts are no longer organized chronologically, like they were online, but thematically. This structure invites readers to establish connections between different topics, allowing them to see the "larger picture" even as they immerse themselves in the analysis of specific issues. The goal is to recognize the broader context framing individual subjects or events and, at the same time, to understand how particular matters shed light on wider trends of our world.

Still, the question of who has the right to pronounce their opinion in our online salon and in its print counterpart remains. Following the spirit of the Enlightenment salons, traditionally assembled around a hostess who, being banned from most public debates, received guest in her house for intellectual exchange, *The Philosophical Salon* endeavored to achieve gender parity and actively sought to make the voices of women thinkers heard. Furthermore, we tried to publish texts by contributors from different backgrounds, from established scholars to young academics, from poets to activists. Far from endorsing a vision of the public intellectual as an auratic figure, one who is ready to dictate an authoritative opinion on any and all topics, the salon aimed to promote an attitude of rigorous thinking that was not tied to given individuals or currents of thought. It was an empty space, or an empty chair, if you like, where anyone could sit, provided she or he had something interesting to share with the audience.

The cultivation of reflection is increasingly needed in an era when thought is straightjacketed between the unabashed apologies of neo-liberal globalization and the nationalist reaction that so often accompanies it. Both political stances are united in the mission of neutralizing thinking, the only remaining threat to the status quo and its knee-jerk inversion. On the side of globalism, we witness the consensual reign of instrumental rationality that replaces ideas with algorithmic functions, "zero-sum games," and other techniques drawn from the sphere of calculation. On the side of resurgent nationalism, the trend is toward the entrenchment of highly exclusive traditional identities, toward which its proponents flee for safe haven (often fantasized as a physical space protected by separation walls) from the leveling economic and cultural logic of globalization. In this latter case, thinking wanes to the extent that its role is transferred to arguments based on the authority of tradition, often immune to the questioning drive. In the face of a two-pronged onslaught, resisting both economism and traditionalism, the task of thinking is to become *ecological*, that is to say, to develop non-parochial languages for, or manners of articulating (*logoi*), the fragile dwellings (*oikoi*) we inhabit, from the planetary to the so-called private. We would like to believe that our salon, inspired in what was initially the most public part of a residence, provided an opportunity for such articulations.

In this sense, too, as an institutional space for the dissemination and exchange of ideas, *The Philosophical Salon* is rather unique. Globalization has its own ideological arm in much of the mainstream media, where analyses of contemporary events are utterly predictable, with more daring suggestions sanctioned. Conservative anti-globalization movements have similarly developed their alternative presses and websites, such as *Breitbart News Network* in the US or *Katehon* in Russia, where often racist or downright fascist opinion pieces thrive. Between the Scylla of the first and the Charybdis of the second, the missing option—resonating with the place of thinking itself—is a context-bound reflection that reaches beyond its specific predicament and forges ties to other contexts, a way of dwelling that opens itself to other modes of inhabiting the world. When we invoked the "empty chair" of the public intellectual, we were not approving of a disembodied, decontextualized space for thought; rather, we referred to the singular universality of thinking that, beginning from its here-and-now, is capable of transcending a particular situation without betraying its immanence.

The texts published in a online version of the salon, a selection of which is now reproduced in this book, invite different strategies of reading. As mentioned above, the digital salon privileged a chronological structure, starting with Jean-Luc Nancy's comment on the Paris attacks on the satirical newspaper Charlie Hebdo, the first article we published in March 2015. This chronological path can still be followed by those who are reading the present volume in order to get an image of the events that marked the past two years. Even though the book version of the salon is organized thematically, we have indicated the date of publication at the end of each article, so that readers would be able to situate a specific text in its context and read chronologically. Such an approach might be appropriate for those who would like, for instance, to trace the debates surrounding the 2016 US elections or the philosophical assessments of "Brexit" before and after the referendum was conducted.

Another possible avenue for reading the essays in this book is to concentrate on topics arising out of the contributors' shared concerns. One could, for example, focus primarily on texts that address environmental issues, among them Kelly Oliver's "Loving the Earth Enough," Gary Francione and Anna Charlton' "Veganism without Animal Rights," Patrícia Vieira's "Is Existentialist a Posthumanism?" and Sarah Conly's "One Child: Do We Have a Right to More?" Or you may decide to concentrate on gender and sexuality issues alone, reading T.M. Murray's "Gay Essentialism in a Eugenic Age," together with Slavoj Žižek's "The Sexual Is Political" and "A Reply to my Critics."

The themes and patterns woven into the texture of the salon move along three general methodological vectors of our thinking relation to contemporaneity. The section *Speculations* includes what are perhaps the most conceptually charged, contemplative pieces that, though relevant to the crucial concerns of our day and age, are not bound to specific events or historical trends. It is as though the authors, whose essays are gathered in this section of the book, zoom out of the minutiae of our preoccupations and, having opened a bird's-eye view on the present, enable us to return to social, economic, political, aesthetic, and other forms of existence with the baggage of richer understanding. Typically, such speculations inquire into the meaning of institutions, phenomena, and expressions that, despite structuring our lives, risk turning into empty buzzwords. They ask, among other things: What is the meaning of politics? Of art? Of enmity? Of clean energy? Of the Anthropocene? Of Europe? The list goes on...

Interventions are the inverse of *Speculations*, and yet, at their best, they achieve a similar outcome, namely a more nuanced appreciation of the complex realities we are a part of. For the articles gathered in this section, a specific occurrence— for instance, hurricane Katrina, the Chernobyl nuclear accident and their respective anniversaries —offers a springboard for a theoretical discussion of the cultural, economic, or political logics, within which it is ensconced. The singularity of the event is, of course, never completely exhausted by these explanatory, semantic nets and the work of mourning it calls for is similarly interminable. But it is only thanks to discerning interventions that we can indeed work through such occurrences, rather than act out, repeating the same tragic errors that have claimed thousands of live (in these cases: the insufficiency of government response to the plight of those who suffered from a severe natural disaster, or our addiction to nuclear power). Zooming in on the singular, the authors who contributed their analyses to this section of *The Philosophical Salon* do not remain mired in infinite details but bring their subject matter to bear on the predicament of being human today.

Reflections, in their turn, experiment with a difficult interplay between the singular and the universal, alternating between those moments when they zoom in on and those when they zoom out of the fine-grains of our world. What does the vehement rejection of gun control in the US do to the very notion of civilization? How, in making reproductive choices, to assume individual responsibility for the environmentally damaging effects of global overpopulation? Can universities still fulfill their critical function in the epoch of their rampant bureaucratization? These are just some of the guiding questions for thinking about the present from the midpoint of what Hegel called "mediation," the in-between of thought that, neither entirely abstract nor wholly concrete, neither conjectural nor empirical, holds a mirror wherein actuality-in-the-making can fleetingly espy itself. Unlike Hegelian dialectics, however, our reflections do not await the moment when the historical process is almost over so as to grasp it; instead, they convey a moving image of rapid developments, their outcomes far from already determined.

The three main sections of *The Philosophical Salon*—Speculations, Reflections and Interventions—are subdivided into thematic clusters, such as "Metapolitics," "Food Matters," "On Refugees," and so on. Each of these subsections and, in fact, each single salon text, constitutes a snapshot of our world, an illustration of a particular issue, problem or event. But these photographs do not stand alone. Every article is both a still and a moving picture that lends depth to the uniqueness of a given image, frames it within a wider context and applies to it the dynamics of thought. Salon articles are thus responses to the provocations of thought. We hope they will be, in turn, thought-provoking for our readers and will provide food for further thought about the pressing issues facing us today.

Part I

Speculations

A. Metapolitics

The Meta-Crisis of Liberalism

JOHN MILBANK AND ADRIAN PABST

The 2008 financial crash and inner-city riots across the West that began in the early 2000s revealed the limitations of the two liberalisms that have dominated Western politics for the past half-century: the social-cultural liberalism of the left since the 1960s and the economic-political liberalism of the right since the 1980s. Both may have provided greater personal freedoms and individual opportunities, but both can now also be seen as arrogant, atomising and authoritarian. For, together they have served the interests of the administrative state and the unfettered market that have collusively brought about an unprecedented centralisation of power and concentration of wealth in the hands of a few. In consequence, a new, rootless oligarchy now combines impersonal technocracy with a manipulative populism, while holding in contempt the genuine priorities of most people.

Historically, each 'face' of liberalism seemed to be the opposite of the other. The liberal left appealed to the state in order to protect the people from the forces of market fundamentalism that the liberal right championed, while the liberal right defended conservative values of family and the nation against the multiculturalism and emancipation that the liberal left celebrated. But far from representing genuine alternatives to one another, the two liberalisms are mutually reinforcing in that they fuse economic-political individualism with bureaucratic-managerial collectivism and social-cultural atomisation—as Max Weber realised better than Karl Marx.

In reality, we have witnessed two revolutions that are but one: the left has advanced a social-cultural liberalism that promotes individual rights and equality of opportunity for self-expression, while the right has advocated an economic-political liberalism that champions the free market liberated from the constricting shackles of the bureaucratic state. We have a 'liberal right' celebrating economic and political negative liberty, and a 'liberal left' celebrating cultural and sexual negative liberty. The two liberalisms were always in tacit, secret alliance. They have now more explicitly fused to proffer the shared creed of the left that recently embraced economic neo-liberalism together with an impersonal statism, and the right that has openly espoused cultural liberalism in scorn of its own natural constituency.

It would be foolish to deny that decades of liberalisation have provided greater opportunities for many and afforded some protection against the worst transgressions upon the liberty of some by the liberty of others, especially given the growing disagreement about substantive notions of justice and the good life. However, economic liberalism has also eroded the social bonds and civic ties on which vibrant democracies and market economies ultimately depend for trust and cooperation. Meanwhile, cultural liberalism, including some modes of middle-class feminism, has carelessly underwritten the new cult of market choice in default of its supposedly radical commitments. And, paradoxically, the two liberalisms have engendered a society that is not just more atomised but also more interdependent in the wrong way—too tied to global financial processes that leave far less scope for individual initiative and the ability to shape one's own life.

The liberal preference for negative freedom is the direct consequence of ruling questions of truth or goodness out of the court of public discussion, because liberals claim that in diverse societies with rival values the pursuit of such and similar shared ends is necessarily intolerant and oppressive. Yet, liberalism's substitution of individual rights and the social contract for the common good ends up creating the very effects that liberals wrongly equate with positive liberty—ideological tyranny, the closing-down of argument, and the ironing-out of plurality. Thus, liberal politics engenders the kind of illiberalism that it ascribes to all non-liberal positions. Without shared ends, individuals are encouraged to maximise their own subjective choice in conditions of growing market anarchy policed by an authoritarian state, as Karl Polanyi diagnosed in his seminal 1944 book *The Great Transformation*. Connected with this is the progressive loss of a 'moral economy' of mutual obligations and the atomisation of society that had hitherto embedded the political and the economic.

Here we can go further than Polanyi to suggest that the triumph of liberalism more and more brings about the 'war of all against all' (Hobbes) and the idea of man as self-proprietary animal (Locke) that were its presuppositions. But this does not thereby prove those presuppositions, because it is only *really existing* liberalism that has produced in practice the circumstances which it originally assumed in theory. Just as liberal thought redefined human nature as isolated individuals who enter into formal contractual ties with other individuals (instead of the ancient and Christian idea of social, political animals), so too liberal practice has replaced the quest for reciprocal recognition and mutual flourishing with the pursuit of wealth, power, and pleasure.

And since in theory and practice liberalism goes against the grain of humanity and the universe we inhabit, we are facing not merely a cyclical crisis (linked, for example, to economic boom and bust or the decline of representative government), nor even just a systemic crisis of capitalism and democracy, but rather a meta-crisis. The meta-crisis of liberalism is the tendency at once to abstract from reality and to reduce everything to its bare materiality, leaving an irreducible aporia between human will and artifice, on the one hand, and unalterable laws of nature and history, on the other.

This can be seen most of all in contemporary capitalism, which operates a simultaneous process of abstraction and materialisation. It subjects the real economy of productive activities to relentless commodification and speculation, while at the same time separating symbolic significance, equated with pure exchange value, from material space which is seen increasingly as just an object for arbitrary division, consumption and destruction. As a result, it renders ecological damage constitutive of our fundamental economic processes. This double conception of wealth as aggregated calculable number and as private consumption cuts out all the relational goods and the 'commons' on which shared prosperity depends. In the long run, the tendency towards abstraction and materialisation leads to destruction that is not creative—as growing economic financialisation exacerbates social dislocation and ecological devastation.

Thus, liberalism undoes itself and, in so doing, it erodes the polity it claims to save from extremes on both the left and the right. After all, the liberal focus on abstract, general standards (such as subjective rights, commercial contracts or formal, procedural justice) is parasitic upon a culture of universal principles and particular practices of virtue that this obsessive and rigid focus undermines, cutting off the branch on which it sits.

04.13.2015

The Politics of Politics

Geoffrey Bennington

Idioms beginning with "the politics of…" are often used to describe a dimension of other activities that is thought to be less than essential to them. "The politics of the university," "the politics of sport," "the politics of art," refer to an apparently extrinsic aspect of activities thought to have their essence elsewhere. Whatever the essence of the university is, the usual thought goes, it cannot reside in its politics, which more or less wastes our time and diverts us from the true academic calling that is ours. Whatever art is truly about, the same thought goes, it surely cannot *essentially* involve the politics of, say, its involvement with galleries, dealers, and the art market.

Similarly, or so it would seem, with "the politics of politics": like other activities, politics is most often thought to have an essential part (however it is defined: participating in the life of the city, discussing, militating, deliberating, voting, enacting and mandating the application of appropriate legislation, protesting, demonstrating, organizing) and an inessential "politics" or "politicking" (what in Paris is called "la politique politicienne" and in Washington "playing politics," or increasingly, in an interesting gesture of disavowal, just "politics"). On this construal, *everyone*, including those most energetically and enthusiastically involved in it, eagerly denounces the politics of politics as a kind of corruption of what politics essentially is or should be, everyone deplores the fact that politics seems to be increasingly bound up in its own politics in this way, and we invest our hopes in figures who seem to be doing politics in the absence of its politics.

But this apparently secondary and supposedly debased dimension of politics (its "politics," then, the politics of politics), cannot satisfactorily

This text is based on the book by Geoffrey Bennington, *Scatter 1: The Politics of Politics in Foucault, Heidegger, and Derrida* (Fordham UP, 2016)

be thought of in this way as merely derivative or parasitic with respect to a true or essential politics. In fact, it is co-extensive with politics from the start. Our fondest desire may be to find or invent a politics unaffected by the politics of politics (a truly moral politics, perhaps, of the kind Kant seems to encourage), but that desire is metaphysical through and through. The *zoon politikon*, or political animal, is engaged in the politics of politics as soon as that *zoon* is engaged in politics, i.e. from the very first, "naturally," as Aristotle put it. The *logos* of politics is irreducibly affected by the kind of distortion and deceit that is usually—moralistically—associated with rhetoric and/or sophistry, with "spin". *Politics is always already the politics of politics.*

This structure is complex enough to impinge on the issue of truth, no less, the truth of truth, even, in its relation to the politics of politics. We might be tempted to call it a question of the politics of truth. This expression "the politics of truth" is of course still relatively indeterminate, and already has an uncomfortable sloganizing feel to it. As it happens, "politics of truth" is one definition Michel Foucault gives of philosophy itself, in the context of his late development of the concept of *parrhēsia*: a kind of freedom of speech or "fearless speech," as it has sometimes been presented, a kind of "telling truth to power" that for Foucault and many of his enthusiastic followers defines the proper role of the philosopher, at least with respect to the political sphere.

But Foucault's concept of *parrhēsia* is, actually, quite unsatisfactory to capture what is at stake here. A quick way of stating why is that Foucault repeatedly and insistently needs to separate *parrhēsia* into a good form and a bad form, the good form being the kind of speaking out that is associated with a famous and seductive image of Foucault himself addressing a crowd through a megaphone; and the bad form being consistently associated by him with rhetoric and sophistry. This attempt to distinguish a good form of *parrhēsia* from a bad obviously opens a question about *parrhēsia* "itself," as it were, prior to its distinction into these good and bad forms. And this will mean that Foucault's analysis founders on a simple fact—that Foucault mentions in passing but never satisfactorily deals with—namely, that *parrhēsia is the name of a rhetorical figure*, a name, in Quintilian, for example, for the figure of rhetoric that claims to eschew all rhetoric and presents itself as the plain unvarnished truth. Far from being a philosophical answer to politics, or the ground on which the philosopher can occupy a salutary position of robust and recalcitrant exteriority with respect to politics (which is what Foucault wants from it), *parrhēsia* describes the basic rhetorical figure of politics itself in its politics. In other words, it reiterates the eminently metaphysical claim (boldly or baldly made by every politician ever, of whatever persuasion) to be simply speaking the plain truth in the absence of rhetoric.

This means that achieving the desired position of exteriority, of truth, with respect to politics and rhetoric is not going to be so easy (if *parrhēsia* itself is a figure of rhetoric, it will follow that rhetoric—like a Moebius strip—*has no outside*), and that by the same token politics has no outside. This does not mean that it is simple or homogeneous, but that it is constitutively doubled up on itself. Again: *politics is always already the politics of politics.*

Political philosophy, that rather disreputable, not very philosophical branch of philosophy (as Giorgio Agamben and Leo Strauss agree), has always wanted to get out of politics, to put an end to this politics of politics, by finally speaking its truth, indulging in that undecidable entanglement of teleology and the death-drive that defines philosophy as such—so that, for a quick and easy example, the best image of Kant's "Perpetual Peace" might always be that of a graveyard. But if politics is constitutively the politics of politics, then this ambition is compromised, and political philosophy needs to be quite radically rethought.

11.16.2015

The Unbearable Slowness of Change:
Protest Politics and the Erotics of Resistance

Nikita Dhawan

In the past decades there has been a proliferation of protest movements that interpellate a global demos, which has been wronged by the neo-liberal beast. From Puerta del Sol to Taksim, from Syntagma to Tahrir Square, from Hong Kong to New Delhi, street politics seem to have transformed the way power, agency and resistance are being perceived and performed. By inserting new actors into the political stage, these counterpublic spheres are displacing the Habermasian idea of public sphere, where rational subjects come together to deliberate over common interests. Instead, counterpublics can be read as affect worlds, where public anger, outrage and frustration reshape the terms of the state-civil society relation.

Despite important differences in goals and strategies, it is claimed that protest movements like the *San Precario* movement, the *Arabellions*, the *indignados*, or *Occupy Wall Street* are all horizontally organized, mostly employing social media like Facebook, blogs and Twitter. Direct action on the streets allegedly brings together heterogeneous groups, inducing "spontaneous solidarity". These bodies on the street are vulnerable to state violence, even as they demand accountability from their political representatives.

The disruptive potentiality of dispossessed masses, as they occupy public spaces to protest economic and political disenfranchisement, can be read as an exercise of popular sovereignty. Political actions on the streets in the form of hunger strikes by asylum seekers in cities like Berlin or self-immolation by a Tunisian fruit vendor have become symbols of global resistance. A number of concepts like "precarity", "wasted lives", "the superfluous", "the outcasts" are mobilized to describe marginal political subjectivities. Despite significant differences in their approaches, all these concepts engage with the condition of dispossession. They outline how the governmentality of efficiency, profitability, accumulation, optimization renders a vast majority of populations expendable and disposable.

Contesting these developments, protest movements in different parts of the world evoke promises of radical political change through shaming powerful states and international financial institutions into good behavior. However, the question remains: How effective are these fantasies of radical change through "Facebook revolutions" and "Twitter insurgencies" in fundamentally transforming social, political and economic relations in the era of postcolonial late capitalism?

There is an intrinsic ambivalence at the heart of today's protest movements. On the one hand, without the desire for and vision of another political order, resistance is not possible. The movements powerfully negate the TINA (There Is No Alternative) principle. On the other hand, current protests unwittingly reproduce processes of subalternization of marginal subjects and collectivities that have a tenuous relation to the state as well as the (international) civil society and counterpublic spheres. The romantic enthusiasm evoked by popular movements erases the exploitative and exclusionary material conditions that make possible the exercise of agency of the dissidents. When, for instance, an anti-capitalist protester tweets with his/her I-Pad, which is produced under super-exploitative working conditions in the global South, the phantasm of subverting capitalism reveals itself as a surreal moment of class-privileged *jouissance*. Such radical politics is marked by a discontinuity between those who resist and those who cannot.

Despite the powerful images evoked by ideas like "bare life" or "disposable lives" that are mobilized by protesters to mirror their vulnerability, in my view, many of these concepts tend to reproduce Eurocentrism. For instance, the recent focus on precarity is closely related to the breakdown of the welfare state in Europe, which conveniently disregards that this situation has been the norm in the global South. The majority of the population was systematically denied access to the formal labor market, health insurance and unemployment benefits, and for decades has been living with the insecurity and anxiety resulting from the system of employment made casual. The irony is that the scene of the crime has expanded. What was done to the global South in the name of Structural Adjustment Programmes (SAPs) is now being implemented in the global North.

My other concern is that enthusiastic discourses about resistance and fantasies of hyper-agency tend to overestimate the scope and influence of current political initiatives, even as they ignore the exclusions they produce. The absurdity of the claim about tweeting one's way out of capitalism is self-evident. Gilles Deleuze and Felix Guattari elaborate the erotics of capitalism: "... the way a bureaucrat fondles his records ... the bourgeosie fucks the proletariat. Flags, nations, armies, banks get a lot of people aroused". I would add that fantasies of radical change through protest politics are getting a lot of urban, class-privileged subjects very aroused. The fact that they are complicit in the very structures they are contesting is conveniently veiled by the rhetorics of the disenfranchised global *demos*.

The fabricated fiction that all bodies are equal on the street or in cyberspace disavows the hierarchies that permeate social and political relations globally. Given that only the elites fulfill the criterion of citizenship invoked in the demographically limited normative concept of civil society, subaltern groups can only unevenly access counterpublics. In response to Michel Foucault's claim "where there is power, there is resistance", I would add "where there is resistance, there is power". There is still a crucial difference between being an unemployed youth in Spain and a farmer in India, who loses his land because of being forced to buy genetically modified Monsanto BT cotton. The former is contesting his precarity on the streets of Madrid as part of the *indignados*, while the later may be one of the nameless thousands who have committed suicide since the enforcement of biological patents. Not as an act of resistance, but because of his inability to make his interests count and make the postcolonial state respond to his subalternization. Against the claim that our common vulnerability brings us together, I would advance a counterargument that deep asymmetries of power and wealth cannot be corrected simply by sharing the street or cyberspace for a common cause or facing police violence together.

It is imperative to rework our understanding of resistance to counteract the seductions of the vocabulary of "tweeting the revolution".

We need to guard against the enthusiastic celebration of radical change through street politics and digital publics. Protest movements are marked by exclusions that are disturbingly overlooked in celebratory discourses about their opposition to the state. The staging of the state as enemy and civil society as agent of salvation can have vicious neocolonial consequences, particularly for subaltern groups. Transnational counterpublics tend to empower civil society actors, whose "will-to-do-good" and "will-to-resist" are marked by feudality and enabled by a neoliberal framing. We need to confront the question whether enthusiastic discourses of resistance really empower disenfranchised communities, or whether they simply reinforce relations of domination between those who act and those on whose behalf these colorful and lively uprisings and revolts are being staged.

The process of de-subalternization is unbearably slow, while the fantasies of revolutions via Twitter and Facebook move at the speed of thought. Gayatri Spivak recommends that the vanguardism of the international civil society be supplanted by the slow, patient work of enabling subaltern access to hegemony. This is not just about teaching subalterns to resist through political indoctrination or consciousness-raising; rather, they must be enabled to exercise intellectual labor, while the class-privileged must unlearn the impulse to monopolize agency in the name of saving the world. Such a development would require a shift from street politics as the site of de-subalternization to other arenas of intervention (e.g., the postcolonial state, which is like a *pharmakon*, both poison and medicine). In contrast to the state-phobic rhetoric of protest movements, the relation between the postcolonial state and the subaltern must be reconfigured, thereby converting poison into counterpoison.

Those on the privileged side of transnationality have to resist becoming self-selected moral entrepreneurs in charge of finding solutions for the world's problems. "The voice of the people" as an act of political speech that authentically expresses the will of the people reveals itself as a phantasm, so that protest movements can ironically subalternize the masses at the very moment that they seem to let them speak. The continued reproduction of subalternity complicates easy notions of transnational alliances, raising troubling questions about the possibilities of post-imperial politics in the era of neoliberal globalization.

09.14.2015

The Dehumanization of the Enemy

Antonio Cerella

The world today appears divided into two opposing camps: the realm of Good and the empire of Evil, the free world against the world of slavery, "crusaders" vs. "martyrs." Yet, this riven field is also crossed by a sort of invisible mirror that deforms one's own reflection. Despite their apparent difference and asymmetry, in fact, the two rivals follow a common strategy: the dehumanization of the enemy.

Behind these metaphors lies a deep crisis of the classical notions of war and peace, guilt and innocence, life and death. It is not merely the loss of the fundamental distinction between combatants and civilians that both suicide bombers and airstrike bombings signal. In the current situation, all the fundamental principles that gave birth to the Laws of War seem to collapse: spatial and temporal limitations of hostilities, proportionality of military actions, discrimination of targets, weapons and the just methods of using them. In this way, the "enemy" is transformed from a juridical concept into an "ideological object." This figure, pushed to a climax from both these "invisible" and "mobile" fronts, becomes absolute and de-humanized.

Obama, Cameron and Hollande's unwillingness to use ground troops against the "uncivilized," as Kerry put it last year, is mirrored by ISIL's call to intensify suicide missions against the "cowards." But what lies behind the asymmetric confrontation between airstrikes and "human-strikes," behind the blurring of the distinctions between the state of war and the state of peace? What notion of humanity are the physical disengagement of the Western powers (with their tele-killing via drones and airstrikes) and the physical engagement of suicide bombers (ready to turn their bodies into a weapon) trying to convey? In other words, how and to what extent is there a connection between the automatization and biopoliticization of war operated by Western powers and the sacrificial nature of the conflict adopted by those who want to fight these powers?

When the enemy is reduced to the empty image of "collateral damage" or the "inverted icon" of the crusader to be destroyed, a frightening abyss—in which all the legal covers sink—opens, leaving room only for naked violence and its intrinsic brutality. German jurist Carl Schmitt warned against this ideological drift. The figures of the enemies, he argued, are our existential reflections, the shaping of ourselves, the embodiment of our own question. Their dehumanization leads to the loss of our most intimate humanity. The dehumanizing mechanism rips human faces from the Others, thus transforming them into what is infinitely identical to itself and yet ontologically different, into the indefinite, abstract, and absolute Enemy of humanity: Islam, the West, America, the French, the Arabs. In this way, individual responsibilities are turned into collective ones: everyone is guilty, and no one is responsible.

Deprived of a face, fear becomes terror. For, terror is faceless presence, the shadow cast by our nightmares upon the Other who is omnipresent precisely because he is invisible, because he does not possess a human, familiar face. Terror is the black sun shining on the landscapes designed by our deepest anxieties, the endless night of our darkest alterity. But what does it mean to deny—un-dialectically erasing—the Other's face?

The dehumanization of the enemy turns the use of violence, from an *extrema ratio* into "just-terror," as the massacres of Paris last November were called by the official organ of the Islamic State; the Other as a less-than-human must "evaporate," as *The Times* has defined the killing of "Jihadi John." The Other is but the Nothingness to be annihilated: only when the last terrorist is wiped out shall we be saved, but our "violent salvation" cannot but produce new "terrorists." Indeed, it is like trying to kill the night by stabbing it with a knife.

This is no moralizing game. What is at stake here is not the justification of a particular use of violence. This conflict—like all conflicts (and the troubled history of Palestine should serve as an example)—is fed by the violent *reciprocity* of weapons, by the ideological and moral figures borrowed from the disfigured or unfigured enemy. To restore the face of one's own enemy is a matter of humanitarian law, if it is true, as Giorgio

Agamben has argued, that "in the silence of the face, and there alone, is mankind truly at home."

One may be skeptical of this enterprise, and there certainly is no lack of reasons for our eventual skepticism as the Syrian war and the occupation of Palestine and Crimea continue to show us. Yet, this conflict—as every struggle—can only be saved by means of law and, above all, of Justice. Franz Kafka, with his life and work, offers us a beautiful metaphor for this.

One afternoon, while walking with Dora Diamant, his girlfriend at the time, in the Steglitz Park on the outskirts of Berlin, Kafka came across a little girl who was crying desperately. Worried, he asked her what had happened. The little girl, sobbing, said she had lost her doll. Seriously concerned, Kafka invented on the spot a long story to explain that absurd disappearance: the doll had left for a long journey; she was now married and lived happily in an exotic country. He knew these things because the doll had delivered a letter to his house. Every morning, for three weeks, Kafka, with total devotion close to exasperation, exercised his fantasy by writing and reading a letter to the little girl in order to give life and consistency to that imaginary world where the absent was present, and she could still live with serenity her dreams, memories and hopes. As Dora Diamant realized, in this beautiful story reported by the jurist Antonio Cassese, to *protect* the child "the lie was to be transformed into truth, through the truth of fiction." Kafka knew that it was necessary to create a world to restore a moral order *with* the other, to each other. Fiction is the instrument by which we fill the abyss opened by our creaturely nullity. Justice, in this sense, is the sharing of our imaginary that restores to the Others their faces.

That is also the fate of international law. It can be seen as an "ethical lie" that must be constantly told and experienced in order to be believed; Law, in other words, must be incarnated in the face of the Other to become "true." Only then does it becomes that "real fiction" which makes the idea of justice meaningful. That is why, to break the bad unity of the world brought about by the dehumanization of the enemy, we need to revive our idea of justice. If we believe in humanity, we must grant it to our enemy.

05.01.2016

The Empire of Solitude

DAVID CASTILLO AND WILLIAM EGGINTON

One attribute of this year's presidential contest that has not gone unnoticed by the press is the apparent insouciance with which the candidates have gone about embellishing their records, denying the embellishment when confronted, and outright fabricating nonsensical facts, all without seeming to suffer any consequences when their lies are called out by the mainstream press. As Michael Barbaro wrote in the *Times*, "Today, it seems, truth is in the eyes of the beholder—and any assertion can be elevated and amplified if yelled loudly enough."

How are we to understand this apparent growing disregard for reality, the ubiquitous presence in politics of an attitude or practice denoted so memorably by Stephen Colbert as "truthiness," or in Webster's definition "the quality of preferring concepts or facts one wishes to be true, rather than concepts of facts known to be true"? Is this perhaps the result of the dismaying rise of cultural relativism, born in the twentieth century and now coming home to roost? Such was Dick Meyer's conclusion in a commentary he wrote in 2006 on the occasion of Merriam-Webster declaring Colbert's coinage the Word of the Year. Truthiness, Meyer writes, "is perfect for the times in every way. It is a fake word invented by a fake person, Stephen Colbert, the comedian whose character, Stephen Colbert, parodies cable news talk shows on his own cable show, 'The Colbert Report.'" Truthiness, Meyer goes on to claim, "is the definitive cultural and comedic acknowledgement of moral relativism."

If we take a second look, though, we should see right away that Republican presidential candidates are no more moral relativists than are the true believers of the Christian Right that they pander to. While they

---

This article is based on the book by David Castillo and William Egginton, *Medialogies: Inflationary Media and the Crisis of Reality* (Bloomsbury, 2016).

may be opportunists in their cooptation of certain political positions, those positions constitute the polar opposite of relativism. The reason truthiness has become such a convincing descriptor in early twenty-first century political life is not because of a widespread realization that one's moral beliefs are culturally and historically determined, but because of a sharp increase in both the proportion of people who believe that their beliefs are direct expressions of reality, and the intensity with which they hold and defend those beliefs. Truthiness, in other words, is not an effect of the rise of relativism; it is an effect of the proliferation of fundamentalism. And fundamentalism is a symptom of today's medialogy, the term we use for the concept of reality determined by a culture's dominant medial form.

The new medialogy is already once removed from the reality concept implied by the prior medialogy, since its prima facie content is now the level of the material media that preceded it: books, bodies, images, and identities are injected with the aura of the real and endowed with a special authenticity. Objects that had become copies of an ineffable real emerge as things in themselves with no further regression required. They are already real and hence require no transcendent reference to ground them. This reification of what had been relegated to the status of copies is the basis for an unconscious fundamentalism that spreads to all walks of life.

In such a medialogical context, the state as the copy of national substance loses that anchoring in the real and becomes a groundless thing, a hollow shell that dissolves into diverse ethnic and religious identifications. Individuals cease to experience themselves as partial perspectives on a shared common ground, and instead start to conceive of themselves as the direct expressions of a particular identity that becomes all-important. In the conditions of the new medialogy, the individual is an unanchored island of solitude connecting via the media to others he or she conceives of as conjoined members of a community with unfettered access to the truth. And as these fellow travelers are always apparently in the minority, others are demonized as at best deluded, or at worst, agents of a sinister plot.

Neoliberalism, the economic model of the new medialogy, profits from this state of affairs. The medialogy's concept of reality, where erstwhile copies are now things, promotes an endless war of unanchored identities; the notion of the commons abandoned, a new commons develops, not "underlying" those identities but "above" them, unseen, syphoning off profits at unprecedented levels on a global scale. Terrorist fundamentalists strengthen rightwing isolationists, who demonize immigrants and hence further reify national, ethnic and religious difference. Governments aren't weakened, though; rather, the constant threat of an irrational other bolsters "democratic" regimes that are little else than symbolic cover for oligarchies whose purpose is the creation and maintenance of rules leading to greater syphoning power.

This picture is reminiscent of the "reality" revealed in the movie *The Matrix* when the virtual reality program that humanity is plugged into is disrupted: thousands of isolated minds each plugged into its own screen, all feeding a system none of them is aware of. And make no mistake about it: the system of global capital benefits from humanity not realizing its common ground or its common plight. In this sense, sociopolitical phenomena like the rise of rightwing, xenophobic parties and candidates in the US and Europe; the apparently ubiquitous threat of terror attacks, often committed by home-grown extremists; or the dramatic rise in school shootings in the US since the nineties, are not disparate cases, examples of a world devolving into chaos. Rather, they are tightly interconnected pieces of a machine that is functioning with great precision, even as it multiplies death and destruction.

Think about a terror organization like the inaptly named Islamic State—inapt because it has neither the attributes normally associated with a state nor is its organizing principle Islam in any theologically recognizably form. In fact, what ISIS most resembles is an online community dedicated to a particularly noxious perversion—like those frequented by the so-called cannibal cop who fantasized online about killing and eating women—the difference being that its members take the next step and carry out the grim fantasies they encourage in one another.

Indeed, this is what we're missing when we point out the racist discrepancy involved in denoting any violence perpetrated by Muslims as terrorism while refusing to use the same term for the shootings committed by non-Muslim white males, despite their often explicitly racist and misogynist reasoning in the manifestos they leave behind. Yes, these are essentially the same as the acts of terror committed by ISIS, but not merely because of the hate that inspires them. They are structurally congruous acts because they are symptoms of a medialogy in which disparate islands of solitude meet in a virtual space to commiserate and share their fantasies, thereby lowering the threshold to enacting these fantasies and hence creating a new reality.

This theory also helps us solve the puzzle of why radicalization fails to track accurately with socio-economic oppression. Many of the young men who kill and blow themselves up come from well-established middle class families. Their allegiance to radical groups is similar to the adherence of the other, isolated young white men to the cult of the black duster. They believe it is about history, religion, and culture, but it is not; it is about an entirely constructed identity whose online proponents proffer it as a solution to all their pain.

This is not to say that there aren't real social and cultural factors underlying the fragmentation of groups according to ethnic and religious identity. France's failure to offer equal opportunity for the full economic integration of its citizens is absolutely central to the sense of exclusion, of being strangers in their own nation, that so many young men of African and Near Eastern descent growing up in the *banlieue* feel. As George Packer reports, "*Banlieue* residents joke that going into Paris requires a visa and a vaccination card." And this is true of young people who are French, born in France, and speak only French. But again, it is vital to note that the alienation of the *banlieue* is not founded on a positive, historical identity.

The *banlieue* as a brewer of extremism and the rise of nationalism in contemporary politics are symptoms of the new medialogy. Categories such as class, nation, religion, or ethnicity have all migrated from the position of copies referring to ineffable substances, and are now self-sustaining, self-referential identities floating free of any history other than fragmentation and alienation.

Such is the ground of fundamentalism. Not a return to the substantial reality of the past, but the frantic desires of an unmoored present. Fundamentalism is fragmentation.

01.04.2016

Trump Metaphysics

Michael Marder

Quite unexpectedly, a whole slew of philosophical—I would even say "metaphysical"—issues have come up on the Republican side of the primaries this election season. How to distinguish the real from the fake? What level of ignorance is simply unacceptable in public affairs? How to view matters of principle, or something like "the inner essence," behind changing appearances? These questions have been, in one way or another, the staples of western philosophy ever since its inception. And most of them have been now linked to the candidacy of Donald Trump.

Take, for instance, the recent GOP debate organized and aired by Fox News. Presenter Megyn Kelly quizzed Trump: "The point I'm going for is you change your tune on so many things, and that has some people saying, what is his core?" Her point goes beyond the usual flip-flopping accusations leveled against presidential candidates. It even overflows the opposition between a politics based on immutable foundational principles, often called the *politics of truth*, and an opportunistic catering to various groups comprising the electorate. Unwittingly, having thrown everything but the kitchen sink at Trump, Kelly has dug up a crucial metaphysical distinction between the stable, selfsame inner essence and fleetingly superficial outward appearances. In his response, Trump insisted that there was no contradiction between his "very strong core," upon which he did not elaborate further, and "a certain degree of flexibility" necessary for learning from past experiences. His inaccessible essence thus reconciled with evanescent appearances, Trump has given himself a meta-excuse for any and all crude inconsistencies in his take on domestic and foreign policies alike.

Along similar lines, Mitt Romney's March 3 verbal assault on the current Republican frontrunner touches on an issue dear to the philosophical heart. The failed 2012 candidate called Trump "a phony, a fraud" as well as "a con man, a fake." Since its inception in ancient Greece, philosophy too has been suspicious of an oratory that substituted a flowery or a fiery rhetoric for the things themselves. Plato's *Republic* associated the political sphere as a whole with such empty and deceptively manipulative strategies, while prescribing a universally valid method for leaving the cave of appearances with the assistance of the philosopher-king. But before identifying Romney with a modern-day (latter-day) Plato or Socrates, we ought to inquire: In the name of what truth is he condemning Trump? The critic overtly assumes that there are Republican politicians who are not fake, those authentically suffused with the bracing tenets of the "conservative movement." Brushing aside Romney's assault, Trump characteristically turned the tables on him and reminded voters of how the former begged for his support as he was running against Barack Obama. Obviously, the accusation "you are a phony, a fraud" loses much of its bite if it comes from someone revealed to be a phony and a fraud in a field populated by similar phonies and frauds.

It is simply futile to chastise Trump from the standpoint of stale metaphysical values, because he embodies a system, which has a long time ago outgrown and abandoned these same values. What does it mean to decry a candidate for the office of president as a "fake" in a country where a Hollywood actor was president (more precisely, enacted the role of president), for two consecutive terms? Does it make sense to bemoan this candidate's ignorance less than eight years after the end of George W. Bush's terms in office? Where is the logic of accusing him of vulgarity when the official pick of the Republican establishment in the presidential race hints at differences in penis sizes as momentous for the outcome of the contest?

The reason behind the fact that Trump is currently leading (in a dismal field, to be sure) is not, as Linda Martín Alcoff has argued in *The Philosophical Salon*, that his own ignorance appeals to certain ignorant white voters. Or, at least, it is not the only reason. Rather, what Trump does most deftly, and what in my view accounts for much of his current success, is that he fully assumes the bankruptcy of the metaphysical ideals such as authenticity, essentiality, or firm principles, and acts accordingly. His rivals, in turn, are aware of the collapse of metaphysics but pretend that it has not happened. In both cases, nothing supplants the outdated value system, except for self-serving private interests or megalomaniac aspirations.

Curtly put, the bygone values are supplanted by nothing—by the nothing, to which everything has been reduced. Whereas Ted Cruz & Co. stand for the consciousness of this nothingness, Trump represents its self-consciousness, and this gives him an unmistakable edge over his rivals. He knows how to use the pure nothing that he represents, even as the other presidential contenders pretend that there is something behind *their* nothing. And so, Trump comes across as much more authentic in his inauthenticity than the others, who are busy drawing, in Plato's words, the "shadow paintings of virtue" all around themselves.

Perhaps, then, a deeper cause for the GOP establishment's concern and dissatisfaction with Trump is that he puts a mirror before it, forcing it to face up to its disavowed reality and exacerbating its tendencies in the process. In order to dissimulate the unpleasant truth, the party has no other choice but to distance itself from the rogue candidate, who uses even this lack of official support for his bid to his advantage, as proof of his outsider status, his non-belonging in the world of "Beltway politics." Any attack can be turned around to serve Trump's purposes, especially if he is censured based on the precepts of metaphysics, which have long become those of "common sense." *Trump trumps metaphysics*: herein lies the recipe to his success so far in the campaign. To oppose him better, more effectively, we would need not to recycle bygone metaphysical slogans but to chart other paths towards what lies beyond metaphysics. Towards a multiplicity free of totalization, a proliferation of differences, and a sense of sharing that has dispensed with the very idea of property.

03.14.2016

B. Interrogating Europe

Homo Europaeus: Does European Culture Exist?

Julia Kristeva

European citizen, of French nationality, Bulgarian by birth and American by adoption, I am not insensitive to harsh critiques of Europe, but I also hear the desire for it and its culture. Despite facing financial crisis, the Greeks, Portuguese, Italians and even the French, do not question their European belonging; they "feel" European. But what does this sentiment mean? I believe European culture can provide the means to lead European nations to a Federal Europe. But this begs the question: which European culture?

In opposition to a certain cult of identity, European culture never ceases to unveil a paradox: there exists an identity—mine, ours, but it is infinitely constructible and de-constructible. To the question "Who am I?" the best European response is obviously not certitude but a love of the question mark. After having succumbed to identity-focused dogmas to the point of criminality, a European "we" is now emerging.

Though Europe resorted in the past to barbaric behavior (something to be remembered and analyzed incessantly), the fact that it has analyzed this behavior better than others perhaps allows it to bring to the world a conception and practice of identity as a questioning inquietude. It is possible to take on European heritage, rethinking it as an antidote to the tensions of identity: ours and others. Without wanting to enumerate all the sources of this questioning identity, let us remember that ongoing interrogation can turn to corrosive doubt and self-hate: a self-destruction that Europe is far from being spared. We often reduce this heritage of identity to a permissive "tolerance" of others. But tolerance is only the zero degree of questioning. When not reduced to simply "welcoming" others, it invites them to question themselves, to carry the culture of questioning and dialogue in encounters that problematize all participants. This reciprocating questioning produces an endless lucidity that provides the sole condition for "living together." Identity thus understood can move us toward a plural identity of the new European citizen.

Whether it be lasting or not, the national character can, like individuals, experience real depression. Europe is losing its image as a world power and its financial, political and existential crises are palpable. But this is also the case of European nations, including France, one of the most prominent, historically.

With a depressed patient, the psychoanalyst begins by shoring up her self-confidence in order to establish a relationship between the two protagonists of the cure in which spoken words become fecund again, allowing for a true critical analysis of the suffering. Similarly, a depressed nation requires an optimal image of itself before being able to take on, for example, industrial expansion or a better reception of immigrants. "Nations, like men, die of imperceptible impoliteness," wrote Giraudoux. A poorly understood universalism and colonial guilt have led politicians and ideologues to behave with "imperceptible impoliteness," often disguised as cosmopolitism. They act with arrogant spite in regard to the nation. They worsen national depression to then infuse it with a maniacal exaltation that is both nationalistic and xenophobic.

European nations are waiting for Europe, and Europe needs national cultures that feel pride in themselves. A national cultural diversity is the only antidote to the evil of banality, this new version of the banality of evil.

The fall of the Berlin Wall in 1989 clearly demarcated the difference between European culture and North American culture. It is a question of two conceptions of freedom played out by democracies. Different but complementary, these two versions are equally present in international institutions and principles both in Europe and North America.

By identifying "liberty" with "self-beginning," Kant opens the way to an apologia of enterprising subjectivity, subordinated to the freedom of Reason (pure or practical) and a Cause (divine or moral). In this order of thought, favored by Protestantism, freedom appears as the liberty to adapt oneself to the logic of cause and effect or, to quote Hannah Arendt, as an adaptation or "calculation of the consequences," to the logic of production, science, or the economy. To be free would be to have the freedom to benefit to the best of one's ability from cause-and-effect relations in order to adapt to the markets and their profits.

But there is another model of freedom, also of European stock. It appears in the Greek world, develops under the pre-Socratics and through Socratic dialogue. Without being subordinated to a cause, this fundamental freedom is deployed in the speaking being who presents and gives herself to herself and to others, and in this sense is liberated. This freedom of the speaking being by and through the encounter between the One and the Other inscribes itself in an infinite question, before freedom gets roped down into a cause-and-effect relation. Poetry, desire and revolt are its privileged experiences, revealing the incommensurable (though shareable) singularity of each man and woman.

One can see the risks of this second model founded on the questioning attitude: ignoring economic reality, isolation in corporatist demands, limiting oneself to tolerance and fearing to question the demands and identity politics of new political and social actors, not standing up to global competition and reverting to archaic behavior and idleness. But one can also see the advantages of this model used by European cultures and which doesn't culminate in a schema but in a taste for human life in its shareable singularity.

In this context, Europe is far from being homogenous and united. First of all, it's imperative that "Old Europe" and France in particular, take the economic and existential difficulties of "New Europe" seriously. But it is also necessary to recognize cultural differences and most particularly religious differences, which are tearing at European countries from the inside and separating them. It is urgent to learn to respect differences better (I'm thinking of the Orthodox and Muslim Europe, of the persistent malaise in the Balkans, of the distress in Greece over the financial crisis.)

Among the multiple causes of the current crisis is one that politicians overlook: it is the denial of what I call the pre-religious, pre-political "need to believe" inherent to speaking subjects and expressing itself as an "ideality illness" specific to the adolescent (be she native or of immigrant origin.)

Contrary to the curious, playful, pleasure-seeking child who wants to know where she comes from, the adolescent is less a researcher than a believer: she needs to believe in ideals to move beyond her parents, separate from them and surpass herself (I've named the adolescent a troubadour, romantic, revolutionary, extremist, fundamentalist, third-world defender). But disappointment leans this malady of ideality towards destruction and self-destruction, by way of exaltation: drug abuse, anorexia, vandalism, attraction to fundamentalist dogmas. Idealism and nihilism—empty drunkenness and martyrdom rewarded by paradise— walk hand-in-hand in this illness of adolescents, which explodes under certain conditions in the most susceptible among them. We see the current manifestation of this in the media: in the cohabitation of Mafia trafficking and the jihadist exaltation raging at our doors, in Africa and Syria.

If a "malady of ideality" is shaking up our youths and with it the world, can Europe possibly offer a remedy? What ideas can she offer? Any religious treatment of this malaise, anguish and revolt proves ineffective before the paradisiacal aspiration of this paradoxical, nihilistic belief held by the de-socialized, disintegrated teen.

Europe finds itself confronted by a historic challenge. Is it able to face this crisis of belief that the religious lid can no longer hold down? The terrible chaos of nihilism-fanaticism linked to the destruction of the capacity to think takes root in different parts of the world and touches the very foundation of the bond between humans. It's the conception of the human forged at the Greek-Jewish-Christian crossroads, with its graft of Islam, this unsteady universality both singular and shareable, that seems threatened. Are we capable of mobilizing all our means—judicial, economic, educational, therapeutic—to accompany with a fine-tuned ear, the necessary training, and generosity the malady of ideality that disenfranchised adolescents, even in Europe, express so dramatically?

At the crossroads of Christianity (Catholic, Protestant, Orthodox), Judaism and Islam, Europe is called to establish pathways between the three monotheisms, beginning with meetings and reciprocating interpretations, but also with elucidations and transvaluations inspired by the Human Sciences. A bastion of secularism for two centuries, Europe is the place *par excellence* to elucidate a need to believe, which the Enlightenment, in its rush to combat obscurantism, greatly underestimated.

Countering the two monsters—the political lockdown by the economy and the threat of ecological destruction—the European cultural space can offer an audacious response. And perhaps the sole response that takes the complexity of the human condition seriously, including the lessons of its history and the risks to its freedom.

05.11.2015

From Outside: A Philosophy for Europe, Part I

ROBERTO ESPOSITO

Interviewed by Diego Ferrante and Marco Piasenter
Translated by Antonio Cerella

Diego Ferrante and Marco Piasenter: Your recent book *From Outside: A Philosophy for Europe* (a translation of *Da Fuori. Una filosofia per l'Europa*, forthcoming with Polity Press) seems to be located at the intersection of two axes: on the one hand, it looks at European philosophies; on the other hand, it explores the idea of a philosophy for Europe. The point of intersection between these two vectors could be the following question: what role should philosophy play in the current debate on Europe?

Roberto Esposito: If you think about it, in the most dramatic moments of its history Europe has always turned to philosophy and, in turn, philosophy has interrogated itself about the destiny of Europe as something that touches its very essence. Why? Which bond holds inseparably together philosophy and Europe? A preliminary answer to this question concerns the European—especially Greek—birth of philosophy. While it was nourished by other traditions of thought, the European connotation marked philosophy indelibly. Even the line of thought that has assumed the name of "analytic philosophy," curiously opposed by some to "continental philosophy," was born in our continent and only subsequently, fleeing Nazism, emigrated elsewhere. But there is something more, something that pertains to the philosophical character of the very constitution of Europe. Not possessing definite geographical boundaries, at least in the East—its distinction from Asia is problematic, considering that two large countries, Russia and Turkey, stretch between the two continents—Europe, from the beginning, has defined itself from the perspective of the constitutive specificity of its philosophical principles: the freedom of the Greek cities as opposed to the Asian despotic regimes.

Although these principles were often contradicted and reversed into their opposite, the idea of Europe is inseparable from them.

The fact is that philosophy has been a decisive source of inspiration in all the great crises that Europe has faced. It has been so in the time that preceded the fall of the Roman Empire, when Augustine of Hippo delineated the features of a new spiritual civilization; in the age of religious wars, when Descartes and Hobbes established the principles of modern science and politics; and at the turn of the French Revolution, interpreted by Kant and Hegel as an event destined to change the history of the world. Finally, it has been so in the deeply philosophical clash between totalitarianism and democracy. If all this is true, why not imagine, even in the crisis that we are currently experiencing, that philosophy can offer Europe, if not a solution to the current crisis, at least a new way of seeing things, a different direction to take? Of course philosophy is not able to impose its own choices on politics, let alone on the economy. Nonetheless, it can help to identify the role of Europe in the global world and the principles that should inform its conduct.

DF & MP: Your book proposes a genealogical analysis of the history of European philosophy in the late twentieth century, identifying three geo-philosophical articulations that develop between them a complex twine of overlays, hegemonic conflicts and cross-references: German critical theory, French post-structuralism, and Italian thought. Each of these theoretical paradigms has reached full development and dissemination through a passage to the outside, a hybridization with what is other than itself. At the same time, however, the crucial distinction between these different 'philosophical streams' depends precisely on the relationship they have established with the outside. How does the thematization of the *outside* vary? And what do its different assumptions entail for the philosophical relevance of these three theoretical horizons?

RE: In the book, the "outside" is understood in its geographical connotation—the Northwest Passage to America—but also in a disciplinary sense, alluding to what does not strictly belong to philosophical self-reflection but to other languages, like those of politics, sociology, and anthropology. Moreover, it can be argued that thought itself always originates from the outside, as Averroes had already realized, for he describes the "possible intellect" as a "separate" and "impersonal competence." If we think about it, all great discoveries and paradigm shifts are always stimulated by an external event. In what I have called "German Philosophy"— referring to the Frankfurt School, which emigrated to America with the advent of Nazism—the philosophical "outside" is essentially represented by the "social," but also, especially for Adorno, by art. In his *Negative Dialectics*—perhaps the last great philosophical work of the 20th century—Adorno refers to the non-conceptual element internal to the concept, thus creating a rigorously 'negative' theory of thought. Regarding "French Theory"—which also passed through America, where it has had its consecration—we should distinguish between a Heideggerian line of thinking represented by Derrida, and a Nietzschean one, which can be traced back to Foucault and Deleuze. For Derrida, the "outside" is essentially writing, which he dialectically opposes to the word, the *logos*. Foucault, however, holds a more radical idea of the "outside," meaning by this notion, on the one hand, the sphere of power, of the real power relations inherent in every discourse and, on the other, the dimension of biological life, as opposed to spiritual interiority, over which humans never have full mastery. As for Italian philosophy—whose origin dates back to Machiavelli—the "outside" is essentially the dimension of the political, thought of as something external to the State. In short, from all points of view and despite all the differences just mentioned, the "outside" constitutes the horizon of meaning and the vital energy of our practice and thought.

DF & MP: The book can be seen as a continuation of your recent work *Living Thought. The Origins and Actuality of Italian Philosophy* (Stanford University Press), devoted to Italian philosophy. In the reconstruction of its different stages, what appears to distinguish Italian thought— from Machiavelli to Vico, from Leopardi and Gramsci up to its most recent developments—is the theme of conflict, the relationship that this thought establishes between origin and actuality, thus offering a more adequate articulation of ontology and politics. How does Italian thought articulate this relationship?

RE: In effect, *From Outside* forms a sort of diptych with *Living Thought*. While the latter is devoted to Italian philosophy, *From Outside* is focused on European philosophy, with the exception of the English tradition, which has long been oriented toward the Atlantic axis. *From Outside* also discusses "Italian theory," or rather "Italian thought," by placing it in a differential relationship with German and French thought. The theme of conflict, in its various meanings, constantly returns in Italian philosophy, from Machiavelli to Gramsci, up to *Operaismo* [Workerism] in the 60s. The fundamental idea that underlies our tradition is that political order does not eliminate conflict, as Hobbes believed, but is indeed entirely crossed by it. It is an idea that is also found in German authors, such as Nietzsche, and French ones, like Foucault. But we can say that the dialectic of order and conflict—their co-belonging—is a distinguishing trait of Italian thought.

The relation between origin and actuality, although connected to the dialectic of order and conflict, is a different matter. It is has to do with the conception of history as perpetual crisis, rather than progressive development. The origin of this conception lies in Vico's work, as can be deduced from the idea underlying his *New Science* (*Scienza Nuova*), based precisely on a continuous alternation of recurring cycles ("corsi" and "ricorsi"). But even Machiavelli believed that when a political organization loses contact with its origin, it declines and risks implosion. After all, if actuality could coincide fully with itself, if it were not inhabited by an element irreducible to it, it would ultimately remain blind to itself. It would lack a critical counterpoint through which to deconstruct its perspective. In the most recent Italian philosophy, categories and terms derived from the archaic tradition, both Greek and Latin, such as *sacertas*, *imperium*, *communitas*, have played a significant role in the international debate. Indeed, the notion of 'contemporaneity' is to be understood not merely as the age that follows the modern one, but rather, as the co-presence, in every age, of different and conflicting times—something that, if radically thought, ends up calling into question the very paradigm of "epoch," the entire epochal economy.

07.11.2016

From Outside: A Philosophy for Europe, Part II

ROBERTO ESPOSITO

Interviewed by Diego Ferrante and Marco Piasenter
Translated by Antonio Cerella

Diego Ferrante and Marco Piasenter: 'Biopolitics' is a recurring term in your work and in your latest book, *From Outside. A Philosophy for Europe.* In it, the European crisis is not only conceptualized as a purely economic or politico-institutional, but also as a bio-political one, since it affects the very life of Europeans. In particular, the increase in migratory flows and terrorist attacks represent two paradigmatic figures of the crisis on the continent. These phenomena reveal an overlap between inside and outside, thus challenging the nexus, which has been taken for granted, between population, territory, and processes of identification. If we look at the legal responses to these crises put in place by the EU and its member states, what emerges is the reactive nature of norms and their casuistic logic. More specifically, regarding the measures to prevent and combat terrorism, intervention has been characterized by a widening of the thresholds of protection and punishment. How it is possible to "disable the apparatuses of negative immunization, and to enable new spaces of the common," as you put it in your article, published in *Angelaki*, "Community, Immunity, Biopolitics"? How do you conceive these spaces, this dimension of the common? And how would it be possible to prevent a deactivation of the apparatuses of control from turning into a form of isolation?

Roberto Esposito: The thesis presented in the book is that the current crisis affecting the whole world, and especially Europe, is not just economic or politico-institutional, but also more dramatically bio-political, since it involves and endangers the biological life of large numbers of human beings. In fact, the effects of the economic crisis have already begun to manifest their thanatopolitical implications to the extent that they have pushed entire populations to the brink of starvation, as was particularly evident in Greece and in the other weakest links of the EU. Moreover, the escalation of Islamic terrorism, on the one hand, and the uncontrollable rise of migration, on the other—in turn caused largely by wars for which the responsibility of Western countries is undeniable— have radically intensified the bio-thanatopolitical character of the crisis. For the first time, the European population is subjected to a pressure that will change profoundly its characteristics, and our ruling classes are not able to deal with the situation, not even to perceive its import. Nowadays, in dealing with immigration, they have to face a decisive biopolitical decision: the extreme choice between keeping alive or abandoning to death a growing number of human beings.

As a matter of fact, European countries have mostly adopted an immunitarian strategy, designed to strengthen or build barriers capable of containing the migratory influx that is often, even intentionally, confused with the risk of terrorism. Certainly, the existence of the EU's external borders is not only inevitable, but also somehow essential—otherwise the Union would no longer exist. Indeed, the opening of its internal borders, established by the Schengen Agreement, which is today called into question, is only possible if the external borders are monitored. But it is completely unrealistic to believe that this would be enough to handle the question of immigration, especially if a number of policies adequate to the importance and extent of the problem are not put in place.

DF & MP: Your trilogy—*Communitas, Immunitas, Bíos*—redefines the issue of inclusion/exclusion in light of the immunization paradigm. To simplify a little, you identify three possible ways of understanding the relationship between inside/outside. On the one hand, there is a dynamics of hyper-immunization activated by the raising of barriers and the intensification of identity politics. On the other hand, a complete absence of immunization spurred by the abolition of all borders and the subsequent loss of identity. Both possibilities are considered politically unacceptable because they cause the annihilation of the body politic (in the first case identity is so self-enclosed that it ends up smothering itself; in the second case it is so open that it ends up dissolving itself). Finally, the third option proposes a form of immunization by means of 'contamination', which both enriches and strengthens identities. This logic of inclusion/exclusion seems to be a bio-logic, as it anchors its ontology in the functioning of the immune system. If German critical theory and French post-structuralism were characterized by a progressive politicization of biology, showing the historico-political character of any definition of the human being, what relation does Italian thought establish between politics and biological life? How would it be possible to avoid both a politicization of biology and a biologization of politics?

RE: As a matter of fact, this is precisely the twofold risk to which Europe, but generally any political and even biological organism, is exposed. The first risk is that of an autoimmune disease—i.e., a process of immunization so strong that it affects the very organism that produced it, eventually ending up by destroying itself. What I mean is that an excess of security apparatuses may constitute a danger in itself, as has often happened in European history. But also the opposite attitude is self-contradictory. The complete abolition of borders, instead of strengthening differences, ends up dissolving them in a total homogenization. Only if taken together, can identity and difference be productive. Drawing on biological dynamics, in my book *Immunitas* I have indicated a path toward a different interpretation of the category of immunization. In this regard, the decisive reference is to the phenomenon of pregnancy. As is well known, the female immune system not only does not reject a foreign element (the fetus, which takes on genetic foreignness from the father) but it also protects and develops the embryo, even though the DNA of the fetus is partly different from her own. If it were possible to apply the same logic—the logic of life—to international relations, things would be much better.

The twofold process of the politicization of biology and the biologization of politics is the outcome of the bio-political dynamics set in motion at the beginning of the twentieth century. On the one hand, it represents a necessity determined by a number of historical, even cultural factors —e.g., the development of the discipline of biology. On the other hand, if left to its own devices, it constitutes a danger. This process, which cannot be avoided, as Nietzsche knew well, should instead be kept under control, since it can easily take thanatopolitical forms, as happened in the most disastrous manner during the Nazi era. In the mid-70s, Michel Foucault was the first to grasp in its full extent both the affirmative and negative sides of this phenomenon. Italian philosophers have worked on the Foucauldian paradigm, developing it in a different direction. Some have insisted on the positive character of the relationship between politics and biological life, while others have emphasized its negative aspects. Personally, I have tried to articulate the biopolitical paradigm in respect to that of immunization, reaching the conclusions that I mentioned earlier. If the processes of the politicization of biology—such as biotechnological practices aimed at controlling and managing births and deaths—and the biologization of politics cannot be stopped, they should at least be governed.

DF & MP: In the final part of the book *From Outside*, you discuss the widespread criticism that the EU lacks legitimacy and suffers from a profound democratic deficit. Contrary to what is imagined by those who expected the spread of supranational forms of identification, we are witnessing a strengthening of national and regional identities: the success of Eurosceptic or anti-European parties and positions slows down the process of constituting a European political subject. The results of the Brexit referendum or the threat by Austria to close its borders with Italy are just recent examples. The EU seems to lack a project that favors a strong identification among its citizens. In your book, you explicitly refer to the notion of 'European people'. What are the philosophical and historical conditions that may lead to the emergence of this political subject? How does democracy fit in with the picture so far presented?

RE: The 'identity syndromes' and the construction of exclusionary barriers, like the results of the Brexit referendum and Austrian nationalism, are the pathological reactions triggered by the dynamics of globalization. Indeed, they are a form of rejection of the 'global contamination.' They are very similar to the autoimmune disease of which we spoke earlier. Naturally, these phenomena not only delay the process of European unification, but jeopardize it, disrupting the integration that has already taken place. And this makes the constitution of a European people all but impossible. Unlike many European countries—such as France, Germany, Italy and many others, whose peoples were formed in parallel with the process of nation-building on the basis of common ideas, languages, and challenges—Europe does not have only one people. Furthermore, the peoples of the various European nations have furiously fought each other until the middle of the last century. In a Europe dominated by the worst nationalist instincts, how could a European people possibly have been born? Of course, as Habermas has argued, the people does not need to be a traditional Volk. It could also constitute itself voluntarily, on the basis of common values and interests, as Europe has tried to do at the end of World War II. But this would require a series of objective and cultural bonds, such as a single language or a common media network, which is exactly what is missing.

How can we get to the bottom of this difficult situation? The decision to prioritize economy, which led to the adoption of the single currency in most EU countries, turned out to be both insufficient and counterproductive, to the extent that it is creating more problems than it solves. The process is now irreversible. For, historically, all U-turns are harbingers of more problems to come. But the negative consequences of financial integration not supported by a political unity are there for all to see. The only way that seems to me to be open is the political construction of a European people. However, this presupposes a harsh confrontation between two ideas of Europe that run across individual nations, which are themselves divided by too many different living conditions to be unified a priori. In this regard, in the book, I refer to the need for a social conflict that restores political strength to the European constituting process. After all, as Hegel pointed out, conflict, if kept within the limits of political confrontation and struggle, has always had a constituent function.

07.18.2016

C. *The Art of Theory*

A Bit on Theory

GAYATRI SPIVAK

"Is Theory Critical?" was a question recently put to some of us publicly. I myself interpreted this question institutionally and practically: how can we ask for continued funding when the humanities have been trivialized and self-trivialized, with something called "theory" at its extreme edge? I quote a sentence from the muscular letter I wrote to the Vice-Chancellor of the University of Toronto: "This kind of training will never generate income for the university directly. Think of it as epistemological and ethical healthcare for the society at large."

Otherwise, it is hard for me to answer any question that pre-asks "What is theory?" I have to rewrite it as "What is it to theorize?" In that mode, I have responded to the Anthropocene—an item included in the original question—by reading the synthetic a priori as rape. This argument will not appeal to responders. Here's a last paragraph from published prose: "Why try to conserve something symptomatically seen as civilized, when the society we live in proves its decrepitude by gated journalism, gated publishing, protected by high walls? Absolutely forget, even the lesson that the literary-ethical suspension in the space of the other is to de-humanize, if humanization from the animal is by way of rape in general, unless we want to mooch over being-human in the face of the Anthropocene."

Globalization was yet another item. I gave back potential funder prose, where the dirty word "theory" lingers under "deep language learning": a global student is one who senses that nation-states are diverse, with history, literature, and philosophical traditions (inclusive of the Law) that can be accessed through deep language learning; that the sciences, though diverse in their beginnings, came to be consolidated in a single trajectory that becomes pluri-dimensional in the world of technology; and that today there is a global simultaneity where these two kinds of diversity can be digitally accessed. The global student comes with an expectation to be introduced into the methodology for accessing this multi-layered reality. As the student matures, s/he gets a rough sense that the Schools of Business and Medicine can make use of digital global-ity in a more direct way, but the preparation outlined above can enhance this use: primary healthcare and chronic disease relief for the Medical School, for example, and real corporate socio-cultural responsibility for the Business School.

To me, neoliberalism and neo-capitalism are closely linked on a chain of displacements. It is "the 'rule of law' that arises because barriers between national capital and global capital are removed, and the state, run to manage the global economy, rather than specifically to look after its citizens, attempts to enhance teaching and learning by producing toolkits that also limit teaching and learning." There, I believe we acknowledge complicity, being folded together, and proceed from this into remember-ing the importance of elementary school teaching.

For me it is the lessons learnt from over fifty years of institutional teaching at Columbia and at reputable universities in the United States but also in the lowest sector of the electorate in India, my country of citi-zenship, landless illiterates, so-called untouchables, people who do not know the word that is used by the upwardly class mobile movement, a Sanskrit classical language word—*Dalit*—which is used outside to rec-ognize such groups. Judging from these two ends, my lesson is: learn to learn how to teach this specific group. I should like to think that I am what in theoretical language would be called the dangerous supplement,[1] showing that the toolkits and templates produced by knowledge manage-ment are incomplete, that they must be exceeded by learning the specific mind-set of a group, opening up homogenizing statistics. There is no computer that can catch the contingent as such. One of the problems with toolkits is that they make teaching "easier." Far away from radical solidarity tourism, teachers of language, as well as the teachers of litera-ture from whom they are hierarchically separated, no longer confront the challenge of the unexpected.

Here are bits written for Occupy Wall Street and for Vincennes-St. Denis. Wall Street first: "Without the general nurturing of the will to justice among the people, no just society can survive. The Occupy Wall Street movement must attend to education—primary through post-tertiary—at the same time as it attends to the uncoupling of the specifically capitalist globalization and the nation-state. This is an almost impossible task to remember, especially when there are such complex and urgent immediate tasks lined up!" And here's Vincennes: "I'm now speaking in the same tone in which, in 1968, we spoke about revolution in the university—except we did not then know that change in elite universities alone will not do the trick. Therefore, now, wherever I go, I repeat the same message. That education has to become holistic, that humanities education especially must not keep compartmentalized primary, secondary, tertiary, post-tertiary and beyond. That is almost impossible in the Western world."

In conclusion: The first part of my answer to the question: "Is Theory Critical?" is institutional. The second part is bits of work. I am not able to answer the question: "Is theory…?" My effort shows to me, yet once again, that theorizing connects to teaching reading, in the broadest sense. Is this "critical"? You tell me. For me, critique remains, vulgarized, a limit to philosophizing. All this is turned around if you consider the tremendous diversity of classed and raced gender-plurality. Try it.

06.15.2015

Notes

1. The phrase is from Rousseau, rewritten in the early work of Jacques Derrida *Of Grammatology*, tr. Spivak, Baltimore: Hopkins Univ. Press, 2016, pp. 153-178).

The Dance of Hermeneutics

LUIS GARAGALZA

The word *hermeneutics* alludes to a way of doing, or of saying, *philo-sophy* as a search for, rather than the possession of, wisdom. It has to do with a *sophia* (wisdom) that always escapes from us, slips between our fingers, and so does not exclude not-knowing, generating a *docta ignorantia* conscious of the limits of our reason, awareness, and language.

As hermeneutists, we are thus in the company of Socrates, Nicholas of Cusa, Montaigne, and the humanists of the Renaissance, among many others, who have reveled in the knowing of not-knowing. For us, their legacy takes the shape of a reflection on interpretation. Hermeneutics presents itself, in effect, as an effort to rethink philosophy after a series of failures, from Plato to Husserlian phenomenology, under the assumption that failure is a constitutive element of human existence, rather than something accidental and secondary. That is why hermeneutics renounces the point of departure in reality, being, or God—characteristic of the Greco-Christian antiquity—as much as in the subject or the human being, whom modernity believes to be in a position to guide the course of history and to control nature through science and technology.

Hermeneutics proposes to begin with the problem of interpretation. It asks what happens when we interpret, realizing that the human is, in fact, an animal that interprets, a weak and clumsy animal that, given its biological deficiencies, needs to interpret its environment and even itself in order to survive. By interpreting, human beings generate cultures, that is to say, myths, languages, the arts, techniques, and sciences, at the same time that they interpret themselves. Interpretation is the mode of being of the human being, an animal that lives off its interpretations and that survives—though we do not know for how much longer—in its interpretations. The human adaptation to our environment consists in culturally interpreting it, converting it into a "world," which the Greeks optimistically named *cosmos* and which remains associated with order and harmony, even if many times in history—indeed, the majority of times—it has rather resembled worldlessness.

Hence, reality is not something closed off in itself, absolute, finished and definitive, independent of human construction. Instead, it is contingent upon our hermeneutical gestures, just as the latter depend on reality. According to this thesis, reality has an open and dynamic character, which is relational or, better yet, co-relational. The reality and its interpreter enter into a relation and dance together: more or less together, as the case may be. The scientific dancer dances alone, keeping his distance; the mytho-poetic dancer seeks more contact, proximity, fusion. Still, this is a special kind of dance, because, in the course of dancing, the dancers are transformed. More than that, we might say, together with Eckhart Tolle, that reality and life are the dancers, and we are the dance that interprets them.

What matters, in any event, is the relation that we keep or, more precisely, that keeps us. Hence, another central thesis of hermeneutics, inherited from phenomenology: the relation is primary, preceding and founding both the subject and the object, both the human and the world. In this manner, *docta ignorantia* is concretized in the becoming-conscious of our interpretations, in the acknowledgement of interpretation as interpretation. Assuming that our relation to the real is a relation of interpretation implies the recognition of a limit, the acceptance of a failure in the intention to capture reality without either touching or staining it, to capture it as it is. We thus renounce Truth, spelled with capital "T." Here, according to Nietzsche, art plays a pedagogic role, insofar as it teaches us to deal with fictions knowing that they are fictional, to play with representations while renouncing the immutable and objective Truth of the metaphysical tradition. (We would do well to recall as an illustration of this point the painting titled *This Is Not a Pipe* by Magritte.)

And yet, the recognition of a limit does not signify an impasse. The consciousness of a limit, whereby we become aware that our interpretations are but interpretations, leads rather to an opening, in which hermeneutical endeavors appear in the plural. Those who know that they are interpreting know that other interpretations are possible and that a great deal escapes from their hermeneutical grasp. In other words, they know that, although interpretations make possible the event of meaning, not one of them exhausts this event.

Once hermeneutics puts our interpretations, symbols, theories and models within their proper limits, it prevents us from conflating them with reality itself and from rendering them dogmatic. This move does not spell out a total annihilation of truth, but only a transgression of literal meaning and of the rationalizations that have "dried it up." Hermeneutics, in turn, enlivens meaning once again, understanding it as a series of anthropological propositions and, thereby, liberating its symbolic dimension.

Interpretation is, in keeping with Gadamer's suggestion, a conversation. If it is to exceed a mere interrogation, a conversation needs to be an adventure, which, despite having a beginning, does not predetermine where and how it will take us. Such an adventuresome conversation is a dance that keeps transforming us, even as it is itself transformed.

10.12.2015

Is Censorship Proof of Art's Political Power?

Gabriel Rockhill

Crews of chisel-bearing operatives were hired to hammer out the auspicious image of Lenin—symbolically gripping the hands of an African-American and a Russian soldier and workers—from a mural prominently displayed on the main floor of the newly constructed Rockefeller Center in 1934. A similar scene repeated itself as recently as 2010, when the Los Angeles Museum of Contemporary Art commissioned an artist for a public mural, only to deface it before its completion. Depicting coffins of war covered by dollar bills instead of flags, Blu's work—like Diego Rivera's sympathetic images of communism—was judged to be inappropriate for the American public.

Although many have claimed that art has little or no real political force, what these examples appear to suggest is that the powers-that-be disagree. The very act of censorship implies, or so it would seem, that the censors resolutely believe in the political and social power of the arts. If they did not, why would they bother to police what people can see, hear and touch? Does not the very existence of censorship prove, in reverse so to speak, that art is a sociopolitical force to be reckoned with? In other words, if censorship exists, isn't it because aesthetics is perceived—at least by those in power—as a very real threat to the social and political order?

Raising these types of questions requires parting ways with a dominant paradigm for thinking the politics of art, which consists in concentrating solely on the motivations of artists and the potential impact of their work. Interpreters often draw up balance sheets weighing the objectives imbued in an artwork (or the politics supposedly inherent in the aesthetic artifact itself) against its ultimate consequences. Such an approach lends itself to bivalent assessments of success or failure, thereby allowing one to reach the conclusion that a particular form of political art is preferable.

The issue of censorship invites us to take a different angle. Instead of relying on a product-centered approach and a linear, instrumentalist logic of means and ends, it encourages us to examine the complexities of aesthetic production as part of a larger force field. Art is never made in a vacuum, and aesthetic immaculate conception is as mythological as other such forms. Creation always takes place through a process of negotiating various constraints and limitations. "We do what we can," the filmmaker Jean-Luc Godard was fond of claiming, "not what we want."

Censorship is a particularly palpable restriction that can draw attention to the other limits operative in aesthetic production. It can function at the level of preproduction to impinge upon what is actually allowed to be created or persist as a work of art. It has the power of making non-art—meaning that which is not permitted to attain the status of art—by prohibiting, destroying or excluding certain creations.

Non-art is an important site of politics. It reveals, to begin with, the political orientation of the establishment, which seeks to control not only what is produced, but also what circulates and is received by the general populace. All three of these dimensions are essential to understanding the social politicity of aesthetic practices, meaning the diverse political aspects of their inscription in an expansive social force field of creation, distribution and interpretation.

If non-art is a nodal point of political and social struggle, it is also because of what we might call *the censorship short-circuit*. Explicit prohibitions often serve to paradoxically guarantee the renown and prominence of whatever is banned. Not unlike the erotic attraction of the forbidden fruit, which was so incisively analyzed by Georges Bataille, proscription runs the risk of both heightening curiosity and fostering fascination. The fame of the infamous can, in certain instances, bring flocks to the forbidden. The sensation around the public display of Gustave Courbet's *L'Origine du monde* (1866), since being bequeathed by Jacques Lacan's estate to the Musée d'Orsay, is a case in point. This highly realistic close-up of a reclining vulva, which Lacan and his wife Sylvia Bataille had obfuscated behind a sliding wooden door painted by André Masson, was rarely seen in public and knew a shadowy existence prior to 1995. It has since been notoriously censored by Facebook.

If the politics of censorship can at least partially backfire by drawing greater attention to whatever is explicitly suppressed—such as in the removal of David Wojnarowicz's "A Fire in My Belly" from the Smithsonian's National Portrait Gallery in 2010, or even the *fatwa* issued against Salman Rushdie—this is not necessarily the case for other types of repression. Soft or indirect censorship is a form of discrete coercion that uses discouragement—often of extreme sorts—rather than prohibition, surely in order to avoid censorship short circuits. Self-suppression is another type, which occurs through acts of conscious or unconscious deference to the sensibilities of authorities. Over time it can evolve into an impalpable bowdlerization that passes itself off as common sense. Corporate-censorship-by-drowning is a particularly insidious and widespread form because it is, strictly speaking, a censorship without censors. A 'market-based solution' to the paradoxes of overt prohibition, it embraces so-called free expression and free speech as long as these take place within the confines of a high-volume and high-speed entertainment industry that is completely dominated by corporate monoculture. Its mantra is: 'create whatever you want, and we will drown it in a sea of profuse and prominent mediocrity!'

Rivera's original mural, of which only dust and a few stolen photographs remain, was presciently and verbosely entitled *Man at the Crossroads Looking with Hope and High Vision to the Choosing of a New and Better Future*. Rockefeller resolved this crossroads by choosing corporate power over anti-fascist art, paradoxically contributing to the prominence of Rivera's message and work, which was immediately exalted in E.B. White's trenchant poem "I Paint What I See." The titan of the Mexican Mural Movement derided the spawn of Standard Oil in a radio interview by asking the following rhetorical question, regarding an imaginary scenario in which an American millionaire purchased Michelangelo's most well-known work: "Would that millionaire have the right to destroy the Sistine Chapel?" The choice of examples could not have been more germane since Michelangelo's work was famously censored by proponents of the Catholic faith, who insisted on having loincloths added to this celestial cornucopia of burgeoning concupiscence, brimming with genitalia and buttocks. Rivera, who later remade his mural in the Palacio de Bellas Artes in Mexico City, surely knew that art is always produced in an intricate force field and that censorship is the malevolent recognition that aesthetics can be a dangerous social and political threat.

06.06.2016

Come Back Aesthetics

DORIS SOMMER

Who needs the Humanities today? Everyone does. Otherwise we give up all hope for freedom, social justice, and general human development in the tradition of enlightened modernity. Modernity hasn't failed, Jürgen Habermas wrote, to nudge us beyond pessimism years ago; the problem is that we haven't achieved it yet. One fundamental reason for the delay has been the demotion of judgment as a core faculty of human understanding. Judgment never gained the ground that Immanuel Kant hoped to win away from imperious reason in his Third Critique; and it hardly interrupts today's personal and collective practices. Getting and spending, surviving, defending, spin out of control to the rhythm of narrow reason, an apparently logical necessity.

To pause for judgment, beyond reason, would be to regain a measure of our humanity, a freedom from the gridlock of mathematical thinking. The Humanities stage that pause; they train the faculty of judgment by pausing to consider works of art, and human creativity in general. It is the faculty that everyone needs in order to stop and to take stock of what one is doing. This is one fundamental motivation for studying culture through the Humanities.

Today more than ever, language, literature, and related fields of cultural constructions strain against the predictable, compact, self-perpetuating and sometimes defensive notion of culture that still informs the social sciences. For humanists as well as artists, culture has an almost opposite value from compactness. It means the interruption of shared practices; and it excites the kind of disconcerting delight that Kant appreciated as the stimulus for free judgment and for candid unscripted conversations. Those disinterested and delightful moments can lead to inter-subjective agreements, to common sense. This faculty for pausing in order to reflect is basic to all disciplines. But the best training ground for judgment is the carefree area of aesthetics. The reason Kant gives in his Third Critique is simple: deciding if something is beautiful responds to an intense experience without obeying any established principles. Therefore, the decision is free from prejudice. Aesthetic judgment is an exercise in unbiased evaluation, a knack that science and civics need as much as art does. So, interpreting art can train us to support urgently needed change. This is not a deviation from humanistic attention to the mechanisms of art production and reception. It is a corollary and a homecoming to civic education.

Asking who needs the Humanities has seemed too long like a rhetorical question. When university administrators ask it, they announce budget cuts and re-structuring. To be fair, students ask it as well, as do their parents concerned about their children's professional futures, including enough solvency to pay off staggering college debt. Voting with their feet, students go elsewhere; enrollments in literature and other Humanities courses continue to fall in departments that survive administrative ravages without disappearing altogether.

Hurt and apparently helpless, we humanists look on, as our field erodes ever nearer to our footing. More petulant than compelling, our defenses have not bothered to argue a case, as if the motives for studying the Humanities were self-evident and only philistines would ask about them. The very lessons we teach students are lost on us. We don't deign to back up claims, nor remember that the first rule of rhetoric is to know one's public. We disdain the public by dismissing its skepticism. And yet, as trainers of judgment, as a vanguard of acknowledging new sensibilities in ways that may mitigate some levels of culture-coded violence, humanists could re-claim our central importance for human development.

All of us would do well to consider art's ripple effects, from producing pleasure to triggering innovation. And recognizing art's work in the world makes us all cultural agents: those who make, comment, buy, sell, reflect, allocate, decorate, vote, don't vote, or otherwise lead social, culturally constructed, lives. But humanist pedagogy can fulfill a special mission by keeping aesthetics in focus, lingering with students over the charmed moments of freely felt delight that enable fresh perceptions and foster new agreements. More apparently practical people rush past pleasure as if it were a temptation to derail reason. We are haunted, it seems, by a Weberian superstition about enjoyment being close to sin and a deterrent to development. But we could learn a countervailing lesson from aesthetic philosophers. Kant knew that sociability and politics begin with delight; and Schiller knew that the passion for art-making, alternating between taking risks and making judgments, was the antidote for the kind of earnest reason that had brought the French Revolution to bloody excess.

Judgment, trained on pleasure, can perhaps save us. Humanists should say so when anyone asks.

04.20.2015

D. Environmental Emergency

Loving the Earth Enough

KELLY OLIVER

What does it mean to love the earth, this rich network of relationality that sustains earthlings, as our shared home? In Darwinian terms, love is the social instinct that drives all sentient beings towards tenderness, compassion and cooperation. Darwin imagines the evolution of tenderness and "sympathy," which become "virtues" that are passed on, initially by a few, until they spread and eventually become "incorporated" into life as we know it. Sympathy not only gives rise to compassion and cooperation, but also to empathy and play. In other words, social bonds are formed through various manifestations of love as the dynamic force of life.

Zoologists and primatologists have confirmed that play is important in establishing empathy and social bonding in many animal species, including humans. For example, recently, psychologist Alison Gopnik proposed that "humans' extended period of imaginative play, along with the traits it develops, has helped select for the big brain and rich neural networks that characterize *Homo sapiens*." And neuroscientist Paul MacLean argues that play is essential in the evolution of empathy in the human species. Moreover, he links play to the formation of a sense of social responsibility. There is increasing evidence that empathy and a sense of ethical responsibility for others within and across species is not only present in the so-called animal kingdom, but also is continuing to evolve in the human species.

Primatologist Frans de Waal's pioneering work on the evolution of morality from, and within, our animal ancestors to humans makes evident that animals are empathic and have a sense of responsibility for others, which can be seen as a proto-ethical, if not also an ethical, response. Studies of rats and monkeys indicate that they would rather go without food themselves than witness pain inflicted on others. Sharing and grooming behavior in animals also indicates a sense of gratitude and reciprocity that could be interpreted as proto-ethical behaviors.

It is becoming clear that our moral sense or conscience has evolved from animal sociability, and that any animal that develops a certain level of intellectual ability will develop moral sensibility. Perhaps, we can learn from nature and from animals about empathy and sharing, lessons that can only help us cooperate in our increasingly globalized world. De Waal's research suggests not only that empathy evolves within species, but also that empathy evolves between or across species. In this case, the biosphere is evolving to be more empathetic. Certainly, humans are becoming more empathic towards other animals.

Increasing concern for animals among human beings, especially in Europe and the United States, signals shifting attitudes towards not only our animal companions, but also other animals with whom we share the planet. In the last few decades, our attitudes towards animals have changed dramatically. Now, in Europe and the U.S., more people live with companion animals than do not; and many consider these as a part of their families. Laws protecting animals and promoting their rights are changing to reflect these changing attitudes, especially recent laws protecting primates in Spain and elsewhere. If this trend continues, within the next few decades we may live in a radically different world where animals are extended empathy, compassion and rights never before imagined appropriate for their kind. Indeed, with technological advances in the production of proteins for human consumption, we may see the end of factory farming. And with continued recognition of the importance that companion animals play in our lives, and their positive impact on mental, emotional and physical health—that is to say our dependence on them—we may see mixed species households and families as the norm and no longer the stuff of science fiction. Indeed this fundamental change in our relationship to other animals, both particular animal species and animals in general, may be the most significant development of our era.

Interspecies sympathy and love may be evolving for the sake of the biosphere. The biodiversity upon which our biosphere depends may require interspecies cooperation and interspecies love. Given what human beings have done to destroy ourselves and to destroy the habitats of various species and slaughter others, human attitudes towards our earthly companions need to evolve if we are to learn to share the planet. Our changing attitudes towards other animals signal a new era of interspecies relationships. The dramatic shift amongst many people in developed countries to consider companion animals as family, and to love and mourn them, is evidence of the evolution of sympathy and love.

Can interspecies cohabitation become the ground for ethical responsibility to the earth and its inhabitants? To say that we are earthbound creatures is to say that we have a special bond to the earth. We belong to the earth, just as it belongs to us. Rather than ownership, this sense of *belonging* harkens back to a more archaic sense of the word that conjures love as longing and companionship. It is not just that we share physical space, or proximity, on the surface of the earth, but more significantly, we share a special bond to the earth as our only dwelling place, whether home or habitat. This singular bond of all living beings to the earth and to other earthlings directly and indirectly obligates us to the sustaining possibility by virtue of which we not only exist and survive, but also live and thrive. Through our relationships with others, human and nonhuman, organic and inorganic, our earthly cohabitation is imbued with meaning. Even if we do not share a world, we do share the earth.

Hannah Arendt said, "Education is the point at which we decide whether we *love the world enough to assume responsibility for it.*" Echoing this sentiment, we might ask, what would it mean to love the earth enough to assume responsibility for it?

06.08.2015

Technologies of Global Warming

SUSANNA LINDBERG

The city of Paris, the host of the Conference of Parties (COP21) whose objective is to slow down global warming, is quite a good illustration of the theme of the meeting. It is a wonderful, witty, elegant city that can prove its modernity by hiring out community bikes (*vélib'*) and even electric citycars (*autolib'*). Still, like all big cities, Paris is entirely enveloped in a permanent curtain of pollution and noise that the drivers of ecological vehicles are not strong enough to disperse. The image of a nice electric city-car fumbling about in a cloud of pollution is also a good image of the role of technology in global warming, which is—so it seems to me—an unprecedented *technological fact*.

Of course, global warming was first discovered and studied as a *natural* phenomenon, which consists in changes of the global climate system because of the increase of CO_2 and other greenhouse gases in the atmosphere. This has led to an increase in global temperature, which, in turn, is responsible for the melting of glaciers and for rising sea levels, flooding and even the future submersion of certain areas (Kiribati, Bangladesh, Louisiana wetlands), causing changes in many ecosystems and the extinction of countless species. Besides, the temperature rise also triggers extreme weather phenomena, soil impoverishment, and so on. Even social changes—like increasing poverty, which instigates new migrations and still more violence at the frontiers of the rich areas of the world (EU, USA)—can be examined as a consequence of natural phenomena.

Global warming is a natural reaction to *human* technological and industrial activity, and seeing that it would not happen without this activity, it can also be analyzed as a *technological fact*. Because technology studies belong to human sciences, rather than to natural sciences, they help to analyze the role of human beings in more detail than simply as a geological or chemical factor among others. Moreover, the examination of global warming as a technological fact provides a healthy challenge to technology studies as well, which are normally more at home among entirely human-made machines and virtual realities. Indeed, global warming appears as a unique technological fact that depicts, in an unprecedented way, the essence of technology as *techno-nature*.

But why precisely "techno-nature"? This term evokes the present situation, in which human activity has become like a natural force. On the one hand, truly wild and unspoiled nature does not exist anymore: all regions of "nature" are marked by human activity (think of modern agriculture, of plastic floating in the oceans, of industrial fallouts on polar glaciers, of chemical additives in our own bodies). On the other hand, this does not mean that the human control of nature has increased. In the middle of the 20th century, techno-industrial activity appeared as our domination over nature through technologies perceived as extensions of human intelligence and will. Today one realizes that this activity is not as conscious and controlled as it was thought; rather, it has in many respects gotten out of hand, and produced a reality of its own. Technology is not only mixed with nature: it has become not only our "second nature" but, quite like nature, it is the *situation in which* we find ourselves and in which, ignoring the whole picture, we try to orient ourselves. Our technological reality has become a domain in which we are but that we do not really know.

This is why understanding global warming as a technological fact allows us to interpret technology in a wholly new manner. Different from the Enlightenment view, contemporary technology cannot be understood primarily as a tool, or as an instrument, that is to say, as an extension of human intentions. It should rather be regarded as a technological world or as the fundamental articulation of a historical situation. Bernard Stiegler considers technique as such to be a fundamental structure of a world in terms of a *pharmakon*: on the one hand, it enables human thought and action but, on the other hand, it induces thoughtlessness and irresponsibility.

Global warming makes it obvious that technology and nature are inextricably mixed. But the same could also be said of technology in general, especially of information and biotechnologies that are often depicted as an intimate part of our (not yet "posthuman") "nature." Contemporary technology consists in multiple networks, or maybe rhizomes, of diverse technologies that grow where they can and interact where they have to, mixing and mingling like vegetation in a jungle. Yet, the whole of technological reality is not a single organization and does not have an overall plan. There is no superior instance that understands and controls the totality. (I suspect that even economy is not such an instance anymore, if even stocks can now be exchanged by mindless algorithms rather than by human minds). Becoming less unitary, technology also appears less totalitarian and alienating, and we generally welcome its help in organizing our lives through close biological and social mediations.

Thick like a jungle, opaque like our own flesh, techno-nature is ontologically (like) *phusis*, the ancient Greek word for "nature." Quoting Heraclitus, German philosopher Martin Heidegger said of *phusis* that it "loves" us and "hides" from us; analogically one can say that contemporary techno-nature "loves us" when it gives itself as the ground of our knowledge and action, but also that it "hides" from us, because we cannot see the ground of this ground. The *why* and the *how* of our own techno-nature withdraw from us. We therefore need to give up the belief in the separate domains of technology and nature, and understand them in terms of mutual co-constitution. As French philosopher Jean-Luc Nancy writes in *Equivalence of Catastrophes*, techno-nature consists in a countless multiplicity of natural, technological, scientific, social, and other singularities, that are equivalent in their power of constituting the world and that are nonetheless incomparable. Everything can act on everything, but without having been built and planned to work as a system. There's no totality, no providence, just events that invent futures and leave histories.

Now, if the ground of techno-nature is a depth out of which anything can emerge, what about its surface that should support knowledge and action? It is good to invent solutions that can make life better, but the entire techno-nature is not a problem that could be solved. The little city-car in Paris is a good invention that makes life better and works against the climatic catastrophe but not even joint efforts of all the city-cars of Paris can dissipate the smog over the city. A similar fate weighs on the contemporary projects of "geoengineering," like capturing CO_2 or the projection of protective particles into the atmosphere: their feasibility and utility are uncertain, while it is certain that they are costly and energy-consuming processes that encourage the use of fossil fuels. Such inventions may be handy on a small scale, but they are not enough to avert global warming. Even in electric city-cars and in CO_2-geoengineering, the old dream of using and controlling nature through technology lives on and continues to shape the horizon of our epoch.

11.30.2015

Is the Anthropocene Upon Us?

PATRÍCIA VIEIRA

We are told that we now live in the Anthropocene, a new geological age marked by human beings' lasting influence on planet earth. In fact, the Anthropocene has become somewhat of a buzzword not only in scientific circles but also in social sciences and the humanities. We can now attend conferences on "Rethinking Race in the Anthropocene" or "Anthropocene Feminism" and read volumes and articles on *The Task of Philosophy in the Anthropocene, Architecture in the Anthropocene, Anthropocene Fictions* or "Anthropology at the Time of the Anthropocene" to name but a few. Both *The Economist* and *Huffington Post* have welcomed us to the Anthropocene and the *New York Times* has even tried to teach us how to die in this novel epoch.

But is all this talk of the Anthropocene much ado about nothing? As far as science goes, we will have to wait and see. The recent history of the term goes back to atmospheric chemist and Nobel Prize winner Paul Crutzen, who co-wrote an article with Eugene Stoermer in 2000 arguing that, due to our extensive impact on the planet, the current geological period should be called the "Anthropocene," the age of humans.

Curzen and Stoermer's idea caught on to the extent that the International Commission on Stratigraphy (ICS) has formed an Anthropocene Working Group. On the table is the possibility that the Holocene, the geological epoch that started at the close of the last ice age approximately 11,700 years ago, has given way to the Anthropocene. There is debate as to when the new period is supposed to have begun: some argue for the expansion of agriculture some 5,000 years ago as a starting date, others for the arrival of Europeans on the American continent, others for the onset of the Industrial Revolution in the 18th century, and others still for the inauguration of the atomic age in 1945. The

Group presented its initial recommendations in 2016, after which any proposal needs to be approved by the ICS and the International Union of Geological Sciences. It will probably still be a while before we know for sure whether we are really living in the Anthropocene.

Ponderous as any verdict on geological time necessarily is, the scientific decision to call ours the age of the Anthropocene does not seal the fate of the term. Even if this designation were, in the end, rejected by the ICS, the expression would most likely continue to be used informally not only in academia but also in the media. It looks like the Anthropocene is here to stay, whether stratigraphers like it or not. But should the rest of us laypeople rejoice in our ingress into this brand new geological era?

At first glance, we seem to have little choice but to accept that the Anthropocene is upon us. Global warming and the impending disappearance of several island-nations, the rampant pollution of the atmosphere that leaves cities like Beijing or Paris in the dark when smog is at its worst, the contamination of waterways by noxious chemicals poisoning all organisms around them, the acidification of the oceans and the concomitant death of marine life, and the staggering rate of species extinction in the last few decades are but a few of the most conspicuous side-effects of humanity's activities on earth. We know of no precedent to such a human-driven hecatomb.

The term Anthropocene brings the disaster-zone that much of our planet has become into a much-needed sharper focus. The shock-effect of realizing that human beings are altering the geological make-up of the earth may jolt the general public out of its habitual complacency. It could serve as a wake-up call to those of us who, while abstractly concerned with environmental issues, are primarily focused on our energy-wasteful, fossil-fuel-driven everyday lives.

"Anthropocene" thus has a performative function: its strategic usefulness as a rallying-point for the environmental movement and as a call to action for politicians and regular citizens goes beyond strictly scientific concerns. It is a battle cry for environmental justice, not only for humans but also for all non-human living beings, who are paying the price for our folly.

Still, deep-seated tensions lurk under the blanket-term "Anthropocene." For one, placing the blame on "anthropos," on humans as a species, hides profound asymmetries in the history and geopolitics of *Homo sapiens*. A fisherman living off his catch on a Mozambican island or a subsistence farmer in Sri Lanka are certainly not as guilty of ushering humankind into the Anthropocene as the average American or European. What is more, the world's poor, deprived of many of the material comforts achieved at nature's expense, lack the means to mitigate the effects of global warming and pollution, therefore bearing the brunt of these scourges.

But the most serious problem with the Anthropocene is that it reaffirms humankind's hubris. By singling ourselves out as the one mover and shaker who determines the fate of the entire planet, are we not falling into the fallacy of human exceptionalism that brought us to our current predicament in the first place? Is there not a certain perverse pride in our quasi-divine ability to shape the earth? In other words, is the use of the term Anthropocene, to a certain extent, not a case of relishing our power, even if it can cause us some misfortunes? After all—so some arguments go—if we are smart enough to almost destroy the planet, we will also be sufficiently clever to save it.

The other side of this hubris-laden defiance is the fatalism that sometimes accompanies the thought of the Anthropocene. Perhaps, some say, our impact on the world is already too significant to be reversed. And maybe humans cannot do otherwise but bring destruction upon ourselves and other inhabitants of the earth. By using this expression, are we not resigning to the *status quo* and accepting that there is nothing each of us can do against such a powerful geological force as the entire human species?

Whether we strategically adopt the term Anthropocene or shun it for endorsing the very larger-than-life view of humanity at the root of the environmental crisis, we would do well to soberly ponder upon our short life on the planet. The earth thrived without us for millions of years and there is no reason to believe that it will not continue to do so once we are gone. Is the Anthropocene the legacy we wish to leave behind? Do we really want to live in a human-crafted geological era? Perhaps, instead of dwelling on thoughts of the Anthropocene, we should strive to leave it behind, once and for all.

05.04.2015

The Meaning of "Clean Energy"

Michael Marder

As the global conference on climate change is taking place in Paris, it is time to contemplate the meaning of "clean energy." In the West, the word *energy* is marked with the force of deadly negativity. It is assumed, for instance, that energy must be extracted, with the greatest degree of violence, by destroying whatever or whoever temporarily contains it. More often than not, it is procured by burning its "source," in the first instance, plants and parts of plants whether they have been chopped down yesterday or have been dead for millions of years, the timescale sufficient for them to be transformed into coal or oil.

Without giving it much thought, one supposes that the only way to obtain energy, be it for external heating or for giving the body enough of that other heat (namely, "caloric intake") necessary for life, is by destroying the integrity of something or someone else. Life itself becomes the privilege of the survivors, who celebrate their Pyrrhic victory on the ashes of past and present vegetation and other forms of life they commit to fire.

Seeing that, for Aristotle (who still maintains a strong hold on *energeia*, a word that he introduced into the philosophical vocabulary), the prototype of matter is *hylē*, or wood, the violent extraction of energy paints a vivid image of the relation between matter and spirit prevalent in the West. A flaming spirit sets itself to work by destroying its other and triumphs over the wooden matter it incinerates. The price for the energy released in the process of combustion is the reduction of what is burnt to the ground. And, unfortunately, the madness of metaphysical spirit, which sets everything on its path aflame, tends to intensify.

It is not that plants are exempt from the general combustibility that, for Schelling, defined the very living of life. They release oxygen, and so provide the elemental conditions of possibility for the burning of fire. But the vegetal mode of obtaining energy—especially that of the solar variety—is non-extractive and non-destructive; the plant receives its energy by tending, by extending itself toward the inaccessible other, with which it does not interfere. That is one of the most important vegetal lesson to be learned: how to energize oneself following the plants, without annihilating the sources of our vitality.

In the meantime, energy extraction means tearing both living and dead things apart, penetrating their core, enucleating them. Energy production is a fury of destruction. It does not relent until the atom is split, until it reaches the nucleus and divides the ostensibly indivisible. Nuclear power and the atomic energy it unbridles is the apotheosis of the contemporary energy paradigm. So is hydraulic fracturing, or fracking, that cracks the earth (particularly shale rocks) open by exerting high water pressure on them from below. Environmentally destructive and shockingly shortsighted as these methods of energy production are, they are not surprising in light of the prevalent conception of energy that involves breaching and laying bare the depth of things (of the atom, of the earth...) and drawing power from this violent and violating exposure.

On the one hand, most approaches to energy presuppose substantial divergence between the inner and the outer, depth and surface. The very language of "storage" and "release" indicates that the energy of everything from galaxies to microbes, economic systems to psychic life, is contained (held inside and prevented from achieving its full actuality) before it is liberated with more or less force.

And the encompassing whole is, likewise, seen as a great container, from which no energy ever escapes; that is what, at bottom, the law of the conservation of energy means. Absent the dimension of interiority, one can no longer explain how things work, how they are put to work, activated, or withheld in potentiality. Energy differentials depend, above all, on the difference between the inside and the outside, on the speed and force with which their boundaries are traversed.

Plants, on the other hand, do not need to devastate the interiority of another being to procure their energy. They set to work the elements they neither control nor dominate nor appropriate. Besides water and the minerals they draw from the soil, they receive what they need from the sun, processing their solar sustenance on their maximally exposed surfaces, the leaves. (Plants can, to be sure, deplete the soil, but this happens only with human inference, due to intensive agriculture and the spread of monocultures. By and large, vegetation returns to the earth much of what it takes in the processes of its decomposition).

Human reliance on solar energy would bespeak our willingness to learn from plants and to accept, *mutatis mutandis*, an essentially superficial mode of existence or, at the very least, to integrate it with the dimension of depth. Although current technical capabilities would sustain a nearly total reliance on renewable energy (solar, wind, hydro, etc.), they do not match the prevalent mindset toward the *essence* of energy, viewed as something destructive-extractive—something to be snatched from the interiority of things.

The focus of attention may, in fact, swing to "clean energy" and that is, in and of itself, laudable. But "cleanness" relates primarily to the effects of its utilization, not to the question of what energy is. That is why oil, coal, and, especially, natural gas companies can claim that they are making the transition to clean energy, without radically modifying the sources of fuel themselves, let alone how they are procured.

Be it labor or truth, we extract value from the core of the human and destroy the material "shell" in the process. On economic spreadsheets, we are accounted for as *human resources*, from which work can be extracted in a mode incompatible with Marx's dream of human self-actualization through labor.

Our epistemologies, too, are consistent with the desire to reveal the inner core of reality, usually by shattering and discarding the outward "mere" appearances that occlude it. Thinking has assumed the shape of mental fracking. Unless we subscribe to the insights of phenomenology, we are quite dissatisfied with the surface of things, with how they present themselves to us in everyday life: with all their imperfections, incompletions, shadowy spots, and stamps of finitude.

For us, superficial actuality, the actuality of the superficies, is never actual enough. As we strive to know what things really are, we break them down to atomic and subatomic, chemical and molecular levels. Why would the framework of energy production and extraction be different from that of the production and extraction of knowledge? The two would have to change in tandem, if the human impact on the world, as well as on ourselves, is to be mitigated.

12.07.2015

Fracking and the Art of Subtext

KARA THOMPSON

Extractive industries condition and are conditioned by narrative structures. The constantly fluctuating demand and supply of "natural" resources begs for a certain kind of narrative energy. Whether striking gold or building a pipeline, narratives condition, validate, backdate: the turns of legality that justify settlement and the removal of Native/Indigenous peoples for the sake of gold, oil fields or pipelines; the narratives about hydraulic fracturing (fracking) that deny environmental impact and degradation or that deploy eminent domain law to allow oil and gas companies to seize control of "private" lands for the sake of the "public."

Resource extraction also parallels and structures the ways we read literature. Those of us who teach literature frequently use terms like *mine* or *dig deep* to talk about acts of close reading, terms that are meant to teach students how to coax something from the text that may not reside on its surface. Perhaps we use the term *fractured* as a metaphor for a structure, or a reader's encounter with a postmodern text. These are also terms that define and describe the procedures of blasting, coaxing, and drawing out natural gas from deep rock.

Compared to surface mining—including mountaintop removal, strip and open-pit mining—fracking is fairly concealed while the surface remains intact. The activity and energy have gone deep underground. In 2015, Oklahoma experienced 907 magnitude 3+ earthquakes; in 2014, 585; and in 2013, 109. The U.S. Geological Survey announced in 2013 that such seismic events are not the result of "typical, random fluctuations in natural seismicity rates" but instead likely caused by the disposal of fracking wastewater. Once the oil and natural gas are pumped out of the rock, the wastewater is extracted and re-injected into the ground at a different site; the injections increase pressure at natural fault lines and cause earthquakes. The process is diffuse and subterranean—the effects perceptible in other, displaced forms, like earthquakes or flammable tap water.

Fracking renders scale and affect ecological and geological. Unlike oil fields with their pumping derricks, mountaintops blasted off and stripped bare, or coal trains rumbling down the tracks, the blasting of rock occurs underground. Fracking obfuscates at the surface. Given its subterranean processes, that first goes deep—7000 feet below the earth's surface—and then horizontally, land owners often don't know their land is being mined for natural gas; nor are people always aware that their fields are being irrigated with fracking waste water, or that the water is being re-injected near their drinking source. Fracking traffics in subtext.

A narrative's subtext is about desire, the unmentionable fantasy or obsession. The text gets most interesting when characters cannot necessarily declare their needs and desires—perhaps they want too much of the wrong thing. From a craft perspective, subtext makes a good story. Charles Baxter puts it this way: "A certain kind of story does not depend so much on what the characters say they want as what they actually want but can't own up to. This inability to be direct creates a subterranean chasm within the story, where genuine desires hide beneath the superficial ones." A character's obsessions might turn manic, thereby creating what Baxter calls in *The Art of Subtext* a "*congested* subtext"—a "complex set of desires and fears that can't be efficiently described, a pile-up of emotions that resists easy articulation." Long after the story is over, the affective accumulation stays with the reader. Baxter's metaphors could be associated with extraction, including fracking—the *subterranean chasm* that can become *congested*. As readers we blast these moments open and are left with the fragments.

While energy extraction has come to resemble subtext, I increasingly direct my students to the text's surface layer, to linger in description and observation, to remain utterly superficial and "simply" describe the poem, or a key scene in the story. But more often than not, they cannot resist excavating, mining for a theme or two that allows them to manage an interpretation. They're utterly committed to the humanist principles of literature, that what makes a poem valid and worth reading is the extent to which it directs the reader *beyond* the textures of language and surfaces of the page. That is, most students who take my literature courses are not interested in subtext *or* surface, but in what they often refer to as "theme" or "meaning"—how a poem might teach us to be better humans, or how a character is a symbol of Christ, or how a complex figure such as Dakota writer Zitkala-Ša (Gertrude Bonnin) "symbolizes" the tragic end of her "noble culture." Not only do many of my settler students resist my insistence (and the evidence) that Dakota people and cultures live and thrive in the present tense, but some students also resist the time it takes to linger on the writer's vivid language, her subtle descriptions of space. I've wondered whether my directing them to the surface makes way for shallow forms of critique, a literary politics that detaches itself from historical context and political accumulation. I simply want them to see the surface, at least at first.

I'm trying to pry apart the deep paradox at play here: the culture that banks our energy futures on deep rock and subterranean extraction also gives us standardized testing in public schools that trains students to be excavators of "meaning." At the very same time that humanities programs are asked to be more streamlined and branded, when we're prompted to justify our existence numerically and many of our students assume that the study of literature must possess value (economic, quantifiable) to be worthy of their own time and energy, energy extraction becomes more elusive and imaginary. Meaning and theme offer a certain kind of extractive value, a portable and useful product that doesn't touch subtext, what's happening underneath the character's surface actions. So too, the traumas of fracking occur so deep underground that we cannot imagine how, when, or where they occur—and it's much easier not to try.

Pauline Matt, co-founder of Blackfeet Women Against Fracking, describes perfectly how fracking relies on subtext: the difference between what the "jolly" and complimentary man with papers at her door *says* and what he most desires, which is unrestricted access to her land, and to sacred sites in Blackfeet homelands, for subterranean drilling. But Matt and other Blackfeet people already know to read for that subtext: "I knew what he was up to right from the minute he walked through the door."

In the last six years, theories of reading have emerged that prompt us to engage with literature horizontally, rather than vertically—I'm thinking here of Sharon Marcus and Stephen Best's work on surface reading.

Then there are microsociological approaches that call for a turn to "thin description," or modes of reading that orient our attention to the text's surfaces, such as those advocated for by Heather Love. Reading practices, in other words, are increasingly oriented to the surface, while energy extraction only digs deeper. What does it mean for us to debate the material depth of reading, the thick and thin of it all, in a moment of fracturing when charges of pressure are forced into the core of rocks, which are the material formations of deep time? Do we need to change the way we read when the earth quakes in Oklahoma and water catches fire?

I suggest that fracking makes way for a different kind of close reading. We might be persuaded both by its depth, and by its shallow imagination. The rock that releases fossil fuel cannot be reducible to its energy function. Rocks do not exist to be fractured, nor are they utterly destroyed by fracking. Rocks buy humans a little more time, but they also steal future time away. The rock is a form on my mind, but it exists before and outside of me too. Rocks are autonomous and noisy; I'm tuned into them now that I recognize how their congested subtexts shake the earth beneath my feet.

06.20.2016

E. Ethics and Responsibility

Are Ethicists an Obstacle to Progress?

Michael Hauskeller

When people who don't know me ask me what I do, I tell them I'm a philosopher. When they ask me what I specialize in, I tell them that I am mostly, even though I've never been entirely comfortable with that label, an ethicist. This used to be a good thing, or at least not a bad one, but things are changing. People like me are now increasingly being described as, at best, a nuisance, and, at worst, a threat to human well-being and possibly even survival.

In this vein, Steven Pinker, the well-known psychologist and bestselling author, has recently (1 August 2015) published an opinion piece in the *Boston Globe*, entitled "The moral imperative for bioethics," in which he chides ethicists for hindering the progress of our species. According to Pinker, biotechnology could do amazing things for us if we only stopped hampering research by raising flimsy ethical concerns about it, which is not helpful at all. Scientific and technological progress is already slow enough as it is, and given the "vast increases in life, health, and flourishing" that biomedical research promises, every day we lose worrying about the ethics of the matter is one day too many. While biotechnological research is urgently needed to rid us of all sorts of terrible diseases, what we most certainly do *not* need are professional worriers who call themselves ethicists, second-guessing every promising new development and thus stalling scientific and technological progress by throwing "nebulous but sweeping principles such as 'dignity', 'sacredness', or 'social justice'" in its way. A *true* ethicist, Pinker decrees, would realize that there is in fact only one valid moral imperative they should promote and follow, namely to "get out of the way."

For Pinker and others like him, ethics is a luxury that we cannot afford. People are dying, people are suffering. The biotech industry is attempting to do something about it, working very hard to succeed, while the "so-called ethicists" are attempting to prevent this from happening. Humanity is painfully pushing a rock up a hill, while all that ethicists are doing is help push it back down again. For Pinker it is as simple as that. Except, of course, it is not. Surprising as it may be, it is in fact *not* the primary goal of us ethicists to make life difficult for those who want nothing but make the world a better place. Ethics is not about issuing "red tape, moratoria, or threats of prosecution" (although ethical reflection *may* occasionally give rise to all that). Instead, ethics is about making sure that we know *what* we are doing and *why* we are doing it, that the path we are following is really the path we *want* to be following and that the place where this path is likely to lead us is really the place where we want to end up being.

We all, naturally, want things to be better than they are, if that is possible. We all want progress. But just as nothing is ever better *as such*, but only ever in certain respects, there is no such thing as progress as such, or in the abstract. We are not sitting in an evolutionary elevator that has only two directions: up and down. Instead, there are many different ways of going up and going forward, many different ways of going down and backwards, and many different ways of going sideways, or around in circles, or of moving without any clear direction at all. Moreover, the ways that lead upwards in *some* way may also lead downwards in some *other* way. Things are usually more complex than we would like, and for this very reason also more complex than we may care to acknowledge. In order to progress, to step forward, you need to have a goal, or at least have made up your mind about a direction. Spending a thought or two on the reasons for choosing that particular goal or direction before you start running doesn't seem like such a bad idea. And that is all we are doing when we are engaging in ethical reflection. The one question that ethicists keep asking is whether the things we do or propose to do *are actually good for us*, all things considered. Would we really prefer that this question be no longer asked?

It is highly naïve to assume that all biomedical research will necessarily benefit some of us, let alone humanity as a whole. What is powerful enough to save us is also powerful enough to harm us. To demand that such research not be regulated in any way because *some* of it might eventually help us find a cure for Alzheimer's and other diseases is like saying that politicians in government should be granted unlimited legislative, judiciary and executive power and not be checked in any way because *some* politicians might actually use that power for the good of the people: we just need to trust that they know best and that they want only what is best for us. But why should we believe that?

I suppose most people would agree that granting such unlimited powers to politicians would be a singularly bad idea, and that, even if scientists and biotech firms were generally smarter and more trustworthy than politicians, they are certainly not trustworthy enough that we could afford not putting any regulations and safeguards in place and thereby retaining some measure of control. Ethical reflection helps us determine the nature and extent of those necessary safeguards. Ideas such as human dignity, sacredness, and social justice may strike tough-minded empiricists like Pinker as decidedly airy-fairy and not worth serious consideration. But even though they *are* a bit airy-fairy, for many of us they do capture something that is both elusive and very real, a sense perhaps that living disease-free and surviving as long as possible is not all that matters, that sometimes more is at stake, that there are other dimensions of our life and experience that are important to us and for us, whatever they may be. Ethicists are the ones who try to figure out what those dimensions are and why they matter to us. They are not the professional doomsayers that some like to depict them as. Their role is more that of psychopomps who guide us from the present to the future, providing secure passage, making sure that we get there safe and sound.

09.28.2015

The Responsibility of Others

Daniel Innerarity

As people in Europe are seeking ways to deal with the fallout from the Greek crisis, a common theme emerges in the discourses of very diverse agents: others are to blame. No matter what happens, we end up repeating something similar to what was affirmed by a character from Goethe's *Torquato Tasso*, who gave us the maxim that is probably the paradigm of all excuses: "whatever one is / other people are to blame." This conviction clarifies nothing, but provides a good deal of relief; its purpose is to reconfirm us as opposed to them. It explains in simple terms the tension between the global and the local, creates a comfortable contrast between states and markets, divides the world into heroes and villains, and provides the basic outline for the relationship between right- and left-wing forces. As we can see, these operations offer a very comfortable simplification when the world has become difficult to understand because of its growing complexity.

Some people say that the fault lies with German hegemony and the harshness of the creditors. They are not mistaken, although if they magnify these faults, they run the risk of forgetting the irresponsibility of the various Greek governments that falsified their public finances (with the assistance, of course, of some of those who are now part of the band of creditors), reneged on many of their commitments and failed to reform a state that was economically unsustainable even before the crisis.

Others blame the crisis on the clichéd irresponsibility of Southern countries, as if they did not know the disastrous end results of previous bailout plans, as well as the economic benefits that the single currency has afforded Northern European countries. In addition, if a member state needs assistance after suffering speculative attacks by market forces based on an arrangement for which it does not hold sole responsibility, it makes no sense for the bailout to be compensated with drastic structural reforms in that member state alone. There are many things that should be reformed in Southern European countries, of course, but also in the incorrect design of the euro and its defective governance.

We are facing a typical case of recursive responsibility in which all criticisms have an element of truth, but none of them reveal the full picture. The bad thing is that, with so many mutual accusations, people find many reasons to stop asking about their own ineptitude, the risks they generate with their decisions or their responsibility toward what we have in common. To the extent that allegations against others increase, self-reflection decreases. When the whole field is filled with conspiratorial explanations, there is no space for interrogation about one's own responsibilities.

We will not get beyond these obstacles until we manage to see our decisions in the context in which they are adopted and that they influence, in ways that can sometimes be catastrophic. Governing involves making every one of the actors who intervene in the process of decision-making aware of the disastrous possibilities that will ensue if they narrow-mindedly pursue their own interests and inviting them to protect themselves against those possibilities with some type of self-limitation. In the end, it is a question of decision-makers realizing that what they must fear is themselves, their unthinking behavior: that a society is not threatened as much by nuclear arms in the hands of the enemy as by its own nuclear power plants; less by the enemy's biological weapons than by certain experiments by its own scientific community; not by the invasion of foreign soldiers as much as its own organized crime; not by the hunger and death caused by war as much as the disabilities and death caused by its own traffic accidents. That what prevents plural societies from freely deciding their destiny is not so much an external impediment—or not only that—as much as their own lack of internal agreement.

As Ulrich Beck noted, contemporary societies cannot attribute everything that threatens them to external causes; they themselves produce what they do not desire. The question about one's own responsibility tends to be glossed over when one finds oneself in the midst of systems whose complexity resides in the fact that there are neither clear and indisputable cause-and-effect relationships nor decisions without side effects. We need to reject the comfortable innocence of conceiving responsibility as something that always falls upon others. This reflexive reversal of the gaze toward one's own conditions is very similar to the personal maturation that consists of replacing external accusations with internal reflection. In the same way that children learn not to interpret their conflicts as the whole world conspiring against them, complex democracies should be capable of discovering the ways in which they themselves produce their own catastrophes.

10.26.2015

In Praise of Suicide

Jeff Love

We seek freedom. Is this not the rallying cry of American democracy, endlessly repeated, endlessly intoned as its most durable credo? We seek freedom to do as we want without fear of reprisal or repression. Indeed, we crave freedom from all reprisal and repression. The society of infinitely expanding wants, the bulwark of consumer dreams—that is America. Be the person you want to be, create yourself! These are exhortations essential to American identity, and they are deeply ambiguous. Once thought to be the property of the progressive left, they belong now increasingly to the many ideological formations of the radical right.

The adoption by the radical right of these once progressive ideals, as well as the insinuation that only the radical right truly respects their content, brings to the fore their surprising malleability. But it also highlights the connection of freedom with unabashed self-interest, the notion that what matters when it comes to freedom is *my* freedom to do as *I* want. The famed American frontier myths come together with the myth of the self-made man as paeans to self-interest. Freedom is first and foremost the freedom to do as I see fit and to acquire enough property and power so that I cannot be gainsaid. Nothing speaks more eloquently of the decay of the communitarian ideal than the rise of this notion of freedom as the final fecund fruit of American democracy.

Perhaps such a rise was inevitable. The philosophical origins of this notion of freedom are a veritable exaltation of selfishness. If we take the thinking of Thomas Hobbes polemically as our foil, the point could not be clearer. For to raise the fear of violent death up to the level of founding principle is to make self-interest the deciding element in a political community. The final irony of this exaltation of self-interest based on the fear of death is that communities exist only to serve or prohibit—they exist only for my benefit, and to the extent they fail to meet my needs, to benefit me, they fail as communities. All are essentially alone, seeking to profit from the community at the expense of others, and this makes perfect sense given the founding principle of fear of death. We may live with others, but everyone dies alone.

There is, however, another, very different way of looking at this notion of freedom that rejects it as a most abject and humiliating form of servitude. According to this view, the supposed freedom of self-interest is based on a largely hidden servitude to the fear of death. What reigns supreme is not my wants as they come clear to me, but, above all, the imperative to self-preservation at any cost. All my wants come down to nothing more than an expression of the imperative to self-preservation, which is merely the "positive" way of describing the fear of death. Put more crudely, what I take for freedom is in reality a grotesque servitude to the body whose pleasures and fears dictate the course of my life.

While there are many precedents for this thinking (Jean-Jacques Rousseau comes to mind), an unusual twentieth-century Russian philosopher, Alexandre Kojève (born Aleksandr Vladimirovich Kozhevnikov, 1902-1968), puts it most sharply and radically. Kojève insists that genuine freedom originates only in our resistance to the imperative of self-preservation. The freest human act is the most radical act of rebellion against the imperative of self-preservation: suicide. Whereas the ostensibly free creation of modern consumer society may deride this proposition as being manifestly absurd, the equation of freedom and suicide emerges as absurd only for those who accept the yoke of self-preservation. Kojève's thinking makes a mockery of the assumption of freedom one might associate with buying power in consumer culture or the freedom "to do as one sees fit." In both these cases, Kojève sees nothing but the slave chained to her desire for the prolongation of a comfortable life.

Does Kojève then counsel us to kill ourselves en masse? What sort of community can he possibly create out of this central claim about what constitutes freedom? The basis of Kojève's thinking fits perfectly well with traditional attempts to create community not through the exaltation but rather the elimination of self-interest, as most purely exemplified by the imperative to self-preservation. The suicide he counsels may thus fit quite nicely with a rhetoric of conversion, whereby one lays down the primacy of the preservation of oneself in favor of the creation of a new communal identity that transcends self-interest by transcending the interest in self-preservation. Kojève may be seen as a Christian philosopher in this sense. But he was manifestly *not* a Christian philosopher. Instead, he supported the notion of a community whose highest ideal is not service to a god but the overcoming of the imperative of self-preservation (and thus of the body) itself.

Kojève dares us to think a community in which the I is We and the We is I. The objections to this way of thinking are predictable. Is this not the drab dream of communism, that we all become the same insofar as none of us has her own identity? Is this the peace of eternal sleep or the night in which all cows are black? Both of these objections seem fair. But, again, they are based on the assumption that difference—and inequality—are to be preferred to a "bland" egalitarianism. Under this objection, of course, one finds a firm rejection of giving up the imperative to self-preservation, which, for some reason, gives us such variety—such as the many crimes, wars and antagonistic differences of culture that have lent history its deliquescent brilliance.

Indeed, Kojève's thought bids us to confront the alternatives: the violence inherent in retaining the imperative to self-preservation or the oppressive peace that arrives from our giving up that urge, to the extent we can. Kojève enjoins us to confront our underlying notions of freedom and, perhaps most powerfully, he forces us to consider what the most thoroughgoing freedom might entail, a freedom indistinguishable from the extirpation of desire. And who can imagine a life with that kind of freedom?

Fortunately, however, we need not imagine the other life, the one that emerges from the exaltation of self-interest: the wondrous pageant of human selfishness surrounds us every day.

04.11.2016

Is Existentialism a Post-Humanism?

PATRÍCIA VIEIRA

It has now been 70 years, almost to the date (October 29, 1945), since Jean-Paul Sartre gave his famous talk "Existentialism is a Humanism," published as a book a short time later. Speaking just a few months after the end of the Second World War, the French philosopher was concerned with ascertaining the meaning of human existence, the value and import of our choices and the weight of humanity's responsibility for its actions. Seven decades after this talk, which came to popularize existentialism as one of the best-known philosophical currents of the twentieth century, with ramifications, for instance, in literature (theater, the novel…) and cinema, the time has come to re-evaluate its legacy.

Sartre, writing in the shadow of the atrocities of the war, peered into the significance of our relations to ourselves and to our fellow human beings. Now, at a time of widespread ecological destruction, we need to consider not only human interactions but also our behavior towards other living and non-living entities. The human propensity to look beyond the present moment into the future and the inevitability of social relations led Sartre to declare that "existentialism is a humanism." But what about our exchanges with other creatures that share the planet with us? What is the role of these beings in existentialism? To put it more pointedly, Sartre established that "existentialism is a humanism;" the question we face today is to determine whether it can also be a posthumanism.

Sartre grounds his existentialism on the distinction between human subjects and mere objects. Objects are created according to a plan to fulfill a specific purpose—in Sartre's example, a paper knife is designed by a craftsman to cut paper. During most of the history of Western thought, humans were considered to be special kinds of objects: they were objects created by a supreme artisan, God Himself. The notion of the human devised by God is thus comparable to the concept of the paper knife in the mind of its manufacturer.

According to Sartre, 18th century-philosophers did away with the idea of God as the ultimate Being responsible for creation. However, they still held on to the belief that humans were the result of a pre-defined human nature, each individual—an instantiation of the universal concept of humanity. Both in the theological paradigm and in the secular worldview of the Enlightenment and post-Enlightenment periods, then, essence precedes existence: each person represents a certain configuration of an essence that was given *a priori*.

The Copernican Revolution that Sartre is proposing, following the philosophy of Martin Heidegger, is that, in the case of human beings, *existence precedes essence*. This simple inversion entails a series of momentous consequences, foremost amongst which is the idea that human beings are, at each moment, responsible for their behavior, one that does not follow a pre-given pattern, or, in Sartre's elegant expression, that humans are "condemned to be free." Values and principles for action are not prescribed by God or by human nature but need to be chosen at every turn of a person's life, which renders each of us fully responsible for our decisions that can no longer be blamed on external factors. Contrary to the paper knife, then, human beings are not created for this or that purpose or to act in a certain way. Thrown into an open-ended existence, our essence—who we really are—will be the sum total of all our actions and responses to the circumstances in which we find ourselves.

What is missing in Sartre's depiction of humankind, as opposed to the realm of material objects? The obvious blind spot in his talk is the rest of the world, namely, those entities that are neither human-made objects built with a certain function in mind, like the paper-knife, nor humans themselves. What is the place of animals, plants, rivers, mountains and deserts in existentialism?

Surely, Sartre cannot claim that animals live only to fulfill a goal pre-established by humans. Formerly considered to have been fashioned by God and, therefore, to have been created, just like humans, by a supreme artisan, where does the death of divinity leave these entities? In the absence of a theologically-inflected *scala naturae*—a ladder of nature that assigned each being a place in the world, with inanimate entities at the bottom, followed by the different plants and animals and reaching, in its higher echelons, humans, angels and, finally God, the guarantor of the system's cohesion and the one who defined every being's *telos* and essence—other entities become just like humans, defined not by a pre-existing essence but by their very lives.

Sartre's conspicuous silence about humanity's co-created beings, emancipated from the role assigned to them by their maker with the death of God, is tied to existentialism's views on human freedom. If he were pressed on this issue, Sartre would probably defend humanity's exceptionalism by pointing out that the non-human elements of creation cannot be responsible for their actions because they are not free. But in regarding humans as the only free entities, is existentialism not condemning the rest of the world to chains? Worse still, is human freedom not dependent upon the yoke of plants, animals and all other beings, put at the service of supposedly free human masters?

The question of humanism is, at its core, a question about the non-human, about what distinguishes *us* from *others*. Humanism is therefore deeply implicated in what has come to be defined as the "environmental crisis." It is pertinent to recall that the ancient Greek word from which our modern "crisis" derives, *krísis*, meant a separation, distinction or election. The environmental crisis is rooted precisely in humanity's separation from the rest of creation, in our conviction that we are inherently better than the rest.

Sartre's existentialist humanism strove to liberate us from the shackles of essentialism and to show that humans are, at each moment, independent beings responsible for their choices. The relevance of existentialism today hinges upon whether it can be not only a humanism but also a posthumanism.

"Posthumanism" should not be interpreted apocalyptically here, as what sequentially follows once humans have died out. Nor should it be regarded as hinting at the obsolescence of the human as we know it, to be replaced by better hybrids such as the half-human, half-machine cyborgs or the genetically modified humanoids of science fiction. I understand posthumanism as a moment within humanism that is a step *beyond* traditional strands of humanism and, at the same time, a revolution (a turning back) of humanism, returning to a more lifelike conception of what being human means.

I would like to finish, then, with seven theses of existentialist posthumanism, one for each decade that has passed since Sartre's talk:

1. Existentialist posthumanism is a recovery of our humanity, lost in abstract conceptions of human exceptionality.

2. Existentialist posthumanism moderates the notion of human freedom and autonomy and recognizes human *heteronomy*, that is, our dependence upon other entities on earth to provide for even the most basic of our needs, such as food and shelter.

3. Existentialist posthumanism is humble, rejecting a larger-than-life view of the human as master of creation.

4. Existentialist posthumanism follows on the footsteps of traditional humanism in releasing all beings from essentialism and granting freedom not only to humans but also to non-humans beings; it recognizes each entity's freedom to be according to its own mode of existence.

5. For existentialist posthumanism, the existence of all beings precedes their essence.

6. For existentialist posthumanism, all beings have their own universe.

7. *Existentialist humanism is a posthumanism.*

11.02.2015

F.   Embodiments

Inside Out

Jean-Luc Nancy

Translated by Michael Marder

The body is nothing but the outside: skin exposed, a network of sentient receivers and transmitters. All outside and nothing like "me" that would be held inside that wrapping. There is no ghost in the machine, no dimensionless point where "I" feel or feel myself feeling. The inside of the envelope is yet another outside, developed (or de-enveloped) otherwise, full of folds, turns, convolutions, and adhesions. Full of invaginations, small heaps, and conglomerations.

It senses just because everything touches it throughout its continuous thickness. Everything is touched and mixed; everything slides into the silence of the organs that provide neither sights nor tastes nor smells nor sounds, but only touch, because the outside is so constant, so thick, so caught up in a compact and solidary mass that the interior body is without organs. Being outside myself as this inside, prohibiting penetration (except by disemboweling or suffocating me), the outside is indefinitely wrapped, absorbed, sunk in its own magma, both fitting it so well and absolutely foreign to that which this magma fills, to that which it sustains and animates, to all this skin exposed with its orifices, mucosa, pores, and hair, all its contacts and communication, all the vibrations of the world, of matter and images, of timbers and resonances, all these gases and squirts, these air currents, these mirrors, these pieces of metal, these other skins, these words, these impressions, depressions, and expressions.

Everything the outside-within sustains with its buttresses, columns, cages, tubes, and membranes, however, also makes an impression on it. Such impressions are expressed in it, and nowhere else. The exposed outside has no other place than this inside to stick its sensations in, as well as its food, the air it breathes, the kisses, the knowledge it sucks in. It is there that it feels and feels itself feeling: it is in the stomach, the intestines, heart palpitations, the filling of the lungs, not to mention the deaf infiltrations channeling nerves in the muscles, the lymphatic vessels in the liver and in pancreatic islets. The skin feels under the skin, the eyes seeing in a frozen socket under the meninges.

But I have said too much, much too much, by saying these words that I have learned from another exterior, that of medicine, physiology, or anatomy, through which the vesicles, tendons, and peristalses receive a determinate, functional sense. As soon as these are presented to me, they signify something completely different from my body, whether inside or out: an apparatus, a piece of equipment plugged into a network of tubes or of chemical products, dissociated and desiccated by a scalpel or needles. It is always intriguing, distracting, or disturbing to see an echography image of one's arteries or of the coronary network, set in a contrast thanks to a special solution and projected onto a screen after a catheter has been introduced into a vein in the groin. But, in the end, this is a representation similar to the results of a blood test or a spirometric measurement that belongs to the complex of physiological representation, computation, and instrumentation.

This complex has to do with something other than that which keeps itself underneath—*sub-jectum, sup-positum, sub-stantia*—and that, in this *underneath*, ingests along with the nutrients their tastes and, with them, the tastes of all the things, the shocks, the frictions, the bells and the trumpets, the moods and their pulsations, the air, spirit, warmth, tenderness, boredom, desire… That subject seems to be subjected to the other, namely, to the character who says "I", and yet it is only a thin contact sheet, almost nothing, an interval between above and below, between these two outsides that make him believe that he can say "inside." But there also, on the inside, it relates to itself, it feels itself, it growls or it bothers, it tightens or it relaxes. Here it makes rumbling sounds; there—the wheezing ones; and there it stands up in erections. At all times, at every opportunity, the skin imprints on its reverse side (muscles, fibers, facial nerves) all the messages (images, foliage, clouds) signaling to me nothing more and nothing less than my presence in the world. But this presence, too, is exposed to my very entrails, to my very intestines that are, according to their name, the insides themselves, not so far from the most intimate, not far at all from the Augustinian *interior intimo meo* and not far from the *interfeces et urinam* from the same book, very close indeed to the perfect god as a flaming excrement. That which comes out and that which enters, shit or thought, speech or saliva, excitation, excoriation: everything goes in pairs and keeps the one outside the other in a constant rustling and movement of the same ensemble in itself, completely outside of me. As for me, I remain an intimate null point of spirit nowhere to be found in this entanglement smeared with pulp, tissues, and fluids that, in their entirety, give place to the soul, which ought to be conceived as extended along the vessels and the teguments, knotted into the lymph nodes, and bathed in plasma.

There is no representation of the outside that is swarming within, except for these cuts on a cover glass, the imagery of magnetic resonance, or whatever issues from tomography scanners. Nonetheless, let us not rush to challenge anatomies, histologies, or physiologies. Their technical strangeness does not allow us to forget that *this* is still us. In some way, it must be the case that my eye is glassy, watery, iridescent and that my finger is bony, tendinous, ungulate. These things are not quite things, and anatomical models play the role of a secret mirror. How is it possible to ignore what the skin molded of orange-red, brown or blue rubber, or the skeleton made of pale plastic with 367 bones stitched in order, tell me something about myself or how they paint me to myself? How, therefore, to ignore to what point I am far away and to what strangely disquieting point I am unrecognizable?

04.04.2016

Do We Own Our Bodies?

Jeff Love and Michael Meng

Ownership is freedom. We may do what we want with what we have. We believe we own our bodies and may do with them as we will. But is that really so? Does this most intimate form of ownership really grant us freedom to do as we will? One has only to take a casual stroll through a hospital to be disabused of that notion—hospitals being little more than horrific prisons where the limits of our ownership, and by extension ownership itself, are all too easy to spot. In a hospital, in room after room equipped with elaborate arrays of equipment that can be joined to the body to keep it in some desired condition, one has to confront a most discomfiting reality: what seems most close and intimate to us is a disorienting stranger. The wondrous forms painted or sketched with consummate mastery by a Leonardo or Michelangelo give way to the disturbing drawings of Vesalius: the body opened up for all to see, a network of tubes and cables that is for some reason much more difficult to look at than those similar networks we find in a building or a car. Why is that so?

We might say that this difficulty is born of deception, the unpleasant encounter with the aspects of the body we would otherwise most wish to hide from ourselves. For all those tubes and lines of cable are fragile and may collapse at any time, possibilities that our regular perception of our own bodies is not likely to emphasize. Of course, we suffer regular breakdowns, and often rather embarrassing ones, that are embarrassing precisely because they reveal how little we own what we think we own. Our capacity to take hold of ourselves proves to be extraordinarily fragile, and there is nothing more estranging, more fundamentally disorienting, perhaps, than a moment when one's body gives out or reacts in such a way that one has no choice but to become aware of a singular fact: "we" (and why is this a "we"?) are strangers in our own body, which is not our own, does not belong to us and cares little or nothing for what is important to us.

Who are we then? We could answer this question in many different ways. We may be mind, we may be body, we may be spirit or flesh, and so on. But, in each case, the contrast arises with the realization that the body is indeed a kind of stranger over which I have utterly no control. Here is the vaunted "mind/body" problem in its least abstract instantiation. While philosophers may discuss this problem in any number of different venues, we each live it and nobody lives this problem more than the patient frozen in fear of the alien taking all she has away in the crepuscular twilight of pain, loneliness and desperate mendacity that is the lot of those whose bodies have decided to collapse.

The myth of ownership collapses along with the body. We are left to face the harsh reality encapsulated in Martin Heidegger's extravagant phrase: "Death is Dasein's ownmost possibility." "Ownmost" is a curious translation of the German "eigenste," an adjective whose root "eigen" denotes ownership, thus suggesting that what we own most (another impossible phrase) is the possibility to die. To put this slightly differently, what we most truly own is death. Of course, this phrase must seem darkly ironic, and it is. For what sort of ownership can this be but ownership that obliterates the inveterate trace of hope secreted away in the notion of ownership itself? A trace intimating that I may be freed of death, that I may own "in perpetuity", that, in other words, I do not have to face the humiliation of death, all my property, my house, my stocks, my cars, proving to be nothing more than an elaborate network of fences that protect me from a ghastly reality, which, having once emerged, will never let me go.

"I did everything correctly and still I must die!" This could be the motto of the main character in Lev Tolstoy's harrowing novella, "The Death of Ivan Il'ich," which Heidegger himself refers to in his discussion of death in *Being and Time*. Ivan Il'ich finds himself secure in what must be the bourgeois version of paradise: he is happily married, has a lucrative career and a lovely house—everything is perfect. But then what is hardly perfect introduces itself into his life, a small pain that becomes more and more severe, that becomes so severe that his entire life becomes nothing but pain, his thoughts scattered, his family distant, his world reduced to nothing more than that. He has discovered his "ownmost" possibility of being. He has come to know himself and, rapidly, all the things he used to claim ownership of fade away in the face of this knowledge.

If ownership is a sordid illusion, a lie we tell ourselves to alleviate the terror of being stuck in a body that finally crushes us in its death throes, is it possible to face that ownmost possibility? If we come to see the illusion of salvation through ownership, what do we do? Is this revelation itself not already a form of death? Can we live without ownership?

06.13.2016

Philosophy as a Bloody Affair

Costica Bradatan

Suppose there is a manner of doing philosophy that, strictly speaking, doesn't involve writing and speech-making, lecturing and teaching—indeed, a form of philosophizing that doesn't even need language. Suppose, further, that this kind of philosophizing is all about performance, *bodily* performance. Philosophers have exhausted all their usual approaches, and now have to put their bodies on the line. The situation doesn't lack irony: an essentially logo-centric discipline finds itself one day in a state where words are useless and arguments futile; no matter how persuasive the philosophers, they will convince no one unless they decide to abandon lecturing and arguing and turn their own flesh into an argument. This is precisely the limit-situation on which I focus in my latest book, *Dying for Ideas: The Dangerous Lives of the Philosophers.*

Socrates was among the first to learn, from personal experience, what the situation entails. His failure to make his fellow Athenians see the worth of his philosophical project, as evidenced especially by his trial and death sentence, must have persuaded him not only that there is a limit as to what language can do for philosophy, but also that the philosopher, if he is not to betray his vocation and himself, needs to take philosophizing beyond that limit. There is a point, Socrates must have realized as he listened to the death sentence the Athenian jury pronounced against him, where philosophy, if it is not to lose face, has to use something stronger than words to do its job. And what is stronger than words, in such a situation, is the philosopher's own death. By the means of his dying

Dying for Ideas was researched while I was a Distinguished Guest Fellow at the Notre Dame Institute for Advanced Study. This essay draws on a research report originally published in the DNIAS Newsletter.

body—and the public spectacle of his death—Socrates communicated to his audience beyond his mastery of the Greek language.

His intuition turned out to be right: by dying the way he did, Socrates accomplished something unique. He managed to solidify a meaningful link between his work and his biography. In the absence of a "philosophical death," not only would Socrates's life have lacked a defining feature, but his work, too, would have been incomplete. Indeed, without a body of written text, it is hard to imagine how his name would have survived in a discipline that, from inception, has been defined by writing.

The message Socrates was sending as he was drinking the hemlock is rather simple, but tremendously powerful: you need to *embody* your philosophy. Primarily, philosophy is not an academic exercise but a matter of *practice*; it is not something you talk about but something you do. To philosophize is to cause a change in yourself, to act upon yourself as if you were some lump of raw material in need of a firm shape. Philosophy is not sheer production of knowledge; its function is not to inform but to form us. Its ultimate object is a project of self-realization, the philosopher's self-fashioning. The place where philosophy dwells, then, is not the academic text, nor the philosopher's speech, but the philosopher's body. Philosophy lives with us. Yet, it hardly dies with us.

Indeed, philosophy *thrives* when the philosopher chooses to die, as a matter of consistence, with his beliefs. Socrates's death was only the beginning of a tremendously influential posterity, which, in the absence of any written work, is nothing short of miraculous. Hypatia, too, has been a very influential figure, even though nothing has come down to us from her. Giordano Bruno is rarely read today but is thought to be one of the greatest Italian philosophers of all time. What makes these figures "great," I argue in *Dying for Ideas*, is the manner of their death. Not only does this particular type of death not annihilate its victims, but it makes them stronger.

These philosophers' ways of life, their being perceived as "out of place" in society, the dramatic build-up that leads to their singling out, the distinct sense of "crisis" that pervades the communities in the midst of which they emerge, then their violent ending—all of these call for a Girardian reading of the event of their death. From René Girard's perspective, they all bear "victimary signs." Committed as they are to "straight talking" (*parrēsía*), to leaving nothing unquestioned, these philosophers are usually incapable of establishing strong ties with others. They remain perpetual outsiders to their own communities; they don't allow themselves to recognize and cultivate those strong bonds of complicity that keep society together. It is telling that these philosophers' remarks often come across as "acidic"; no bonds can stand the corroding effect of their *parrēsía*. And in times of crises they become easy targets because their philosophy has made them fundamentally vulnerable.

Girard's theory of the "scapegoat mechanism" explains not only why martyr-philosophers are killed, but also why they become so influential after their death: by dying the kind of death they die they are made "sacred." They become "founding figures" because their annihilation was caused by what Girard calls a "founding murder." Due to the powerful mix of guilt and shame that remains in the collective memory, the tradition processes these philosophers' deaths along the lines of myth-making. We end up elevating them to a mythical status and make them part of our mythic imagination.

This may explain why we tend to misinterpret what these philosophers did or said or who they were while they were alive. We regard Socrates as the "founder" of Western philosophy. This is not entirely true, as there were other philosophers before him. Tellingly, we call them "pre-Socratics." Hypatia is often seen as having founded the tradition of women in philosophy, even though there certainly were women philosophers before her. She is also associated with the foundation of philosophical feminism (at least two feminist journals bear her name), even though, since her work has not survived, it is difficult to tell exactly what was feminist about it. The death of these philosophers simply "blinds" us. Our reception of them is not strictly rational; it's tinted by mythology.

The case of martyr-philosophers points to an important fact: the formation of intellectual and philosophical traditions is not governed by strictly rational patterns but sometimes by forms of mythic thinking and imagination. Typically, we tend to think that myth and reason are opposites and that one subverts the other. This may be a simplistic picture, though. Sometimes myth complements reason: myth-making and mythic imagination can bring to philosophy a level of depth and sophistication that reason alone cannot secure.

05.18.2015

Asceticism Reimagined

Daniel Kunitz

I don't need to tell anyone reading this how technology, ease of movement, and relative wealth have opened up myriad ways for us to spend
or waste our time; or how readily we can feel ourselves adrift in oceanic
abundance, buffeted by the possibilities swelling about us while goaded
by commercial entities to indulge our every desire and whim. Less
noticed, however, is the fact that, in the face of hyper-abundance, many of
us are adopting programs of self-discipline that have evolved along with
new conceptions of fitness and wellness.

Consider L., the founder and CEO of a successful start-up. With long
work days and stacked responsibilities, she has nevertheless ordered her
life around a set of strictures meant to boost her physical performance
and overall well-being. She manages to work out six days a week, sometimes twice a day, which means that L. has given up the hours often
reserved for carousing or binge-watching television. Beyond this, she
also restricts the foods she allows herself to eat, so as to maximize her
energy levels and recovery, both of which are also boosted by her precise
sleep schedule. L. has even set aside specific days to rest physically and
mentally—a self-imposed secular Sabbath, if you will. Although L. is at
the avant-garde of today's austerity practices, her example suggests the
dizzying variety of types of self-denial that people get up to. Some leave
off tracking their Instagram or Facebook feed while tanning at the park in
favor of working through yoga postures, which has in turn driven them to
abstain from processed foods and added sugars. Others carve away their
morning television in order to meditate, and maybe in addition to that
practice they've given up meat for vegetarianism. Some might be training
for an obstacle race at the same hour that they used to devote to post-
work drinks, and they too sleep and eat in a manner that is calibrated for

athletic performance. There is a growing movement of people who regularly fast, for other than religious reasons.

These are not the sackcloth-wearing, world-renouncing hermits we tend to associate with asceticism; they are people we know and live among. It seems to me they are fulfilling a wish, voiced over a century ago by Friedrich Nietzsche, when he wrote that he wanted to make asceticism "natural again." Nietzsche believed religious—more specifically, Christian—asceticism, the mortification of the flesh with whips and gruel, is unnatural because it aims at abnegation of the self and, ultimately, the world. He looked instead to an older, Classical and pre-Christian, model.

The word *ascetic* derives from the ancient Greek *askesis*, which means exercise or training. For the Greeks, the foundational model of askesis was inculcated in the *gymnasion* (from which we derive the word *gymnasium*), such as Plato's Academy, where the training was athletic, intellectual, and ethical. Throughout the Classical era, a number of forms of ascetic training developed. Perhaps the best-known of these technologies of the self, to borrow Michel Foucault's term, is Stoic philosophy, which has enjoyed a not-so-quiet revival in recent years. (Articles on those adopting it have appeared in numerous outlets, from *Forbes* to *The New York Times*). Classical *askesis* was oriented toward self-mastery, to live in the world better. At the end of the Classical era, the first Christian monks took this notion of *askesis*—alluding to the centrality of physical exercises by calling themselves "athletes for Christ"—and morphed it into an asceticism that sought to free the soul from the body. Self-mastery gave way to self-abnegation, physical training to a denigration of the physical, worldliness to otherworldliness. This is the form of asceticism that we in the West have been familiar with for nearly two millennia. (Eastern forms differ by not separating mind and body, but not so much that they don't still seek spiritual purity through self-abnegation and disciplining the mind-body.)

To make asceticism natural again means embracing the world and the body; it means renouncing certain luxuries and indulgences in an affirmative mode—not because particular foods or ways of spending time are inherently evil but because we prefer, on ethical grounds, other foods and activities. "I abhor all those moralities which say: 'Do not do this!

Renounce!…' writes Nietzsche. "But I am well disposed toward those moralities which goad me to do something and do it again, from morning till evening, and then to dream of it at night… When one lives like that, one thing after another that simply does not belong to such a life drops off… What we do should determine what we forego; by doing we forego." When, at a restaurant, my sister teasingly accuses me of having orthorexia for waving away the bread basket, she is not identifying in me some moral denunciation of wheat; she's inadvertently registering my joyful anticipation of waking up the next morning feeling energized, my body recovered from the previous day's exertions. Eschewing bread is a happy choice: if I want to load up on—relatively—empty carbs, I'll eat a pint of ice cream.

However, embracing the world and its sweets also entails an implicit rejection of the old, Western division of mind and body. When we practice such disciplines as yoga and meditation in their contemporary forms, we are, like Walt Whitman, asking: "if the body were not the soul, what is the soul?"

But if the point is no longer spiritual purification, what is the appeal of such regimes? The Stoics, I think, gave the answer most pertinent to our lives today. "We ought not to make our exercises consist in means contrary to nature," says Epictetus. Rather the goal of our self-mastering exercises is: "Neither to be disappointed in that which you desire, nor to fall into anything which you would avoid." If ascetics today subject their minds and bodies to rigorous discipline, it is because these exercises provide both the means and the model for training our faculty of choice—for helping us to know ourselves well enough to know what to desire and, most critically, how to spend our ever shrinking time. Having a set of practices that aid us in filtering out the noise of marketing, in navigating the maze of goods placed before us, and in saying yes or no to various leisure activities is like having a sharp knife that we can use to whittle our lives into an artfully deliberate shape.

10.24.2016

Part II

Reflections

A. The End of Civilization

What Are We Talking About When We Talk About Zombies?

WILLIAM EGGINTON

Legions of cultural critics are focusing the beam of Marxist-inflected critical theory on the mass-cultural phenomenon of zombies. And what a phenomenon they have become! Zombies—the rambling, post-apocalyptic, multitudinous variety, as opposed to the voodoo-induced loners of Caribbean lore—have spread like a virulent contagion since their introduction in George Romero's 1963 *Night of the Living Dead*, itself an adaptation of the novel from a decade earlier *I Am Legend*. Indeed, my own quick survey on the Google Ngram viewer shows a steep incline in English-language mentions starting in the year that seminal slasher was released, amounting to a more than one thousand percent increase in the appearance of zombies in print by 2008, the last year surveyed.

In light of this explosion in zombie cultural production, but also in critical examinations of those cultural artefacts, it behooves us both to ask what zombies mean in late capitalist society *and* what it can possibly mean for zombies to mean something.

Such interpretations entail the critical use of zombies in particular or monsters in general as a metaphor for representing some aspect, usually socio-political, of society, such as when Henry Giroux writes that "the metaphor [of the zombie] is particularly apt for drawing attention to the ways in which political culture and power in American society now work in the interests of bare survival, if not disposability, for the vast majority of people."

This piece is excerpted from the afterword to the volume *Zombie Talk: Culture, History, Politics*. Eds. David R. Castillo, David Schmid, David A. Reilly, and John Edgar Browning, London: Palgrave, 2016. All quotes in the article are from this book.

For David Schmid, writing in a forthcoming volume on zombies, while monsters in general and zombies in particular can be read metaphorically as reminders of the monstrous aspects of neoliberalism, the concomitant risk such readings carry with them is that the very same monsters, in the "excessive visibility" of the "subjective violence" that they commit and that is committed against them, can blind us to the very real "objective violence" of a neoliberal political economy whose devastation continues unabated.

Yet, while zombies commit subjective violence in excessively visible ways on our screens, critically informed attention to their role on those screens and the appeal they generate need not be distracted by that visibility from the hidden but almost universal violence that is, using T. S. Eliot's term, their objective correlative. In other words, a reading attuned to such objective violence can give us clues as to how the undeniable *appeal* of zombies responds to an implicit knowledge on the part of the consumers of that hidden violence, and how the cloistered, suburban lives of late capitalist consumers rest uneasily over the shallow grave of abject multitudes. This is why the consumer class of the culture industry, on the one hand, seeks to erase the suffering legions produced by an economy of extraction, while, on the other, greedily devouring their avatars in fictional form.

In fact, it is exactly because zombies stand in such conflicted relation to the socio-historical reality they emerge from that they exert such a fascination on their consumers. As David Castillo puts it, "zombie masses are us in more ways than one: they are our dark mirror image, our sweat shops, our garbage, our landfills, our pollution, the face of globalization, an infinitely reproducible and exportable product of the mass-culture industry, and also, paradoxically, a built-in site of contestation against this same phenomenon."

This paradox is what lies at the heart of the cultural symptom, and what gives it its force. It represents the socio-historical reality at the same time as it articulates an unconscious knowledge and a concomitant desire. In this case that knowledge is that we are the agents of our own demise; like the slave Jacques Lacan spoke of bearing the order for his own execution tattooed to his scalp, our destruction is ensured by the very fulfillment of our functioning as autonomous consumers in a late capitalist economy. Zombies literalize that image in their relentless and cannibalistic drive to consume the human survivors; at the same time, as Dave Reilly has argued, the cells of human survivors evince the desire imbricated with that knowledge, a desire for freedom and self-determination from the economic forces that situate us as the agents of our own destruction. For as producers proudly turn to new technologies (including and even especially information technologies) to obviate the need for employees, those of us still employed happily purchase their products, thereby contributing to the very economy that, according to Martin Ford's analysis in *Rise of the Robots: Technology and the Threat of a Jobless Future*, will inevitably drive us to obsolescence as well.

In some ways, then, the ultimate zombie movie of the twenty-first century was a pre-millennial release that technically had no zombies in it. Nevertheless, the fantasy scenario painted by the 1999 film *The Matrix* firmly encapsulates the paradoxes and appeal of our fascination with the undead. For can it not be said that we, the citizens of the early twenty-first-century industrialized world, are like so many coppertop batteries, our brains plugged into a virtual world in which we live, play, and dream, while our bodies, that is, our economic livelihood, are kept on life-support to be drained dry in the service of that economy? Everything is constructed so that we avert our gaze from this reality. We become zombie consumers of media—zombies because we are animate without anima; we believe we are alive, real, autonomous, but in reality we are already dead, plugged into the relentless machine of capital hell-bent on our destruction.

07.06.2015

Gun Control or the End of Civilization

Jay M. Bernstein

Just the numbers are terrible. More Americans have been killed by a gun since 1970 than in all the wars America has fought since the American Revolution: roughly 1.5 million versus 1.4 million. On average 32,000 individuals are killed by gun each year, and in 2015 there was on average one mass shooting (a shooting involving four or more persons) a day.

The National Rifle Association's (NRA) relentless rejection of every gun control measure, including the proposal—supported by the vast majority of NRA members—of requiring background checks prior to the purchase of a gun, concerns more than the good of public safety versus the profits of the gun industry. At stake is whether America is about to break the great civilizational contract with its basic tenet that, in place of each individual judging and executing the law himself, we agree to hand over to the state a monopoly over the use of force. Whatever the failures of the modern state, and they abound, and whatever the excruciating failures of the American criminal justice system, the idea of the state possessing a monopoly over the use of force represents both the modern state's moral core and its enduring civilizational achievement.

The notion of a state monopoly over the use of force had its initial outing in John Locke's arguments for the state's right to punish. For Locke, the major inconvenience of the state of nature was that each man was entitled to be judge, jury, and executioner in his own case. Hence, leaving the state of nature entailed handing over the right of punishment to a central government. One might argue that the state's right to punish is weaker than the thesis that the state should have a monopoly over the use force. But what legitimate use of force might remain after the right to punish has been centralized?

It is, oddly and surprisingly, in Hans Kelsen's positivist legal philosophy that we catch the fiercest defense of the state having a monopoly over the use of force. In his 1944 *Peace Through Law*, Kelsen states that it is "an essential characteristic of the law as a coercive order to establish a community monopoly of force" since without such a monopoly individuals would be entitled to use force based solely on their private judgment. He then goes on to state that the "modern state is the most perfect type of a social order establishing a community monopoly of force. Its perfection is due to the centralization of the employment of force... Within the state, pacification of inter-individual relations—that is, *national* peace— is attained in the highest degree." He completes this elaboration thus: "Except under certain extraordinary circumstances, such as revolution or civil war, the employment of force is eliminated from the relations between citizens and reserved for central agencies... that are authorized to use force as sanctions against illegal acts."

Kelsen is aware that peace through law is both less than justice and not quite ideal: the long history of slavery, marital rape, domestic abuse, police interrogation methods, and brutal prison regimes all represent areas of tolerated violence against the person. Nonetheless, it is his claim that the very idea of a legal-state, a state under law, the *absolute minimum conception of a modern state* involves a monopoly over the legitimate use of force. Force, he argues, is either a delict, a wrong, or a sanction for a wrong; the idea of force being either delict or sanction must be exhaustive if the threat of force is going to be removed for ordinary social interactions. To give up on that idea is to give up on the notion of a legal order altogether, to relinquish the hope that we might secure *mutual trust* among the vast majority of law-abiding citizens by having reasonable confidence that there is a system of protection against criminal activity and that when such activity occurs those responsible will be apprehended and punished, with each act of punishment involving a mix of retribution, deterrence, and collective expression.

Yet, *tacitly* in the NRA's opposition to all proposals for gun control, *tacitly* in the suggestion that it is the right of every citizen to keep and bear arms, and *explicitly* in the statements of Republican candidates for presidency that the best solution to gun violence is for all citizens to be armed, this minimum conception of the modern state has come under direct threat. I am unsure when, precisely, our national conversation about gun control shifted from a debate about the meaning of the Second Amendment to, in effect, a debate about whether or not we are committed to the civilizational contract prohibiting punitive self-help. But my sense is that the conversation has now shifted, that, through small concessions and failures of collective action, it has become about something more like the shape and limits of a self-policing society than one about the right of gun ownership in a society where there remains a state monopoly on the use of force.

Of course, there is more than a hint of anxiety about state monopoly over the use of force in the Second Amendment. But even the most vociferous defense of that amendment understood it not as a challenge to the state monopoly over the use of force, but as a component of the right to self-defense. That wedge, the needs of self-defense, has become a wrecking ball, and we should have seen it coming. If the NRA were serious about self-defense but not about abandoning the civilization contract, then there would be no reason for them to resist background checks, making combat weapons and high caliber arms illegal, or, clearly the most promising proposal around, the development of guns that require PIN numbers or fingerprint activation devices. That all these propositions are repudiated as a threat to gun ownership should alert us to what the stakes of the conversation now are.

I hope it is obvious that peace is a great civil good, and that a form of life in which peace is central to its self-conception involves the deepest respect for the freedom and bodily integrity of each and every citizen. Whatever other goods are necessary for a worthwhile life and whatever other rights we require as citizens, we *minimally* require, in Kelsen's words, "mutual conduct" in which all "refrain from forcibly depriving one another of life, health, freedom, or property." Such is the condition of peace made possible by a state monopoly over force: "Law and force must not be understood as absolutely at variance with each other. Law is an organization of force." To be committed to law in this sense is to be committed to a form of life. It is just this form of life that is under immanent threat in America today.

03.07.2016

Is Ours a Post-Utopia World?

Patrícia Vieira

It is five hundred years since Thomas More published his book *Utopia* in Leuven, Belgium, under the patronage of his fellow humanist Erasmus. The text is a fictional account of an island nation more perfect than the conflict-ridden European countries of the time, rife with inequality and corruption. Utopian society practiced communal ownership and religious tolerance, came close to gender parity and strove to provide for the well-being of all its citizens. A word coined by More based upon Greek, the term *utopia*—meaning "no place" (ou-topos) or, in an alternative interpretation, "good place" (eu-topos)—came to signify an idealized perfect community that does not exist in the present and whose coming into being is often projected into the future.

After enjoying great success and spawning a veritable avalanche of proposals for perfect societies in the centuries that followed, utopia has, of late, acquired something of a bad rap. Perhaps this had to do with the understanding of communism as the ultimate utopia. The creation of a classless society where all workers shared in the decision-making process about and in the profits of their labor, therefore being able substantially to reduce the amount of time spent in useless toil, seemed to be the culmination of centuries of utopian thought. But the results of actually existing communism disheartened many supports of utopianism. From Stalin's purges to the massacres perpetrated by the Cambodian Khmer Rouge, historical communism fell short of its theoretical ideal.

Five hundred years after the creation of utopia, is it time to finally ditch the concept and get real? Many thinkers believe so. In his ominously titled volume *Black Mass. Apocalyptic Religion and the Death of Utopia* British philosopher John Gray, for instance, argues that utopias work as normative models used to justify violent acts perpetrated by religious or political groups and concludes that they necessarily lead to totalitarian political regimes. French philosopher Jean-Luc Nancy also distances himself from utopian thought in an interview published in my co-edited book *Existential Utopia*. For Nancy, utopia is, at best, a beautiful albeit unreachable fantasy and, at worst, a distraction from our efforts to address real problems.

In literature, as in philosophy and political thought, utopia seems to have been replaced by much bleaker views on society. While the focus used to be on imagining a better community in a different place, at a future time, or both, the twentieth century witnessed the rise of dystopian narratives. From George Orwell's *1984* (1949) to the popular *Hunger Games* trilogy (2008-10) by Suzanne Collins, from catastrophic climate change scenarios like the one described in J. G. Ballard's *The Drought* (1965) to gender-relations nightmares such as Margaret Atwood's *The Handmaid's* Tale (1985), dystopias are here to stay. To be sure, dystopian thought shares utopia's goal of criticizing present society. But while utopias show how the world can be improved by comparing it to a better one, dystopias draw attention to the ills of our time by exacerbating them, imagining what would happen if our worst fears came true.

It is worth pondering the reasons for our move into a post-utopian world. Utopia feeds upon what German thinker Ernst Bloch called the "principle of hope," the idea that the current situation can improve thanks to human ingenuity. It is not by chance that the concept was born at the dawn of modernity. Utopian thought is tied to a linear understanding of time and to a belief in human-led progress towards an increasingly perfect polity, ideas that started to coalesce during the Renaissance. Unlike utopia, dystopia has abandoned the "principle of hope." Remaining at the deconstructive, destructive level, it pointedly criticizes the problems of our time without offering alternative options or possible solutions. It is a fitting corollary, in the sphere of the imagination and of speculative thought, to a society on the verge of ecological disaster. If utopia signaled the belief in new beginnings, dystopia belongs in a world that sees itself as being not only at the end of history but at the end of all existence.

What are the political implications of abandoning the "principle of hope" and of embracing dystopia as our official creed? Current technocratic democracies are one possible instantiation of a politics of hopelessness. Economic imperatives determine political choices made by a managerial class of legislators. Instead of real decisions about the common good, a concept that, in and of itself, should be open to debate, politics is reduced to the administration of the status quo. We are told that our lives cannot be otherwise and political action is turned into a mere reaction to events—the 2008 economic crisis, climate change, and so on. The current "business as usual" model of politics prevalent in the European Union is an example of hopelessness turned into technocracy, as was the political platform of Hillary Clinton in the US elections. Promising nothing but a continuation of the same, a glaring unwillingness or inability to tackle current problems, both the European Union and Clinton were jolted out of complacency by the Brexit vote in the UK and by the victory of Donald Trump in the US.

The correlation between the Brexit and Trump phenomena has been pointed out by a variety of commentators. They represent an alternative instantiation of the politics of hopelessness that I would define as authoritarian reactionarism. Though arising from the same wellspring as technocracy, authoritarian reactionarism does not defend the status quo but advocates instead for its overhaul. Still, its seemingly radical political action—the UK leaving the EU; the US building a wall on its Southern border and preventing Muslims from entering the country, etc.—does not spell out real political change. Corporate interests will remain intact after Brexit, and the billionaire Donald Trump is clearly not interested in lifting destitute Americans out of poverty. Political action is in this case also a reaction, albeit not so much to current events, as in technocracy, but to hopelessness itself.

The rise of authoritarian figures within other democratic regimes around the world—Recep Erdoğan in Turkey, Rodrigo Duterte in the Philippines—is a political expression of the electorate's hopelessness that leads it to turn to extreme figures and ideology when all else has failed. The enduring popularity of Vladimir Putin in his native Russia is, *mutatis mutandis*, another expression of a hopeless political climate. As Russians so often acknowledge, Putin is bad but the alternative could be much worse.

Straightjacketed between technocracy and authoritarian reactionarism, between hopeless, reactive stasis and hopeless, reactionary change, we would do well to go back to More and his five hundred-year-old utopia. The communitarian society he described might bring back some hope to a world in dire need of the belief that a better future is still possible.

28.11.2016

The Politics of Hope and Fear

Hasana Sharp

Emotions are contagious. Because everyone feels this, everyone knows this. When philosophers refer to humans as social animals, part of what they mean is that there is an irrepressible mimetic aspect to our psychic and physical existence (of course, as Aristotle observed, this is true of many animals). We cannot but imitate others, transmit feelings to others and undergo their feelings. This is how we learn, love, and grow. Whether we are affected by others, or whether we affect them escapes our control. This makes possible circuits of care and knowledge, as well as circuits of abuse and illusion.

This communicability of affect is often a cause for concern, however, especially in the domain of politics. We worry that people can be made to feel anything by a successful manipulator. Media are blamed for rendering "us" both increasingly afraid and increasingly inured to violence. It is not the case, however, that charismatic figures or the "media" simply implant the feelings they intend into masses of people. Artists, teachers, orators, commanders, and politicians aspire to move masses in certain ways, but the masses—that is, we—are only sometimes and unpredictably responsive. Of course, seats of power and widely circulating representations matter, but the general public is not the passive effect of them. Who and what gets uptake depends upon the incalculably diverse passions and actions of a vast multitude.

The current election prompts acute attention to the emotional medium of politics. Candidate Donald Trump stokes the fears of audience, such that fear and xenophobia are now synonymous with official Republican party platform. In contrast, Hillary Clinton heralds a message of hope, elaborating Barack Obama's branding of himself and the Democratic party as forces of steady progress and optimism. We are told that the political "choice" is between fear and hope. But feeling is not something we select at a ballot box. Emotions are not objects in circulation that we might pick up or put down. And, as Benedict de Spinoza (1632-1677) once remarked, "there is neither hope without fear, nor fear without hope."

The political polarity of hope and fear is traditional. Spinoza is among the many political thinkers of the Renaissance and early modern period to reflect upon political emotions and government, as well as upon the government of political emotions. Like Hobbes and Machiavelli, he picks out fear as an especially salient collective feeling to which those in government must be acutely sensitive. Those engaged in the arts of government—ideological as well as repressive—must be aware of how they galvanize fears, such as the fear of punishment. A state depends for its existence upon fear of its "sword." States by necessity strive to move their own subjects toward obedience and other peoples toward alliance or submission. No party or candidate can govern without operationalizing fear.

Yet the fears at play in the government are not only those of its subjects. Governments exist only as long as subjects are, as Spinoza says, "attached" to them, admiring their constitution, laws, and leaders. Governors must fear the dissolution of popular support. The various institutions of government stoke and mobilize fears, but also feel and respond to their own fears. Thus, as we watch the election unfold, which is, in essence, a series of calls for popular support, we ought to be reminded not just of the power of aspirant leaders to shape our future, but of how our hopes and fears can be a source of leverage against government. So when increasingly many subjects fear law enforcement agents as executors of arbitrary violence, detention, and deprivation, the admiration for the law upon which the state depends is threatened. This fear can be a source of power. It should not simply be replaced with the hope, however audacious, that moderates will rise to power and restrain the repressive state apparatus. We should not assuage the government's fears nor should we relax our fear of government agents.

This is not a call for fear. Nor is it in any way a defense of "the party of fear"—indeed, there is no one party of fear. It is an observation—or rather, a Spinoza-guided conviction—that political life is structured necessarily by a complex dynamic of affective communication, in which fear and hope play key roles. Let us discuss the dynamic of affective communication, while recognizing that we cannot hope to be freed from fear from above. So, at least as much as we talk about how our aspirant leaders make us feel, we should be talking about how we want to make them feel. The question is not about choosing between hope or fear. And it is not only about what we ought to hope for or what we ought to fear. Let's ask, while they're paying attention and every day afterward, what kinds of hopes and fears we want to inspire in our governors.

29.08.2016

Algorithms of Taste

Daniel Innerarity

The cultural section of newspapers is one of the traditional bastions of criticism. It is here that books, music and theater plays are reviewed and judged. We are all aware that the Internet has changed the nature of newspapers, and that the advent of the "digital realm" has had a major impact on the function of criticism as a cultural practice. For some time now, criticism has ceased to be something carried out by professional critics, and the plethora of forums, blogs, and other platforms all contribute to generating a dense murmur of ongoing assessment.

Whereas before we turned to Bloom, Pivot, or Reich-Ranicki for literary reviews, to Parker for an expert opinion on wine, the Michelin Guide for sage advice about fine dining, and official dictionaries for general information about our language and spelling, we now check what Tripadvisor has to say, read the recommendations of Spotfire and Amazon, and use automatic spell checkers in all our writing tasks. In the open, amorphous space of the web and social media, with a simple click of the "like button", people pass vague, non-specific judgments backed up by no explanations or qualifiers.

On the Internet, nothing is safe from a rejoinder. Any news report or expert opinion is open to comments and criticism from anyone. Our tastes are no longer defined in the vertical space of authority, but in the midst of a Babel of voices in which the view of an expert is just one amongst many, supported or opposed by the opinions of other experts, connoisseurs, enthusiasts, and even simple users. In this transformed context, the function of a "critic" as someone responsible for defining good taste, laying down canons, and deciding what is (and what is not) culturally valuable seems, at best, unnecessary, if not downright ridiculous.

Thus, the hierarchy of the media begins to wobble, and the high priests (the critics) are in danger of falling from their pedestals. Expert knowledge is no longer something static that can only be found in one specific place, but rather something fluid, flowing through a wide range of diverse channels.

All this has given rise to a heated debate between two diametrically opposed groups: those who applaud the new online era, characterized by the democratization of criticism and taste; and those who lament the loss of individual sovereignty.

For the first group, democratization is the logical consequence of the fact that, thanks to the Internet, the general public has now recovered something that had been taken away from it and announced in the cultural sections of newspapers as a kind of Official Gazette, laying down the laws of culture. We are no longer living in the golden age of criticism, when supreme authorities were the only bridge over the abyss that separated high culture from the masses. Nowadays, anyone can pass judgment in matters of taste. Critics abounding on the web, as well as the possibility of being able to post a comment on a news article, have opened up an arena for debate and protest that, despite being oftentimes banal, have the effect of undermining the authority of the original written word. The emergence of the figure of an unqualified commentator has introduced an element of horizontality into a medium that was built on the basis of an eminently vertical structure. The public arena has become fragmented, broken up into taste-based communities, and there is no longer any authority capable of imposing one single canon to which everyone must adhere.

From the other side of the fence, negative views of this new era have given rise to a wide variety of arguments, ranging from those that complain about banality to those that herald imminent doom and complex conspiracy theories. In our everyday lives, our judgments and tastes are formed by recommendations compiled by aggregation algorithms ("customers who bought this, also… "). Consumers are kings, and any suggestions made to them are based on an attempt to guess their preferences. Is there any better example of sovereignty? And yet, can good taste be based solely on what we already like?

Critics of the Internet include those who denounce a logic which, instead of broadening our horizons, simply confirms our prejudices, as well as those who espouse the apocalyptic visions of having discovered a sinister conspiracy that lurks behind this apparently amiable wooing of online customers. To my mind, what people who make both these arguments fail to understand, is that the whole process is at the same time dialectical and ambivalent, as it opens the doors to future developments that may ensure greater freedom and more information.

They also seem to have forgotten the existence of filters, without which we could not possibly survive in an environment that is so densely saturated with information. We cannot hope to defend our online independence unless we strive to understand the nature of these filters and learn to manage them. And what's more, these filters can always be improved: they can be rendered more neutral or better able to specify our chosen selection criteria.

Can we conclude, then, that algorithm-based advice to users has rendered criticism in the traditional sense unnecessary? Surely not. For a start, because the proliferation of these procedures does not spell out the death of criticism. Quite the opposite, in fact: The critics have multiplied. There is now *more* criticism, not less, with all that this increase entails. The Internet has triggered a huge rise in criticism: People write hitherto unimaginable reams of reviews on all manner of things, covering an immense range of tastes and qualities in accordance with different niches. In this quagmire of opinions, the media has indeed lost its old monopolistic position, or, in other words, its power to regulate access to the public discourse and set the terms, conditions, and main players of cultural debate.

The general public has taken a firm hold of the reins of its own sphere of attention. However, this context also offers criticism the chance to return to what it once was: a set of judgments issued by experts who do not limit themselves to merely recording or reproducing dominant tastes, but who rather take us out of our comfort zone with new, unexpected proposals. Experts who do not focus on any one particular reader or customer, but, instead, strive to say something with a universal value. In this way, critics could free themselves of the shackles of having to tell users what, at heart, they already know.

03.16.2015

B. Rights and Wrongs

Why Human Rights Are So Often Unenforced?

Michael Gillespie

Imagine you are walking through the woods with a hunting rifle and come upon a clearing where two terrorists with large swords are about to cut the heads off ten hostages. You realize your only chance to save them is to kill the two terrorists—what would you do?

Now imagine a similar scenario in which a birdwatcher with a camera runs up to you and says "Two hundred meters ahead of you, there are two terrorists with swords about to kill ten hostages, you need to save them." What would you do then? In the first instance, almost everyone recognizes that they have a moral duty to save the innocent and can be convinced that they should kill the terrorists.

Most don't want to do it, but they recognize that morally they have to do so. Once they admit their moral responsibility in the first case, they almost invariably accept their responsibility in the second case, even with the added two hundred meter walk. But once they do, it is difficult for them to deny their responsibility in a third and much more realistic case: "Right now somewhere in the world there are ten hostages about to be murdered by terrorists and you are obligated to save or at least try to save them." At this point almost everyone becomes very reluctant to agree. They recognize their moral responsibility and yet don't like the conclusion that they have been led to. They feel that it is wrong but at the same time they have a great deal of trouble explaining why they are unwilling to do what their own moral sensibilities tell them they should do.

Why do they hesitate? It can't just be the greater distance, since that would suggest that there is some measurable space within which we have moral responsibility. It also can't be that we can't save everyone in such situations, because that doesn't prevent us from saving some of them. Moreover, acting collectively through our governments and NGOs we can almost certainly save many. It also can't be because we might be making a mistake or might make things worse, since error is possible in every situation. In the original scenario, for example, the "terrorists" and "victims" might simply have been filming a movie. In that case you may have tragically killed two innocents but neither the law nor your own conscience would tell you you had acted wrongly or immorally.

It also can't be because the sovereign state in which this scenario takes place doesn't want you there, since the "terrorists" may in fact be agents of that state itself. There is no moral difference between a terrorist state and individual terrorists. It also can't be that it costs too much, since it is hard to imagine anyone seriously arguing that their big screen TV is worth more than a human life. What then is going on?

The liberal democratic order of the Western world is rooted in a notion of rights. These rights have corresponding duties, but these duties in the first instance are merely negative—I have a duty not to violate your rights and we enter into an agreement (explicit or implicit) to set up and enforce a system of rules to protect these rights. The group that is formed may be small or large but that agreement imposes a moral burden upon me to defend others' rights. But not the rights of all others, only those within my group.

But what of the rights of those outside my group? What of the human rights of those in the rest of the world? I am certainly obligated not to violate their rights, but do I have an obligation to defend them from those who violate them? Here is where our moral reasoning begins to stumble and where we see the first glimmerings of the fundamental differences between the moral and the political. Christianity asserted that it was a sacred duty to love, protect, and care for one's neighbor and this doctrine remains strong in the modern secular West.

Who are our neighbors? And how far does our neighborhood extend? Certainly to our immediate family, and most likely to our extended family and friends. We at least feel some kinship in these situations. Perhaps to a somewhat lesser extent to our fellow believers or to other members of our ethnic group, although here many would raise questions. In large states, legally but almost certainly not affectively, to all of our fellow citizens. But what about foreigners, resident aliens, or strangers? In these cases we are much less willing to provide positive assistance. They do not feel like our neighbors and while we generally recognize their basic humanity and our duty not to violate their rights, we also generally are unwilling to come to their assistance, at least not unless it is in our interest to do so.

The world, however, is shrinking. Globalization and particularly a globalized media make even the most distant places seem near, bringing the victims of violence into our living rooms on a daily (or even hourly) basis. They seem nearer to us in many respects than the ten victims in our second example. We are thus increasingly unwilling to say, "Thank God we do not live in such a place," and increasingly more likely to say "Something must be done." And given the globalization of our interests we are much more likely to do something, or to let our government do something. But the mixture of our motives, the conflict between our legitimate desire to fulfill our moral duty and the suspicion that our moral claims merely mask a rapacious self-interest is inevitable.

The notion of the universality of human rights is morally undeniable but the idea of defending such rights requires a step beyond mere non-interference that leaves us hopelessly entangled in questions of our own motivations and reemphasizes the enduring differences of morality and politics.

07.20.2015

On Privacing

RICHARD POLT

Was privacy—as an idea and a reality—only a brief interlude, available to a few prosperous, modern Westerners? They could afford rooms of their own where they might experience genuine solitude, solitude without the certainty that family, society, government, or God were looking over their shoulder. But now that we have invented an artificial God, seemingly omnipresent and omniscient, such solitude is scarce. "A child born today," warns Edward Snowden, "will grow up with no conception of privacy at all." Coming generations will inhabit a world where (to quote Dave Eggers's *The Circle*) "all that happens must be known."

As I was researching the use of typewriters in the 21st century for my book *The Typewriter Revolution*, I learned that these humble devices are used by the Kremlin and MI6 to outwit the most sophisticated espionage techniques. No hacker can remotely access a typescript in a filing cabinet. Citizens, too, turn to typewriters when they want to communicate securely: although our government scans the exterior of every envelope, its contents remain relatively safe, and the typewritten letter you open from your friend has probably been read only by you and her.

Such quaint artifacts as postal letters have new significance in a time when free, instant, global, indelible publishing is available to us all—when the default setting for our existence is public, so much so that the term "publishing" has begun to sound obsolete. What we need in a time of consummate publicity is *privacing*: deliberate steps to create pockets of privacy in our overexposed lives.

Privacing is more than simply ensuring that information won't fall into the wrong hands. Obviously, we don't want thieves to use our credit cards. We all have something to hide from someone. But by the same token, the self-styled forces of good can always promise to protect us from those who would misuse our data. And if we don't trust the forces of good—what's wrong with us? What do we have to hide?

Even if we have nothing to be ashamed of, and even if those who store and analyze our data are just as secure and benevolent as they claim to be, we have lost something when we behave in a way that is open to such analysis. With the sense that our words and acts are under constant, automatic surveillance, we tend, consciously or not, to polish our persona, to behave as we want others to see us behaving. Whether we want to be perceived as harmless nobodies, as glamorous winners, or as fearless rebels, to be seen—and not to be—becomes our priority.

Privacing is not the protection of information, but the choice of being over seeming. It happens whenever we find occasions to have experiences that will be meaningful even if no one else ever learns of them, even if we tell no one about them, even if we take them with us to that place that so few secrets today survive long enough to reach: our grave.

Privacing can take the form of writing with a secure, nondigital tool, writing that need not be communicated to anyone. Privacing can consist in making music that is never recorded, sketching a scene and tearing up the sketch, or sinking into a novel that you read on that insensitive and oblivious old medium, paper. Privacing takes place when you explore an empty beach or a busy city without making any external record—nothing that could be published at all—but only your memories.

In her wistful reflection on "the day of the postman," Rebecca Solnit writes that our digitized lives inhabit "a shallow between two deep zones, a safe spot between the dangers of contact with ourselves, with others." Ever exchanging images with our accumulating "friends," we drift away from love and from self. Privacing not only reacquaints you with yourself but also opens doors to intimacy, should you choose to mail your letter or tell someone about your walk on the beach.

Privacing can even serve as a source of ideas that you choose to make public in a deliberate and thoughtful way, restoring significance to the word "publishing"—as when some of today's typists "typecast" by posting images of their typescripts online.

Playwright and filmmaker Patrick Wang describes the heart of privacing on his typecast blog. Turning off his divisive devices —"expert dividers, of our attention, our understandings, our lives"—Wang establishes "digital quiet": "But then in my mind, all things begin to flash and cry for attention. Enough abandoned memories to trip over, today's passions beginning to smoke. It appears the housework of the soul has gone neglected. There is a chaos demanding a worthy opponent. There is feeling looking for form. God, even without our devices, we were already in pieces. But with time and the spaciousness of solitude, we can pull ourselves together."

Who knows? We may even manage to keep the concept of privacy alive a bit longer.

12.14.2015

One Child: Do we Have a Right to More?

Sarah Conly

We need to talk about population. If you are like most people, you don't want to. But the truth is that at present, given the danger of environmental disaster, we don't have the right to have more than one child, and this is something that needs to be discussed. We're not living sustainably with our present population of 7.3 billion, and the United Nations' most recent estimate is that our numbers will reach 9.7 billion by 2050, and then a hard-to-imagine 11.2 billion by 2100. And this is when the global average for women is to have about two children. Yes, population would eventually stabilize, but if it becomes stable at an astronomically high number it will still be a disaster. This isn't something we have a right to bring about.

Almost no one wants to interfere with people having children. A common reaction is to say it just isn't a problem. Critics dismiss fears about overpopulation as "neo-Malthusian." The idea is that since Thomas Malthus was wrong in 1798 when he wrote that population would soon outgrow food production, the current gloomy estimates about population are also wrong. However, we are obviously better at science than we were in 1798. Demographers at the U.N. aren't a lot of mad-eyed tree-huggers. They are scientists, whose job in life is to study fertility trends around the world. If they say 9.7 billion by 2050, they didn't pull that figure out of a hat. Meanwhile, the International Panel on Climate Change, also a pretty reputable organization, has said that we need to cut back our emissions between 40 and 70% to keep global warming within 2° Celsius. That's a lot. It's going to be hard enough to do with the number of people we have now, but almost unimaginable with 11.2 billion, or even the more modest 9.7 billion we'll have by 2050—within the lifetime of many who are living today.

So what should we do? This is the question I address in *One Child: Do We Have a Right to More?* (Oxford University Press, 2016.) Some have realized that rising population is a danger. The problem is that they have found themselves without a solution, because they believe that people have a right to have as many children as they want, and so there is nothing we can do. Instead of focusing on population, they concentrate on reducing consumption.

Reducing consumption is, of course, a good idea for those of us who can do it (which isn't everyone. Cutting back just isn't an option for the one third of the world who live in absolute poverty, and who direly need more stuff, not less.) All the evidence, though, is that we just won't cut back. Since the 1997 Kyoto Protocol, with its relatively modest goal of reducing the emission of greenhouse gases by 5% relative to 1990 by 2012, we have, as a planet, increased emissions significantly—in an age where we *know* the effects of consumption. Will we do better when we need to cut back at least 40%?

Having more than one child when we know that consumption won't be significantly reduced is like throwing a match on a house soaked with gasoline. It's not the match alone that does the damage, but if you know the gasoline is there, and then you throw the match, you have done something you don't have a right to do.

At the same time, we have shown that we are willing to cut back on how many children we have. The fertility rate has, after all, fallen over the past decades, simply because many people prefer to have fewer children. What we need to do now is accelerate that process.

But again, won't this violate rights?

No. The truth is that there is no reason to think we have a right to have more than one child. Sometimes we say we have a right to what we need for basic subsistence, which is why many people think that we have a right to food. Fair enough—but this doesn't give us a right to more than one child, because of course we can live good lives with just one child. We do want the human race to continue, which gives us a reason to have children, and we have a basic interest in equal treatment, which would give each of us an equal right to have a child, but we certainly don't need more than one child for that interest to be met.

Other people will say that we have more general rights—rights to live our lives as we want. We have a right to live according to our own values, to make our own life plans. Again, fair enough. But this only goes so far. As Oliver Wendell Holmes said, my right to swing my fist ends at the other man's nose. The right to live as you want doesn't mean you can live in a way that does dire harm to others. When the world wasn't threatened with catastrophic climate change, soil depletion, over-fishing, the extinction of species, and a growing shortage of fresh water, you could suit yourself when it came to deciding how many children to have. That's not the world we're in, though, and when circumstances change we need to change what we do.

Does this mean we must allow forced abortions and sterilizations? No. Those are assaults, and do violate rights. They are also completely unnecessary. All the evidence is that we can change the fertility rate with a combination of incentives and disincentives. We can educate. We can make contraception free and easy to get. We can reward having fewer children with tax breaks, or disincentivize having more with tax penalties. These are likely to be successful measures, but one of the things we need to talk about is how best to discourage people from having too many children. To do that, though, we need to address the problem, and we need to start now.

02.15.2016

Social Media and the Lack of Consent

KELLY OLIVER

Social media such as Facebook, Snapchat, and Tinder were invented as part of a culture that objectifies and denigrates girls and women. It is well known that the Facebook founder and Harvard graduate, now one of the richest men in the country, invented the social media site Facebook to post pictures of girls for his college buddies to rate and berate. Reportedly, Evan Spiegel, Stanford graduate and inventor of Snapchat, sent messages during his days in a fraternity referring to women as "bitches," "sororis-luts" to be "peed on," and discussed getting girls drunk to have sex with them. And the founders of the wildly popular hook-up site Tinder were both involved in a sexual harassment suit involving their former Vice President of marketing, who claims she received harassing sexist messages calling her a "slut," a "gold-digger," and a "whore."

Given the continued use of social media to target, harass, and humiliate young women, it is telling that these technologies were born out of sexist attitudes. In their inception, some of the most popular social media sites were designed to denigrate women. Of course, lots of social media sites, like other forms of traditional media, bank on pictures of attractive girls and women looking sexy or cute, along with pornographic images. Creepshot sites in particular are a telling example of a new phenomenon, namely, the valorization and popularization of lack of consent.

"Creepshots" are photographs of women's bodies taken without their consent. Lack of consent is essential, as is outlined on websites that specialize in creepshots such as tumblr's *creepshooter, creepshots. com*, and metareddit's *creepshots*, which insists photos must not be posed and should not be taken with the subject's knowledge. Clearly, girls and women are seen as unsuspecting "targets," prey to be "shot" and "captured" on film. Some creepshot videos end up on pornographic sites.

Creepshots are explicitly valued because of the lack of consent on the part of the subjects. Indeed, insofar as they are unaware they are being photographed, subjects of creepshots cannot give consent... unless women moving through the world in their everyday activities wearing their everyday clothes (see *yoga pants* as a subcategory of creepshots) constitute consent, as if women were public property.

The same valorization of lack of consent can be seen on college campuses, especially in fraternity culture where chants and signs endorsing sexual assault with unconscious women, and fraternity Facebook sites filled with pictures of unsuspecting naked or partially clothed women, have become commonplace. For example, in 2010 at Yale, fraternity brothers marched around the freshman dorms chanting, "No means yes, yes means anal." In 2013, a fraternity at St. Mary's University in Halifax welcome new students: "SMU boys, we like them young. Y is for your sister, O is for oh so tight, U is for underage, N is for no consent, G is for grab that ass," and a fraternity was suspended from Texas Tech for flying a banner that read "No Means Yes." That same year, another frat was suspended at Georgia Tech for distributing an email with the subject line "Luring your *rapebait*," which ended, "I want to see everyone succeed at the next couple parties." And, in 2014 at William and Mary, fraternity members sent around an email message, "never mind the extremities that surround it, the 99% of horrendously illogical bullshit that makes up the modern woman, consider only the 1%, the snatch." Last year a fraternity at Virginia's Old Dominion was sanctioned for posting sexist signs, including "Drop off your freshman daughter here." The list goes on and on.

These examples suggest an aggressive campaign on the part of some fraternities to insist "No" means "Yes," and consent is not only irrelevant, but also undesired. In the St. Mary's chant, lack of consent is openly valued, "N is for no consent." Actively seeking sex without consent, sometimes even admitting it is rape, is what they claim they want. Whatever their actual desires, these college men are *saying* that they want nonconsensual sex.

Fraternities around the country have been sanctioned for posting creepshot photographs of unconscious naked or semi-clothed women, some in embarrassing sexual positions. The women involved did not know or consent, and some of these photographs may be evidence of sexual assault or nonconsensual sex, as well as illegal in their own right. Obviously, these fraternity boys think that pictures of naked women and their body parts, circulated to hundreds on Facebook, are fun and funny.

In the highly visible cases of Steubenville and Vanderbilt, along with the rapes, taking creepshot photographs of unconscious naked girls or women and distributing these were an important part of the sexual assaults. The boys and men smiled and clowned for the camera, joked and jeered for posterity, and took pleasure not only in sexually abusing their victims, but also in capturing it on film, and then sharing it with friends. Reportedly, in the Vanderbilt case, Corey Batey told Brandon Vandenburg to "get this on camera," as he assaulted their unconscious victim. Serial rapists and sexual predators who seek out vulnerable girls, drug them, or prey on intoxicated girls, and then view their rapes as conquests, are increasingly photographing them as a new form of trophy.

While boys and men bragging about their sexual exploits is not new, posting "creepshot" pictures on social media is. While rape and debasement of women are not new, the use of social media to do so is. The use of ubiquitous cellphone cameras to take creepshots of unsuspecting women makes it clear that contemporary mainstream youth culture values lack of consent. In other words, it is not just that some men will take pictures, or have sex, without a woman's consent, but also that photographs and "sex" are valued more where there is no consent. Of course, this makes an unconscious woman the perfect subject for creepshots and sexual assault.

Candid camera, and humor in humiliating photos, has been around since photography itself, and so has the penetration of pornographic images into mainstream culture. If men and boys used to secretly share pictures of naked women, now they do so publicly. And whereas, in the past, pornographic images were produced for mass consumption but sold privately, even wrapped in brown paper, and only to adults, now the Internet is filled with selfie porn, sexting photos, and creepshots. Rapists hamming for the camera, and taking creepshots of unconscious girls, are part and parcel of the patriarchal pornutopia in the age of social media.

04.18.2016

Universities' Bureaucratic Rule

Ágnes Heller

University has not always been the unwieldy bureaucratic machine that it is now. From the end of the eighteenth century onwards, European gymnasiums and universities were supposed to establish norms of social behavior, instill in students ethical concepts, as well as sound judgments of taste, and develop codes of honor for practicing one's trade. On the one hand, they offered education in the art of living; in Berlin, the closing words Hegel uttered to his students in their last class on the history of philosophy were "I wish you to live a good life". On the other hand, they became essential for the creation of a bourgeois and national identity, allied to good scientific training in the then developing nation states.

The task of the university was to form a new bourgeois elite that served simultaneously as a cultural elite. Ranks inherited at birth were replaced by social classes, and wealthy parents, even if uneducated, wanted their sons (and, later, daughters) to receive a good education. Whereas in the United States intellectuals did not enjoy great prestige, they did in Europe. Not all diplomas had the same worth, but political leadership required one, preferably issued by a respected faculty, such as Law.

As class societies were slowly transformed into mass societies, the old bourgeois forms of life crumbled, and the so-called civilizing process stopped or was even reversed. The task of universities in mass societies was no longer to prepare students for living a decent, good life.

Because of this social transformation, the mission of universities assumed a paradoxical form. The modern society is a functional society, which means that the kind of education appropriate to it is one that allows students to establish their places in the social hierarchy by performing a function. Thus, in our mass societies, institutions of higher education, especially elite universities, teach the performance of the better-paid functions.

Three tendencies characterize modern education, especially at the university level: first, the loss of academic authority; second, a special school certificate as the entry ticket of most positions; and, third, bureaucratization.

First, liberalization. As a result of the 1968 student-movement, students acquired the ability to participate in the life of their school. They can choose among schoolbooks, among subject matters; at universities, they can also choose their classes and their professors. The power of a professor depends more on his or her *personal* authority than before, and that authority depends on the professors' teaching style and their ability to establish human relations with students.

This development, namely, the liberalization of universities and the greater power of students, which is desirable in and of itself, went together with some, in my mind, less desirable outcomes. Several new subject matters without significant academic worth were included in the curriculum, partly due to political correctness, partly due to the students' wish to get a grade without mental effort, and finally due to the goal of some teachers to get an academic position at all.

The second tendency that gained momentum was to tie many occupations and positions to a certificate from universities or, at least, to a high school certificate. Several occupations that were well practiced without degrees or certificates, cannot be practiced without them now, even if those certificates do not prove that their holders are more able to perform the task in question. Many young men and women, who do not need a diploma or certificate at all, must spend many years in schools, where they study something they could learn just by practicing the skill, or learn something they cannot use at all. They just need a piece of paper as a condition to be employed.

Finally, the last thirty or forty years witnessed an unprecedented growth of bureaucracy in the university system and in many institutions of research. Peter Murphy showed statistically that, whereas in the 1980s universities all around the globe spent 40 percent of their funds on bureaucracy, by now they spend 60 percent of all their funds on it. Thus, less than half of the funding remains for everything else, student stipends and professor salaries included. From this, it follows that growing tuition fees are not spent on education, but on the upkeep of administration. The main task of professors is no longer to teach but to fill out hundreds of papers, to document all their actions and the actions of their students. I presume that in all universities at least ten, if not more, people are hired to create useless questionnaires, to collect answers from professors, to group them, and to give a report on them. Why? For no other reason than to keep bureaucracy growing and swallowing up all the rest.

What can be the reason behind this unreason? The total loss of trust in personal honesty. Everyone needs to be controlled many times over. At a mass university there are so many students that one cannot know them, nor talk to them. One can only "process" or register them. Moreover, it is presumed that students do not enroll in order to learn something, to hear something that interests them, but for the sole reason of getting a good job in order to earn considerable amounts of money. Since motivations cannot be controlled and tested except through a mind-reading machine, administration controls what can be controlled, namely the data. As if the data could tell anything about motives!

All this is not meant as an indictment against mass universities, much less as a defense of traditional universities. But what I strongly suggest, by way of reforming institutions of higher learning, is to get rid of half of the bureaucracy and to vest more trust into individuals. From the money at the university's disposal much more should be spent on student grants and stipends. I suggest more freedom for students and young faculty to develop their best abilities, to pursue their potentials and talents. I would also suggest more concern for general culture, or for what can be termed "universalism".

Surely, at a music school, a violin student must concentrate on learning how to play well; at a science faculty, a chemistry student must learn the principles of scientific inquiry, and so on and so forth. But the old recipe for higher education needs to accompany these projects. To understand history, to get a view on the state of the world in general, to become interested in fine arts… All those contribute to the students' ability, to their readiness to play an active part as well-informed citizens and to participate in society as concerned and thinking individuals, not just as members of one or another pressure group.

I do not know whether the tendency toward the bureaucratic rule of universities and of many research institutes can be reversed. I only recommend that it *should* be reversed. For, if it is not, the creativity of our cultures will get entirely lost, and so will upward mobility. Political activity will be limited to professional politicians. A new iron age will set in.

03.30.2015

The University and Us: A Question of Who We Are

Todd May

It will not be news to anyone who reads this column that the university is in crisis, which is felt particularly in the humanities, where the closing of departments and the larger question of what the discipline has to offer has become fodder for public discussion. This crisis is not solely a US phenomenon: last year over two dozen Japanese universities announced cuts or closings of humanities and social sciences departments. In the UK, universities are being severely restricted. Similar pressures are being felt at other academic institutions in Europe and elsewhere. And so, although my focus here is primarily on the US, we should bear in mind the larger context in which these reflections take place.

It would be short-sighted to account for the current crisis solely in terms of the post-2008 economic crunch. One should go further back, perhaps locating its origins in the withdrawal of public financial support for institutions of higher learning by the Reagan administration and the subsequent "corporatization" of university financial operations. In fact, one might argue in a more general vein that crises of universities are almost as old as the university itself. Think back to the 1960s and the student revolts in favor of more "relevant" education, one of the products of which was the increase in programs in Women's Studies and African-American Studies. If one were in an ironic frame of mind, one might say that with the recent challenges to the university the question of relevance has returned, although in a very different guise.

The current crisis once again raises the question of the character and purpose of a university. In this case, it does so with particular acuteness for those areas of study without immediate, or at least immediately recognizable, vocational relevance. This includes not only the humanities but also some areas of science such as theoretical physics and advanced mathematics. These are large questions. However, the dilemmas raised by the recent challenges to the university are of far greater scope than the university itself. What is at stake here is the issue of who we are, both as a people and as people.

The question of who we are *as a people* is about us as Americans. What is it to be an American? Does it include the embrace and reproduction of certain cultural forms? Are the writings of William Faulkner or William James or Walt Whitman or the paintings of Edward Hopper important elements of who we are? To ask this does not mean asking whether everyone has to be familiar with these writings in order to be a "real" American. It is to ask instead whether having these writings, paintings, etc. circulating in one form or another, being discussed and kept alive, is an important aspect of American life, an aspect of what it is for us to be us. It is to ask whether our collective life remains recognizably American without them.

"Who are we *as people*?" is like the previous question, only wider. What does it mean to be a human being in this day and age? Does the wider human culture include the work of Chinua Achebe, string theory in physics, Gödel's theorem, Kant's ethical theory? Again, at issue is not whether every human must be conversant with all of these things in order to be fully human. (If so, I would fail on at least two of the examples I've just offered.) It is a question of whether it matters that these contributions be preserved in a systematic way and passed on to others. It is a question of whether it is important that they be sustained and available to following generations, not only as texts in an archive but as living legacies for current engagement.

The university is, for better or worse, the primary institutional site at which these various cultural elements, both American and otherwise, are cultivated and passed on in a systematic way. It is the site that allows professors to engage with these cultural elements and to introduce students to them. Is it a good life for those of us who are able to attain a permanent position at a university? For the most part, it is (although one aspect of the crisis is that fewer of us are able to attain permanency). Is this good life one that is often unavailable to those who cannot afford the years of education required to take part in it? Yes again, and more should be done to address this. The university is not a terribly efficient place, and not always a terribly equitable one. But it is the place in which many of the cultural aspects of our collective life are engaged with, preserved, and passed along.

The current challenges to the university are challenges not simply to its equity or efficiency but to the character of who we are and what we value. They raise the question, and I mean it to be a question, of who we are. Should our collective life be determined by market values and our culture by what people are currently interested in or willing to pay for? Should these, in turn, become our values? I do not believe so, but that is not what I am arguing. I am arguing that we need to ask the question, forthrightly and without flinching.

These are indeed difficult economic times. For the university, difficult economic times are not merely of recent vintage. But for those of us who fund the university, the severity of the latest economic downturn presses upon us to order our priorities more rigorously than we otherwise might. We must recognize, however, that the changes we make to the university today are not momentary. We are defining the cultural legacy for our children and our grandchildren. We must ask ourselves what is important enough that we ensure it is available to them. Are the cultural elements of much of current university life merely a legacy of the past, an anachronism to be done away with in the name of a university that responds more closely to economic imperatives? Or are the aspects of the university that are currently in jeopardy worth preserving? These are questions we must consider for the sake of those who are to come after us, because they cannot raise them themselves and because our answer cannot but answer it for them.

We are at a defining moment in our cultural history. I have my own view about the answers to these questions. But I am only one person, and a humanities professor at that. It seems to me that it would be a shame to lose the elements of our culture that I have called attention to here. But it would also be a shame, perhaps even a greater one, if we were to lose them without ever asking ourselves, straightforwardly and sincerely, whether indeed that is what we ought to do, and whether who we are without them is a people that we ought to be.

09.12.2016

C. *The Politics of Sexuality*

The Sexual Is Political

SLAVOJ ŽIŽEK

Segregated toilet doors are today at the center of a big legal and ideological struggle. On March 29, 2016, a group of 80 predominantly Silicon Valley-based business executives, headlined by Facebook CEO Mark Zuckerberg and Apple CEO Tim Cook, signed a letter to North Carolina Governor Pat McCrory denouncing a law that prohibits transgender people from using public facilities intended for the opposite sex. "We are disappointed in your decision to sign this discriminatory legislation into law," the letter says. "The business community, by and large, has consistently communicated to lawmakers at every level that such laws are bad for our employees and bad for business." So it is clear where big capital stands. Tim Cook can easily forget about hundreds of thousands of Foxconn workers in China assembling Apple products in slave conditions; he made his big gesture of solidarity with the underprivileged, demanding the abolition of gender segregation ... As is often the case, big business stands proudly united with politically correct theory.

So what is "transgenderism"? It occurs when an individual experiences discord between his/her biological sex (and the corresponding gender, male or female, assigned to him/her by society at birth) and his/her subjective identity. *As such, it does not concern only "men who feel and act like women" and vice versa but a complex structure of additional "genderqueer" positions which are outside the very binary opposition of masculine and feminine: bigender, trigender, pangender, genderfluid, up to agender.* The vision of social relations that sustains transgenderism is the so-called postgenderism: a social, political and cultural movement whose adherents advocate a voluntary abolition of gender, rendered possible by recent scientific progress in biotechnology and reproductive technologies. Their proposal not only concerns scientific possibility, but is also ethically grounded.

The premise of postgenderism is that the social, emotional and cognitive consequences of fixed gender roles are an obstacle to full human emancipation. A society in which reproduction through sex is eliminated (or in which other versions will be possible: a woman can also "father" her child, etc.) will open unheard-of new possibilities of freedom, social and emotional experimenting. It will eliminate the crucial distinction that sustains all subsequent social hierarchies and exploitations.

One can argue that postgenderism is the truth of transgenderism. The universal fluidification of sexual identities unavoidably reaches its apogee in the cancellation of sex as such. Recall Marx's brilliant analysis of how, in the French revolution of 1848, the conservative-republican Party of Order functioned as the coalition of the two branches of royalism (orleanists and legitimists) in the "anonymous kingdom of the Republic." The only way to be a royalist in general was to be a republican, and, in the same sense, the only way to be sexualized in general is to be asexual.

The first thing to note here is that transgenderism goes together with the general tendency in today's predominant ideology to reject any particular "belonging" and to celebrate the "fluidification" of all forms of identity. Thinkers like Frederic Lordon have recently demonstrated the inconsistency of "cosmopolitan" anti-nationalist intellectuals who advocate "liberation from a belonging" and *in extremis* tend to dismiss every search for roots and every attachment to a particular ethnic or cultural identity as an almost proto-Fascist stance. Lordon contrasts this hidden belonging of self-proclaimed rootless universalists with the nightmarish reality of refugees and illegal immigrants who, deprived of basic rights, desperately search for some kind of belonging (like a new citizenship). Lordon is quite right here: it is easy to see how the "cosmopolitan" intellectual elites despising local people who cling to their roots belong to their own quite exclusive circles of rootless elites, how their cosmopolitan rootlessness is the marker of a deep and strong belonging. This is why it is an utter obscenity to put together elite "nomads" flying around the world and refugees desperately searching for a safe place where they would belong—the same obscenity as that of putting together a dieting upper-class Western woman and a starving refugee woman.

Furthermore, we encounter here the old paradox: the more marginal and excluded one is, the more one is allowed to assert one's ethnic identity and exclusive way of life. This is how the politically correct land-scape is structured. People far from the Western world are allowed to fully assert their particular ethnic identity without being proclaimed essentialist racist identitarians (native Americans, blacks...). The closer one gets to the notorious white heterosexual males, the more problem-atic this assertion is: Asians are still OK; Italians and Irish—maybe; with Germans and Scandinavians it is already problematic... However, such a prohibition on asserting the particular identity of white men (as the model of oppression of others), although it presents itself as the admis-sion of their guilt, nonetheless confers on them a central position. This very prohibition makes them into the universal-neutral medium, the place from which the truth about the others' oppression is accessible. The imbalance weighs also in the opposite direction: impoverished European countries expect the developed West European ones to bear the full bur-den of multicultural openness, while they can afford patriotism.

And a similar tension is present in transgenderism. Transgender sub-jects who appear as transgressive, defying all prohibitions, simultane-ously behave in a hyper-sensitive way insofar as they feel oppressed by enforced choice ("Why should I decide if I am man or woman?") and need a place where they could recognize themselves. If they so proudly insist on their "trans-," beyond all classification, why do they display such an urgent demand for a proper place? Why, when they find themselves in front of gendered toilets, don't they act with heroic indifference—"I am transgendered, a bit of this and that, a man dressed as a woman, etc., so I can well choose whatever door I want!"? Furthermore, do "normal" het-erosexuals not face a similar problem? Do they also not often find it dif-ficult to recognize themselves in prescribed sexual identities? One could even say that "man" (or "woman") is not a certain identity but more like a certain mode of avoiding an identity... And we can safely predict that new anti-discriminatory demands will emerge: why not marriages among multiple persons? What justifies the limitation to the binary form of marriage? Why not even a marriage with animals? After all we already know about the finesse of animal emotions. Is to exclude marriage with an animal not a clear case of "speciesism," an unjust privileging of the human species?

Insofar as the other great antagonism is that of classes, could we not also imagine a homologous critical rejection of the class binary? The "binary" class struggle and exploitation should also be supplemented by a "gay" position (exploitation among members of the ruling class itself, e.g., bankers and lawyers exploiting the "honest" productive capitalists), a "lesbian" position (beggars stealing from honest workers, etc.), a "bisexual" position (as a self-employed worker, I act as both capitalist and worker), an "asexual" one (I remain outside capitalist production), and so forth.

This deadlock of classification is clearly discernible in the need to expand the formula: the basic LGBT (Lesbian, Gay, Bisexual, Transgender) becomes LGBTQIA (Lesbian, Gay, Bisexual, Transgender, Questioning, Intersex, Asexual) or even LGBTQQIAAP (Lesbian, Gay, Bisexual, Transgender, Queer, Questioning, Intersex, Asexual, Allies, Pansexual). To resolve the problem, one often simply adds a + which serves to include all other communities associated with the LGBT community, as in LGBT+. This, however, raises the question: is + just a stand-in for missing positions like "and others," or can one be directly a +? The properly dialectical answer is "yes," because in a series there is always one exceptional element which clearly does not belong to it and thereby gives body to +. It can be "allies" ("honest" non-LGBT individuals), "asexuals" (negating the entire field of sexuality) or "questioning" (floating around, unable to adopt a determinate position).

Consequently, there is only one solution to this deadlock, the one we find in another field of disposing waste, that of trash bins. Public trash bins are more and more differentiated today. There are special bins for paper, glass, metal cans, cardboard package, plastic, etc. Here, already, things sometimes get complicated. If I have to dispose of a paper bag or a notebook with a tiny plastic band, where does it belong? To paper or to plastic? No wonder that we often get detailed instruction on the bins, right beneath the general designation: PAPER—books, newspapers, etc., but NOT hardcover books or books with plasticized covers, etc. In such cases, proper waste disposal would have taken up to half an hour or more of detailed reading and tough decisions. To make things easier, we then get a supplementary trash bin for GENERAL WASTE where we throw everything that did not meet the specific criteria of other bins, as if, once again, apart from paper trash, plastic trash, and so on, there is trash as such, universal trash.

Should we not do the same with toilets? Since no classification can satisfy all identities, should we not add to the two usual gender slots (MEN, WOMEN) a door for GENERAL GENDER? Is this not the only way to inscribe into an order of symbolic differences its constitutive antagonism? Lacan already pointed out that the "formula" of the sexual relationship as impossible/real is 1+1+a, i.e., the two sexes plus the "bone in the throat" that prevents its translation into a symbolic difference. This third element does not stand for what is excluded from the domain of difference; it stands, instead, for (the real of) difference as such.

The reason for this failure of every classification that tries to be exhaustive is not the empirical wealth of identities that defy classification but, on the contrary, the persistence of sexual difference as real, as "impossible" (defying every categorization) and simultaneously unavoidable. The multiplicity of gender positions (male, female, gay, lesbian, bigender, transgender…) circulates around an antagonism that forever eludes it. Gays are male, lesbians female; transsexuals enforce a passage from one to another; cross-dressing combines the two; bigender floats between the two… Whichever way we turn, the two lurks beneath.

This brings us back to what one could call the primal scene of anxiety that defines transgenderism. I stand in front of standard bi-gender toilets with two doors, LADIES and GENTLEMEN, and I am caught up in anxiety, not recognizing myself in any of the two choices. Again, do "normal" heterosexuals not have a similar problem? Do they also not often find it difficult to recognize themselves in prescribed sexual identities? Which man has not caught himself in momentary doubt: "Do I really have the right to enter GENTLEMEN? Am I really a man?"

We can now see clearly what the anxiety of this confrontation really amounts to. Namely, it is the anxiety of (symbolic) castration. Whatever choice I make, I will lose something, and this something is NOT what the other sex has. Both sexes together do not form a whole since something is irretrievably lost in the very division of sexes. We can even say that, in making the choice, I assume *the loss of what the other sex doesn't have*, i.e., I have to renounce the illusion that the Other has that X which would fill in my lack. And one can well guess that transgenderism is ultimately an attempt to avoid (the anxiety of) castration: thanks to it, a flat space is created in which the multiple choices that I can make do not bear the mark of castration. As Alenka Zupančič expressed it in a piece of personal communication: "One is usually timid in asserting the existence of two genders, but when passing to the multitude this timidity disappears, and their existence is firmly asserted. If sexual difference is considered in terms of gender, it is made—at least in principle—compatible with mechanisms of its full ontologization."

Therein resides the crux of the matter. The LGBT trend is right in "deconstructing" the standard normative sexual opposition, in de-ontologizing it, in recognizing in it a contingent historical construct full of tensions and inconsistencies. However, this trend reduces this tension to the fact that the plurality of sexual positions are forcefully narrowed down to the normative straightjacket of the binary opposition of masculine and feminine, with the idea that, if we get away from this straightjacket, we will get a full blossoming multiplicity of sexual positions (LGBT, etc.), each of them with its complete ontological consistency. It assumes that once we get rid of the binary straightjacket, I can fully recognize myself as gay, bisexual, or whatever. From the Lacanian standpoint, nonetheless, the antagonistic tension is irreducible, as it is constitutive of the sexual as such, and no amount of classificatory diversification and multiplication can save us from it.

The same goes for class antagonism. The division introduced and sustained by the emancipatory ("class") struggle is *not* between the two particular classes of the whole, but between the whole-in-its-parts and its remainder which, within the particulars, stands for the universal, for the whole "as such," opposed to its parts. Or, to put it in yet another way, one should bear in mind here the two aspects of the notion of remnant: the rest as what remains after the subtraction of all particular content (elements, specific parts of the whole), and the rest as the ultimate result of the subdivision of the whole into its parts, when, in the final act of subdivision, we no longer get two particular parts or elements, two somethings, but a something (the rest) and a nothing.

In Lacan's precise sense of the term, the third element (the Kierkegaardian chimney sweeper) effectively stands for the phallic element. How so? Insofar as it stands for pure difference: the officer, the maid, and the chimney sweeper are the male, the female, *plus their differ-ence as such*, as a particular contingent object. Again, why? Because not only is difference differential, but, in an antagonistic (non)relationship, it precedes the terms it differentiates. Not only is woman not-man and *vice versa*, but woman is what prevents man from being fully man and *vice versa*. It is like the difference between the Left and the Right in the political space: their difference is the difference in the very way difference is perceived. The whole political space appears differently structured if we look at it from the Left or from the Right; there is no third "objec-tive" way (for a Leftist, the political divide cuts across the entire social body, while for a Rightist, society is a hierarchic whole disturbed by mar-ginal intruders).

Difference "in itself" is thus not symbolic-differential, but real-impos-sible—something that eludes and resists the symbolic grasp. This differ-ence is the universal as such, that is, the universal not as a neutral frame elevated above its two species, but as their constitutive antagonism. And the third element (the chimney sweeper, the Jew, *object a*) stands for difference as such, for the "pure" difference/antagonism which pre-cedes the differentiated terms. If the division of the social body into two classes were complete, without the excessive element (Jew, rabble...), there would have been no class struggle, just two clearly divided classes. This third element is not the mark of an empirical remainder that escapes class classification (the pure division of society into two classes), but *the materialization of their antagonistic difference itself*, insofar as this differ-ence precedes the differentiated terms. In the space of anti-Semitism, the "Jew" stands for social antagonism as such: without the Jewish intruder, the two classes would live in harmony... Thus, we can observe how the third intruding element is eventual: it is not just another positive entity, but it stands for what is forever unsettling the harmony of the two, open-ing it up to an incessant process of re-accommodation.

A supreme example of this third element, *objet a*, which supplements the couple, is provided by a weird incident that occurred in Kemalist Turkey in 1926. Part of the Kemalist modernization was to enforce new "European" models for women, for how they should dress, talk and act, in order to get rid of the oppressive Oriental traditions. As is well known, there indeed was a Hat Law prescribing how men and women, at least in big cities, should cover their heads. Then, "in Erzurum in 1926 there was a woman among the people who were executed under the pretext of 'opposing the Hat Law.' She was a very tall (almost 2 m.) and very masculine-looking woman who peddled shawls for a living (hence her name 'Şalcı Bacı' [Shawl Sister]). Reporter Nimet Arzık described her as, 'two meters tall, with a sooty face and snakelike thin dreadlocks [...] and with manlike steps.' Of course as a woman she was not supposed to wear the fedora, so she could not have been 'guilty' of anything, but probably in their haste the gendarmes mistook her for a man and hurried her to the scaffold. Şalcı Bacı was the first woman to be executed by hanging in Turkish history. She was definitely not 'normal' since the description by Arzık does not fit in any framework of feminine normalcy at that particular time, and she probably belonged to the old tradition of tolerated and culturally included 'special people' with some kind of genetic 'disorder.' The coerced and hasty transition to 'modernity,' however, did not allow for such an inclusion to exist, and therefore she had to be eliminated, crossed out of the equation. 'Would a woman wear a hat that she be hanged?' were the last words she was reported to have muttered on the way to the scaffold. Apart from making no sense at all, these words represented a semantic void and only indicated that this was definitely a scene from the Real, subverting the rules of semiotics: she was first emasculated (in its primary etymological sense of 'making masculine'), so that she could be 'emasculated.'"[1]

How are we to interpret this weird and ridiculously excessive act of killing? The obvious reading would have been a Butlerian one: through her provocative trans-sexual appearance and acting, Şalcı Bacı rendered visible the contingent character of sexual difference, of how it is symbolically constructed. In this way, she was a threat to normatively established sexual identities... My reading is slightly (or not so slightly) different. Rather than undermine sexual difference, Şalcı Bacı stood for this difference as such, in all its traumatic Real, irreducible to any clear symbolic opposition. Her disturbing appearance transforms clear symbolic difference into the impossible-Real of antagonism. So, again, in the same way as class struggle is not just "complicated" when other classes that do not enter the clear division of the ruling class and the oppressed class appear (this excess is, on the contrary, the very element which makes class antagonism real and not just a symbolic opposition), the formula of sexual antagonism is not M/F (the clear opposition between male and female) but MF+, where + stands for the excessive element which transforms the symbolic opposition into the Real of antagonism.

This brings us back to our topic, the big opposition that is emerging today between, on the one hand, the violent imposition of a fixed symbolic form of sexual difference as the basic gesture of counteracting social disintegration and, on the other hand, the total transgender "fluidification" of gender, the dispersal of sexual difference into multiple configurations. While, in one part of the world, abortion and gay marriages are endorsed as a clear sign of moral progress, in other parts, homophobia and anti-abortion campaigns are exploding. In June 2016, *Al-Jazeera* reported that a 22-year-old Dutch woman complained to the police that she had been raped after being drugged in an upmarket nightclub in Doha. And the result was that she was convicted of having illicit sex by a Qatari court and given a one-year suspended sentence. On the opposite end, what counts as harassment in the PC environs is also getting extended. The following case comes to mind. A woman walked on a street with a bag in her hand, and a black man was walking 15 yards behind her. Becoming aware of it, the woman (unconsciously, automatically?) tightened her grip on the bag, and the black man reported that he experienced the woman's gesture as a case of racist harassment...

What goes on is also the result of neglecting the class and race dimension by the PC proponents of women's and gay rights: "In '10 Hours of Walking in NYC as a Woman' created by a video marketing company in 2014, an actress dressed in jeans, black t-shirt, and tennis shoes walked through various Manhattan neighborhoods, recording the actions and comments of men she encountered with a hidden camera and microphone. Throughout the walk the camera recorded over 100 instances coded as verbal harassment, ranging from friendly greetings to sexualized remarks about her body, including threats of rape. While the video was hailed as a document of street harassment and the fear of violence that are a daily part of women's lives, it ignored race and class. The largest proportion of the men presented in the video belonged to minority communities, and, in a number of instances, the men commenting on the actress were standing against buildings, resting on fire hydrants, or sitting on folding chairs on the sidewalk, postures used to characterize lower class and unemployed men, or, as a reader commented on it: 'The video was meant to generate outrage … and it used crypto-racism to do it.'"[2]

The great mistake in dealing with this opposition is to search for a proper measure between two extremes. What one should do instead is to bring out what both extremes share: the fantasy of a peaceful world where the agonistic tension of sexual difference disappears, either in a clear and stable hierarchic distinction of sexes or in the happy fluidity of a desexualized universe. And it is not difficult to discern in this fantasy of a peaceful world the fantasy of a society without social antagonisms, in short, without class struggle.

08.01.2016

Notes

1. Bulent Somay, "L'Orient n'existe pas," doctoral thesis defended at Birkbeck College, University of London, on November 29, 2013.

2. See https://thesocietypages.org/sociologylens/2014/11/18/nice-bag-discussing-race-class-and-sexuality-in-examining-street-harassment/.

A Reply to my Critics

Slavoj Žižek

Lately I am getting used to attacks that not only render my position in a totally wrong way but also practice slander pure and simple, so that, at this level, any minimally rational debate becomes meaningless. Among many examples, suffice it to mention Hamid Dabashi, who begins his book *Can Non-Europeans Think?* with: "'Fuck you, Walter Mignolo!' With those grandiloquent words and the gesture they must have occasioned and accompanied, the distinguished and renowned European philosopher Slavoj Žižek begins his response to a piece that Walter Mignolo wrote..."[1] No wonder that no reference is given, since I never uttered the phrase "Fuck you, Walter Mignolo!". In a public talk in which I responded to Mignolo's attack on me, I did use the words "fuck you," but they did not refer to Mignolo: his name was not mentioned in conjunction with them; they were a general exclamation addressed (if at anyone) at my public. From here, it is just one step to elevating my exclamation into "Slavoj Žižek's famous 'Fuck you, Walter Mignolo,'" as Dan Glazerbrook did.[2]

Back to Dabashi's book. On page 8, the comedy reaches its peak: a long quoted passage is attributed to me (it follows "Žižek claims:"), and after the quote the text goes on: "This is all fine and dandy—for Žižek. He can make any claim he wishes. All power to him. But the point is..." There is just one tiny problem: the passage quoted and attributed to me and then mocked as an example of my European racism and of my misreading of Fanon is from Fanon himself (again, no reference is given in Dabashi's book—the quoted passage is from Frantz Fanon, *Black Skin, White Masks*, New York: Grove Press 2008, p. 201-206.)

So, I thought we had reached the lowest point, although in a more recent contribution to *Al-Jazeera*, Dabashi puts me into the same line with Breivik, the Norwegian racist mass murderer.[3] But the reactions to my "The Sexual Is Political" demonstrate that one can go even lower. Browsing through numerous tweets and email blogs, I searched in vain for a minimum of argumentation. The attackers mostly just make fun of a position, which is simply not mine.

Here is a relatively decent example: "I know that this is difficult to understand, mostly because it draws from his big Daddy the contemptible Lacan. Really though, all Žižek is saying is that opposition to transgender people represents an anxiety which in his theory occurs because of sexual difference; i.e. transgender people disrupt the binaries we construct in order to place ourselves into discrete genders. What Žižek tries to say, he's not a very good writer in English at least, is that the antagonism will exist even if we completely accept LGBT people as members of our community because they always exist as a threat to the binary. I don't think that Žižek ultimately thinks social antagonism against LGBT people is something we can move beyond as long as the binary system exist. This is why he cites the story of Şalcı Bacı, to Žižek she represented an existential threat to people's identities. In a sense you can say it is a right-wing concept, because it's essentially saying that transgender people are indeed the threat to society they're portrayed to be. The question would be, does Žižek approve of threats to society as the revolutionary he supposes himself to be?"[4]

I have to admit that I couldn't believe my eyes when I was reading these lines. Is it really so difficult to follow the thread of my argumentation? First claim: "all Žižek is saying is that opposition to transgender people represents an anxiety which in his theory occurs because of sexual difference; i.e. transgender people disrupt the binaries we construct in order to place ourselves into discrete genders..." No, I'm not saying that at all: I don't talk about the anxiety experienced by heterosexuals when they confront transgender people. My starting point is the anxiety transgender people themselves experience when they confront a forced choice where they don't recognize themselves in any of its exclusive terms ("man," "woman"). And then I generalize this anxiety as a feature of every sexual identification. It is not transgender people who disrupt the heterosexual gender binaries; these binaries are always-already disrupted by the antagonistic nature of sexual difference itself. This is the basic distinction on which I repeatedly insist and which is ignored by my critics: in the human-symbolic universe, sexual difference/antagonism is not he same as the difference of gender roles. Transgender people are not traumatic for heterosexuals because they pose a threat to the established binary of gender roles but because they bring out the antagonistic tension which is constitutive of sexuality. Şalcı Bacı is not a threat to sexual difference; rather, she is this difference as irreducible to the opposition of gender identities.

In short, transgender people are not simply marginals who disturb the hegemonic heterosexual gender norm; their message is universal, it concerns us all, they bring out the anxiety that underlies every sexual identification, its constructed/unstable character. This, of course, does not entail a cheap generalization which would cut the edge of the suffering of transgender people ("we all have anxieties and suffer in some way"); it is in transgender people that anxiety and antagonism, which otherwise remain mostly latent, break open. So, in the same way in which, for Marx, if one wants to understand the "normal" functioning of capitalism, one should take as a starting point economic crises, if one wants to analyze "normal" heterosexuality, one should begin with the anxieties that explode in transgender people.

This is why it makes no sense to talk about "social antagonism against LGBT people" (incidentally, a symptomatically clumsy and weird expression: "antagonism against"?). Antagonism (or, as Lacan put it, the fact that "there is no sexual relationship") is at work in the very core of normative heterosexuality, and it is what the violent imposition of gender norms endeavors to contain and obfuscate. It is here that my parallel with the anti-Semitic figure of the Jew enters. The (anti-Semitic figure of the) "Jew" as the threat to the organic order of a society, as the element which brings into it from the outside corruption and decay, is a fetish whose function is to mask the fact that antagonism does not come from the outside but is immanent to every class society. Anti-Semitism "reifies" (embodies in a particular group of people) the inherent social antagonism: it treats "Jews" as the Thing which, from outside, intrudes into the social body and disturbs its balance. What happens in the passage from the position of class struggle to Fascist anti-Semitism is not just the replacement of one figure of the enemy (bourgeoisie, the ruling class) with another (Jews); the logic of the struggle is totally different. In class struggle, the classes themselves are caught in the antagonism inherent to social structure, while the Jew is a foreign intruder who causes social antagonism, so that all we need in order to restore social harmony, according to Fascist anti-Semitism, is to annihilate Jews. This is the old standard Marxist thesis: when my critic writes about my line of thought "In a sense you can say it is a right-wing concept," I would really like to know what precise sense he has in mind.

So, what is the anxiety I refer to about? For a brief moment, let me ignore my primitive critics and engage in a brief theoretical exercise. The underlying structure is here that of a failed interpellation (where "interpellation" refers to the basic ideological mechanism described by Louis Althusser). In the case of interpellation, Althusser's own example contains more than his own theorization gets out of it. Althusser evokes an individual who, while carelessly walking down the street, is suddenly addressed by a policeman: "Hey, you there!" By answering the call—that is, by stopping and turning round towards the policeman—the individual recognizes-constitutes himself as the subject of Power, of the big Other-Subject. Ideology "'transforms' the individuals into subjects (it transforms them all) by that very precise operation which I have called interpellation or hailing, and which can be imagined along the lines of the most commonplace everyday police (or other) hailing: 'Hey, you there!'.

Assuming that the theoretical scene I have imagined takes place in the street, the hailed individual will turn round. By this mere one-hundred-and-eighty-degree physical conversion, he becomes a subject. Why? Because he has recognized that the hail was 'really' addressed to him, and that 'it was really him who was hailed' (and not someone else). Experience shows that the practical transmission of hailings is such that they hardly ever miss their man: verbal call or whistle, the one hailed always recognizes that it is really him who is being hailed. And yet it is a strange phenomenon, and one which cannot be explained solely by 'guilt feelings,' despite the large numbers who 'have something on their consciences.'

Naturally for the convenience and clarity of my little theoretical theatre I have had to present things in the form of a sequence, with a before and an after, and thus in the form of a temporal succession. There are individuals walking along. Somewhere (usually behind them) the hail rings out: 'Hey, you there!' One individual (nine times out of ten it is the right one) turns round, believing/suspecting/knowing that it is for him, i.e. recognizing that 'it really is he' who is meant by the hailing. But in reality these things happen without any succession. The existence of ideology and the hailing or interpellation of individuals as subjects are one and the same thing."[5]

The first thing that strikes the eye in this passage is Althusser's implicit reference to Lacan's thesis on a letter that "always arrives at its destination": the interpellative letter cannot miss its addressee since, on account of its "timeless" character, it is only the addressee's recognition/acceptance that constitutes it as a letter. The crucial feature of the quoted passage, however, is the double denial at work in it: the denial of the explanation of interpellative recognition by means of a "guilt feeling," as well as the denial of the temporality of the process of interpellation (strictly speaking, individuals do not "become" subjects, they "always-already" are subjects).[6] This double denial is to be read as a Freudian denial: what the "timeless" character of interpellation renders invisible is a kind of atemporal sequentiality that is far more complex than the "theoretical theatre" staged by Althusser on behalf of a suspicious alibi of "convenience and clarity." This "repressed" sequence concerns a "guilt feeling" of a purely formal, "non-pathological" (in the Kantian sense) nature, a guilt which, for that very reason, weighs most heavily upon those individuals who "have nothing on their consciences." To ask differently: In what, precisely, does the individual's first reaction to the policeman's "Hey, you there!" consist? In an inconsistent mixture of two elements: (1) why me? what does the policeman want from me? I'm innocent, I was just minding my own business and strolling around...; however, this perplexed protestation of innocence is always accompanied by (2) an indeterminate Kafkaesque feeling of "abstract" guilt, a feeling that, in the eyes of Power, I am a priori terribly guilty of something, though it is not possible for me to know what precisely I am guilty of. And for that reason—since I don't know what I am guilty of—I am even more guilty; or, more pointedly, it is in this very ignorance of mine that my true guilt consists.[7]

What we thus have here is the entire Lacanian structure of the subject split between innocence and abstract, indeterminate guilt, confronted with a non-transparent call emanating from the Other ("Hey, you there!"), a call where it is not clear to the subject what the Other actually wants from him (*"Che vuoi?"*). In short, what we encounter here is interpellation prior to identification. Prior to the recognition in the call of the Other by means of which the individual constitutes himself as "always-already"-subject, we are obliged to acknowledge this "timeless" instant of the impasse, when innocence coincides with indeterminate guilt: the ideological identification by means of which I assume a symbolic mandate and recognize myself as the subject of Power takes place only as an answer to this impasse. So what remains "unthought" in Althusser's theory of interpellation is the fact that prior to ideological recognition we have an intermediate moment of obscene, impenetrable interpellation without identification, a kind of vanishing mediator that has to become invisible if the subject is to achieve symbolic identity, i.e., to accomplish the gesture of subjectivization. In short, the "unthought" of Althusser is that there is already an uncanny subject preceding the gesture of subjectivization.

And the same goes in a much stronger way for sexual interpellation. My identification as "man" or "woman" is always a secondary reaction to the "castrative" anxiety of what I am. One—traditional—way to avoid this anxiety is to impose a heterosexual norm, which specifies the role of each gender, and the other is to advocate the overcoming of sexuality as such (the postgender position). As for the relationship between transgender and postgender, my point is simply that the universal fluidification of sexual identities unavoidably reaches its apogee in the cancellation of sex as such. In the same way as, for Marx, the only way to be a royalist in general is to be a republican, the only way to be sexualized in general is to be asexual. This ambiguity characterizes the conjunction of sexuality and freedom throughout the twentieth century: the more radical attempts to liberate sexuality get, the more they approximate their self-overcoming and turn into attempts to enact a liberation from sexuality, or, as Aaron Schuster put it (in personal communication): "If part of the twentieth century's revolutionary program to create a radically new social relation and a New Man was the liberation of sexuality, this aspiration was marked by a fundamental ambiguity: Is it sexuality that is to be liberated, delivered from moral prejudices and legal prohibitions, so that the drives are allowed a more open and fluid expression, or is humanity to be liberated from sexuality, finally freed from its obscure dependencies and tyrannical constraints? Will the revolution bring an efflorescence of libidinal energy or, seeing it as a dangerous distraction to the arduous task of building a new world, demand its suppression? In a word, is sexuality the object of or the obstacle to emancipation?"

The oscillation between these two extremes is clearly discernible already in the first decade after the October Revolution, when feminist calls for the liberation of sexuality were soon supplemented by the gnostic-cosmological calls for a New Man who would leave behind sexuality itself as the ultimate bourgeois trap. Today, with the rise of the "Internet of Things" and biogenetics, this perspective got a new boost. And, as a part of this new perspective, I predict that new demands for overcoming old limitations will emerge. Among them there will be demands for legalizing multiple marriages (which already existed, not only as polygamy but also as polyandry, especially in the Himalayan region), as well as demands for some kind of legalization of intense emotional ties with animals. I am not talking about sex with animals (although I remember from my youth, from the time of the late 1960s, the widespread tendency to practice sex with animals), even less about "bestiality," but about a tendency to recognize some animals (say, a faithful dog) as legitimate partners. It's not about "bestiality," but about the "culturalization" of animals, their elevation to a legal partner.

To recapitulate, not only do I fully support the struggle of transgender people against their legal segregation, but I am also deeply affected by their reports of their suffering, and I see them not as a marginal group, which should be "tolerated," but as a group whose message is radically universal: it concerns us all; it tells the truth about all of us as sexual beings. I differ from the predominant opinion in two interconnected points that concern theory: (1) I see the anxiety apropos sexual identities as a universal feature of human sexuality, not just as a specific effect of sexual exclusions and segregations, which is why one should not expect it to disappear with the progress of sexual desegregation; (2) I draw a strict distinction between sexual difference (as the antagonism constitutive of human sexuality) and the binary (or plurality) of genders. Both these points are, of course, totally misread or ignored by my critics.

Concerning my "class reductionism," anyone minimally acquainted with my work knows that one of the problems I am dealing with is precisely how to bring the struggle of Third World people against neo-colonial oppression and the struggle for sexual emancipation (women and gay rights) in the developed West together. Some Leftists claim that we should focus on the universal anti-capitalist struggle, allowing each ethnic or religious group to retain its particular culture or "way of life." I see a problem in this easy solution: one cannot distinguish in a direct way the universal dimension of the emancipatory project and the identity of a particular way of life, so that while we are all together engaged in a universal struggle, we simultaneously fully respect the right of each group to its particular way of life. One should never forget that, to a subject who lives a particular way of life, all universals appear "colored" by this way of life. Each identity (way of life) comprises also a specific way to relate to other ways of life. So, when we posit as a guideline that each group should be left to enact its particular identity, to practice its own way of life, the problem immediately arises: where do customs that form my identity stop and where does injustice begin? Are woman's rights just our custom, or is the struggle for women's rights also universal (and part of the emancipatory struggle, as it was in the entire Socialist tradition from Engels to Mao)? Is homophobia just a thing of a particular culture to be tolerated as a component of its identity? Should arranged marriages (which form the very core of the kinship structures of some societies) also be accepted as part of a particular identity? Etc.

This "mediation" of the universal with the particular (way of life) holds for all cultures, ours (Western) included, of course. The "universal" principles advocated by the West are also colored by the Western way of life, plus we should never forget the rise of religious-nationalist fundamentalism in countries like Poland, Hungary and Croatia. In the last decades, Poland was one of the few European definitive success stories. After the fall of Socialism, the per capita gross domestic product more than doubled, and, for the last couple of years, the moderate liberal-centrist government of Donald Tusk ruled. And then, almost out of nowhere, without any great corruption scandals as in Hungary, the extreme Right took over, and there is now a widespread movement to prohibit abortions even in the limit-cases of the mortal danger to the mother's health, rape, and deformities of the foetus. A whole series of problems emerge here: what if equality among humans is in tension with equality among cultures (insofar as some cultures neglect equality)?

The task is thus to bring the struggle into every particular way of life. Each particular "way of life" is antagonistic, full of inner tensions and inconsistencies, and the only way to proceed is to work for an alliance of struggles in different cultures. From here I would like to return to the project of the alliance between progressive middle classes and nomad proletarians: In terms of a concrete problematic, this means that the politico-economic struggle against global capitalism and the struggle for women's rights, etc. have to be conceived as two moments of the same emancipatory struggle for equality.

These two aspects—the imposition of Western values such as universal human rights, and respect for different cultures independently of the horrors that can be part of these cultures—are the two sides of the same ideological mystification. A lot has been written about how the universality of universal human rights is twisted, how they secretly give preference to Western cultural values and norms (the priority of the individual over his/her community, and so on). But we should add to this insight that the multiculturalist, anti-colonialist defence of the multiplicity of ways of life is also false: it covers up the antagonisms within each of these particular ways of life, justifying acts of brutality, sexism and racism as expressions of a particular culture that we have no right to judge by foreign Western values.

This aspect should in no way be dismissed as marginal. From Boko Haram and Mugabe to Putin, anti-colonialist critique of the West more and more appears as the rejection of Western "sexual" confusion and as the demand for returning to traditional sexual hierarchy. It is, of course, true that the immediate export of Western feminism and individual human rights can serve as a tool of ideological and economic neo-colonialism. (We all remember how some American feminists supported the US intervention in Iraq as a way to liberate women there, while the result is exactly the opposite). But one should nonetheless absolutely reject to draw from this the conclusion that Western Leftists should make here a "strategic compromise," silently tolerating "customs" of humiliating women and gays on behalf of the "greater" anti-imperialist struggle.

The communist struggle for universal emancipation means a struggle which cuts into each particular identity, dividing it from within. When there is racism, when there is domination over women, it is always an integral part of a particular "way of life," a barbarian integral underside of a particular culture. In the "developed" Western world, Communist struggle means a brutal and principled struggle against all ideological formations which, even if they present themselves as "progressive," serve as an obstacle to universal emancipation (liberal feminism, etc.). It means not only attacking our own racist and religious fundamentalisms, but also demonstrating how they arise out of the inconsistencies of the predominant liberalism. And in Muslim countries, Communist strategy should in no way be to endorse their traditional "way of life" which includes honor killings, etc.; it should not only collaborate with the forces in these countries which fight traditional patriarchy, but it should also make a crucial step forward and demonstrate how, far from serving as a point of resistance against global capitalism, such traditional ideology is a direct tool of imperialist neocolonialism.

08.05.2016

Notes

1.   Hamid Dabashi, *Can Non-Europeans Think?*, London: Zed Books 2015, p. 1.

2.   Quoted from http://www.counterpunch.org/2015/03/16/ with-enemies-like-this-imperialism-doesnt-need-friends/.

3.   See http://www.aljazeera.com/indepth/opinion/2016/06/europe-creation-world-160613063926420.html.

4.   Quoted from: https://m.reddit.com/r/GamerGhazi/comments/4vxmfk/ philosopher_slavoj_zizek_knows_next_to_nothing/.

5.   Louis Althusser, "Ideology and Ideological State Apparatuses," in *Essays in Ideology*, London: Verso 1984, p. 163.

6.   I resume here a more detailed critical reading of Althusser's notion of ideology from Chapter 3 of Slavoj Žižek, *The Metastases of Enjoyment*, London: Verso Books, 2006.

7.   Here I follow the perspicacious observations of Henry Krips. See his excellent unpublished manuscript *The Subject of Althusser and Lacan*.

Gay Essentialism in a Eugenic Age

T. M. Murray

The search for a gay gene has intensified since the publication in the early 90's of the now famous research by Simon LeVay and Dean Hamer. Their findings were reconfirmed only last year with the release of a study from Dr. Alan Sanders, who analyzed the genes on 409 pairs of gay brothers and found they shared notable patterns in two regions of the human genome, on the X chromosome and chromosome 8.

Yet the importance and significance of a genetic explanation for human sexual orientation is hotly contested within LGBT academia, where a rift has opened between those who view the essentialist ("born that way") thesis as a vindication of LGBT human rights and those who see it as both irrelevant and dangerous. In the latter camp is Julie Bindel, who claims that resting human rights "on the basis that we can't help who we are is counter-productive." She sees those who embrace the gay essentialist thesis as attempting to vindicate homosexual behavior (which is a choice) on the grounds of biological difference, which would put gay rights on the same basis as anti-racist or feminist politics.

Many gay people are sympathetic to Bindel's claim that homosexuality is not due to genes but to "a mix of opportunity, luck, chance, and, quite frankly, bravery." But what Bindel means by "homosexuality" is homosexual *behavior*, not the involuntary experience of homosexual attraction or desire, which can be expressed or repressed. Essentialists may agree with Bindel that homosexual conduct is a choice. The essentialist thesis is not determinism and does not require that homosexuals have no choice about their sexual expression. Indeed, Bindel is right to say that sexual behavior is down to a variety of factors and not simply reducible to biological sexual attraction. Perhaps not surprisingly, Dean Hamer expressly rejected any sort of "gay gene determinism" after publishing his study on the gay gene back in 1993.

No one is claiming that *all* people who identify as lesbian or gay were born that way. For a variety of personal reasons, some people simply prefer to share intimate partnership with someone of the same sex. Even if people are "born that way" this would not entail that they necessarily behave in exclusively homosexual ways. Some might even pretend to be straight for their entire lives. Nor is anyone claiming that being "born that way" is a necessary condition for granting full legal acceptance of homosexuality. In a liberal democracy, bisexuals and people not born with a predisposition to same-sex attraction ought to be free to participate in homoerotic (or any) sexual behavior, so long as it is consenting and between adults.

However, the essentialist thesis still has significance for LGBT human rights because research into the biological causes of sexual orientation continues unabated. If private companies can profit from offering prospective parents a eugenic "treatment" for homosexual orientation, we can be sure they will lobby hard for the liberty to do so. They are already laying the discursive groundwork for a eugenic age.

The traditional nexus between acknowledging that some people have no choice in being "born that way" and social tolerance of homosexual behavior has broken down. So Bindel is right that pinning one's hopes for justice and equal rights on gay biology is a lost cause.

Back in 1992, only months after Simon LeVay published his "gay gene" theory, the Roman Catholic Congregation for the Doctrine of the Faith reiterated its position that the homosexual inclination must be seen as an "objective disorder." From the 1990s onwards a variety of religious and social conservative bioethicists began publishing widely in support of interpreting homosexuality as a pathology and used pseudo-medical language with a view to the future when reprogenetics—the merging of reproductive and genetic technologies—or some similar treatment scenario will be viable. These authors were frighteningly well placed to influence public policy.

Nowadays, instead of describing given aspects of natural "creation" as the very benchmark of God's design and plan, Christian bioethicists such as Ronald Cole-Turner, Michael J. Reiss, Nigel M. de S. Cameron, Dr.

Roger Straughan and Ted Peters emphasize how biotechnology might facilitate human interventions into "fallen creation" in order to "restore" it to "its full glory." They argue in support of treating homosexual orientation as a target for biomedical intervention.

Whether or not there is a biological substrate that determines patterns of sexual attraction is a question of fact, not one of value. So, if it turns out that there *is* a "gay gene(s)," denying its existence *in theory* will not prevent big biotech firms from providing the means to eliminate it *in fact*. Therefore, forming an anti-eugenic lobby to advocate for laws that would prevent the misuse of biotech is preferable to treating gay biology as a chimera.

Liberal eugenicists are already arguing for unlimited and unregulated use of reprogenetics. They distinguish it from eugenics in that the latter implies state coercion with the presumption of benefit. The former would be voluntarily pursued by individual parents with the aim of improving their children according to their preferences. This is a form of privatized or free-market eugenics, so there is of course a financial incentive to promote its use.

Liberal eugenics leaves eugenic decisions to the market, driven by parental preferences and consumer demand. This seems to qualify as "liberal" because the state does not impose any single vision of "the good life" upon future generations of individuals subject to it. Rather, it leaves individuals the "moral space" within which to make value judgments for themselves (and for their offspring). Consequently, proponents like Nicholas Agar and Gregory Stock argue that the future direction of human nature will be determined not by a dictator with utopian plans for social engineering, but by parents and what they perceive to be in the best interests of their offspring. Though not a Christian invention, the liberal eugenics movement provides an ideological Trojan horse by means of which Christian (or any) eugenics can get a legitimate foothold in a liberal democracy.

Against this view, it should be noted that allowing a patient's "disease" status to be defined (and treated without his consent) not only fails to protect the individual from the tyranny of the majority; it legitimizes subjecting individuals to such a tyranny by new, more powerful, and irrevocable means. Unlike the indoctrinated child who can, if given adequate alternatives, rebel against a controlling parent, the genetically modified child would simply not wish to rebel. Medicine will be enlisted to do the work that punishment and moral exhortation did in the past. But providing new, more efficient and permanent ways of expressing the majority's intolerance for perceived "social ills" is anything but liberal.

Reducing the biological substrate for homosexual attraction (if one exists) will almost certainly reduce homosexual behavior. The purpose of the reprogenetic interventions will be to eliminate individuals' voluntary homosexuality by eliminating their involuntary biological predisposition for it. This will happen not by taking away the individual's free will, but by biologically steering the direction in which it is most likely to be expressed. To deny this is to pretend that voluntary sexual acts are unrelated to involuntary sexual attraction.

05.23.2016

Feminine Monstrosity in the 2016 Presidential Campaign

MARTHA PATTERSON

In 1897, the popular humor magazine *Life* featured the William Walker cartoon "The Inauguration of the Future," in which a portly, spectacled, middle-aged mannish woman delivers her presidential acceptance speech. On the right appear similarly corpulent women in robes and military attire, while on the left, cross-armed, gaunt, spectacled women sit in top hats. The only man on the podium holds a squalling baby.

Walker's caricature typified for many the prevailing anxiety about women's changing roles in American society in the late nineteenth century. If allowed to enter political life, particularly as a suffragette, the New Woman risked becoming manly, browbeating, and neglectful of her proper role as mother and wife.

And yet at the same time that *Life* satirized the New Woman as political activist, it also celebrated the statuesque white American girl by one of the most popular artists of his time, Charles Dana Gibson. With her abundant upswept hair, corseted waist, pert nose, and towering persona, Gibson's iconographic "Gibson Girl" quickly became the *de rigueur* of American femininity in the late nineteenth and early twentieth century that young women, regardless of race, ethnicity or class, often tried to emulate. Appearing on calendars, glove boxes, popular illustrated novels, decorative plates, and weekly magazines, the Gibson Girl affirmed women's desire for greater freedom, but only as a personal, rather than political, freedom. Her youthful beauty, then, sanctioned her greater athleticism—swimming in the sea or exclaiming "Fore" to the world on the golf course; her greater autonomy in the marriage market—juggling prospective suitors unchaperoned; or, even, occasionally, her desire for higher education—wearing a cap and gown. Hers was a transgression that shoppers would want to buy.

Indeed, while Gibson disavowed the presence of women in political settings, he extolled the American girl as the catalyst for a new consumer-based economy and as a representative of the nation. As Columbia, she was an icon of American power and seeming invincibility during a period of U.S. imperial expansion. Gibson's illustrations for *Life* featured the "joke" that the Gibson Girl was a trophy to be won, and as such, the money needed to sustain her shopping sprees should be indulged if they propelled the Gibson Man to work harder.

Both the mannish suffragette turned president and the Gibson Girl turned consumer became two sides of the New Woman coin: one a symbol of derision, the other a symbol to emulate.

The pages of that early version of *Life* offer an important frame to understand the historic moment of Hillary Clinton as the first woman to become the nominee for president from a major political party. Initially, it appears, her presence seems to offer, at last, a definitive refutation of anti-New Woman arguments typified in Walker's illustration. Neither fat, ugly, nor spectacled, Hilary has not reduced her husband to the role of nanny nor driven her female supporters to expressions of manliness.

On the one hand, Hillary's candidacy initially seemed to have provoked less of a misogynist backlash than her 2008 run. We aren't watching *Saturday Night Live* skits about her cankles or reading that she eschewed an appearance in *Vogue* lest she would appear too feminine, a decline that prompted Anna Wintour to remark, "The notion that a contemporary woman must look mannish in order to be taken seriously as a seeker of power is frankly dismaying."

And, in some ways, even though Hillary's hawkish approach to foreign policy suggests a need to assert masculine toughness, she seems to have dodged Walker's satire of maternal abandonment by being a mother and grandmother, which she noted in her presumptive Democratic nomination acceptance speech. She has watched her weight, in a way that a male presidential candidate could forego. She declared herself a "bottle blonde" who wouldn't "shrink from a fight"—thereby appearing younger but still tough enough to lead a nation.

And yet, a sexist backlash still frames Hillary's candidacy, especially to the extent that arguments against her focus on how her behavior defies that which is positively but subordinately feminine—namely that her overwhelming political ambition leads her to break the rules.

If Obama, as the first president to overcome the color barrier, is accused of being foreign-born and secretly Muslim—in effect, profiting from the unpoliced borders of nation and religion—Hillary, as the first woman to break the barrier of sex, is accused, albeit indirectly, of being manly in her ambition and womanly both in her cowardice and deception. As man/woman she is inherently "crooked"—a term before this election season typically applied to men—in the very way that the corseted Gibson Girl is straight. Rather than smiling to please, she yells, presenting herself, in the words of Republican National Committee chairman, Reince Priebus, as "angry and defensive." Pandora-like, she lies to mask the extent to which she is to blame for the world's ills. In that hybrid of masculine ambition and feminine deception, she becomes, as we heard in the Republican Convention, monstrous, deceitful, criminal, murderous even. Her legacy, according to Trump in his acceptance speech, is "death, destruction and weakness."

In the view of Trump's supporters, Hillary is the candidate of transgression, the crossing of gender, legal, national and economic borders, as Trump is the candidate of walls—traditional gender roles, tight border security, and high tariff barriers. He is clearly the patriarch; the chooser of desirable women, the father of five children. His authoritarian style, exemplified by his admiration for Vladimir Putin, is an extension of that patriarchal role. Commanding other nations to bow to his authority, he would order Mexico to pay for the construction of a border wall and would somehow compel other countries to acquiesce to trade agreements more favorable to the United States.

Making American Great Again offers in Melania Trump a revival of the Gibson Girl, a figure more often seen than heard as beauty icon and trophy wife.

And yet, of course, the open/closed dichotomy is messy, just as the New Woman/Gibson Girl icon was. Trump has clearly benefitted from free trade and a globalized labor force; his wife is a first generation immigrant from Slovenia; his daughter Ivanka, more visible on the campaign than his wife, is an accomplished businesswoman.

But the historical parallel does offer us an important reminder of the lenses that still color how we view this first female presidential nominee and the zeal of her antagonist's followers, even as it points to the irony of Trump as the disciplined border-control, tough-on-terrorism and law-and-order candidate. The quest for the Gibson Girl, as Columbia, was supposed to inspire a rigorous, but sedulous male counterpart in the clean shaven, prosperous, well-disposed Gibson Man. Trump's impulsivity, petulance, and narcissism evoke long-held stereotypes of women as they suggest a body and mind governed by emotion rather than reason.

Changing who takes charge of the wailing baby and who assumes the office of the presidency is still, for many Americans, an uncomfortable upending of traditional mores, and raises an intriguing question. When Trump declared his candidacy in June of 2015, most Americans anticipated that Hillary Clinton would probably be the Democratic nominee. Had the Democratic frontrunner and eventual nominee been a white male, would the Republican nominee have been different? Perhaps not, but given the history of American New Woman iconography, it is no surprise that her rival for the presidency offers Americans such a dramatic contrast, in gender politics as much as political vision.

09.26.2016

Rape Is Torture

Jay M. Bernstein

In an excruciating *New York Times* article, Rukmini Callimachi details in painful and exact terms the system of sex slavery of Yazidi women and girls that ISIS has set in place. Without any boundaries of sexual permissibility apart from the prohibition against sex with pregnant women, ISIS warriors and followers pray to God before and after raping and sexually destroying their Yazidi captives as if they were thereby fulfilling a deeply religious obligation. If we possess any sense that there are absolute moral boundaries, ISIS's practices of torture, slavery, and rape cross them, defiantly.

Let us look at those boundaries for a moment. After saying everyone has the "right to life, liberty and security of person," there occurs the first substantive and specific article of the *Universal Declaration of Human Rights*: "No one shall be held in slavery or servitude; slavery and the slave trade shall be prohibited in all their forms." To enslave an individual is the systematic denial that they possess equal human dignity; enslaving is now the paradigm act of what it means to deny others equal human worth. To be a slave is either to be a mere thing, a tool, for the other; or a peculiar kind of 'human-thing,' a human that qua human has no worth in him or herself and exists solely for the benefit of the enslaver. In this respect, the link between enslaving and religious rape could not be more perspicuous: Yazidi religion is taken by ISIS to fall outside the pale of those religious practices suitable for humans, peoples of the Book, who are God's creatures; slavery and sexual abuse is the use proper to the less than fully human.

Given the easy path from slavery to rape, and rape's persistence as a fundamental form of degradation and dehumanization, one might have thought that the next article of the *Declaration* would mention rape. But rape is not mentioned in the next article; instead one finds (Article 5): "No one shall be subjected to torture or to cruel, inhuman or degrading treatment or punishment." Despite much argument concerning women's rights and equality, I know of no discussion of rape in the run-up to the *Declaration*. A reasonable hypothesis for this lacuna is that the authors of the *Declaration* considered rape as one, explicit form of torture—an hypothesis that easily falls in place when we recall that, since ancient times, rape has been used as a form of torture, as if corporeal torture and rape were nothing other than the sexual division of torturous labor's objects.

ISIS's religious rape practices would be morally heinous and abominable even if they were not part of a system of slavery. Part of the awfulness of slavery is, precisely, its function as mechanism for licensing rape and torture, or, better, rape as torture. Rape is torture: it is this thought that has been missing from recent discussions of rape. Getting this idea into view is complicated because sex is complicated, and all things being considered, while we officially revile rape, we also—secretly, sotto voce, unconsciously—consider it the dark side of sex, part of the danger of sex, the underside of sex's threading together of pleasure and pain. Rape is none of these things, however; rape is torture.

Let me begin again. Sex is always complex and risky. In it we physically expose ourselves to the touch of another in ways we do not otherwise allow. And, at least at its heights, sex involves letting go of the prerogatives of will, control, and mastery in order to surrender to bodily involuntariness: we are overcome and undone, we *quiver* with delight. And sex is messy. Mixed in with all the excitement and joy, sexual life is laced with failure and unhappiness. There are all sorts of unhappy and bad sex: sex we regret from the first kiss, or halfway through ("This feels weird"), or the morning after, or years later ("Why did I sleep with him?"). There is also just bad sex, sex in which we feel we are being used, in bed with someone who is utterly self-absorbed, or who has no clue how to give sexual pleasure, or who is into stuff we find disgusting.

However messy sex is, rape is not a form of bad sex—say, very bad sex, terrible sex, the worst sex ever. Rape is not sex at all from the perspective of the victim, even as it exploits the victim's powers for sexual pleasure. It is, rather, torture.

Consider this: The torturer's strategy and goal is to reduce his victim to his body. What is it for a human to be "reduced" to his body given that we are anyway bodily beings?

Human embodiment has a dual structure: we are the kinds of beings that both *are* our bodies and *have* our bodies. More precisely, the human body must be conceived as having both voluntary and involuntary dimensions. The involuntary body is the body that sweats, blushes, hiccups, excretes, menstruates, gets pregnant, lactates, feels pains and pleasures, the body that rages with anger and quakes with fear, the body that feels the touch of every object, and too the body that laughs hysterically and cries uncontrollably. The voluntary body, the body I have, is the body that is a vehicle for action, the body that intends the world through action, the body that can be so absorbed in its doing that it disappears from focal consciousness, with only the object of the activity present: my fingers dashing over the keyboard as I simply play the sonata, only the sonata itself as the object of consciousness.

All human experience involves a coordination of the voluntary and involuntary body, where the correct or appropriate relation between the voluntary and involuntary body is set in place by social rules. Torture depends on working the difference between the involuntary and the voluntary body differently. In torture, the victim is reduced to her involuntary body, while the torturer effectively takes possession of all voluntariness and agency; the torturer has the victim's body. Hence the victim's body is no longer hers; she is a being who can suffer and weep and cry out and sweat and excrete—but these involuntary happenings occur beyond any possibility of control.

If in torture I can no longer call my body "mine," then torture dispossesses me of my body. And it is just this that rape is about: a radical act of dispossession through violation. What torture accomplishes through pain, rape accomplishes through violation—penetration without consent. Rape too is a medium of communication, typically between a man and a woman, in which the message is that bodily voluntariness belongs essentially to the man and bodily involuntariness belongs to the woman as what is proper to her. The work of rape is to make the difference between bodily voluntariness and bodily involuntariness into a sexual and moral fate: the man appropriating all voluntariness to himself as he deposits the woman in bodily involuntariness. In insisting that his victim is only her involuntary body, he is insisting her body is *his*. Not only does slavery license torturous rape, but rape enacts the fundamental act of possession that constitutes slavery. Rape cultures are slave cultures in waiting.

Rape is a weapon in the sexual wars, and is meant at such; rape remains patriarchy's most brutal means and a standing assertion of its end. Legal reform is important but does not answer to the persistence of rape in a presumptively liberal culture in which it has no place. Until there is a pervasive and overwhelming *culture of intolerance for rape*, it will continue; until, say, fellow soldiers and fraternity members take full moral responsibility for their communities—by not permitting rape to occur when it can be prevented, and turning in and testifying against rapists—rape will continue. The slave trade and rape practices of ISIS are indeed horrific; our condemnation of their barbarism would be more convincing if the implicit tolerance for rape in our own culture were not so pervasive.

02.01.2016

Rape on Campus: The *Title IX* Revolution

KELLY OLIVER

Title IX legislation, associated primarily with equal opportunities for girls in high school and college athletics, has become a turning point in discussions of sexual assault. Until recently, the greatest impact of the 1972 Title IX legislation had been to ensure girls and women had access to sports. Although introduced to stop discrimination in higher education, Title IX became the hallmark of women's athletics, to the point that today there is a women's sporting clothing company named *Title Nine*, and last year President Obama spoke about the importance of Title IX for girls in terms of his own experience coaching his daughters' basketball team and the confidence it gave them. Initially, Title IX was used to secure funding for girls and women's sports, which had been lacking until required by this federal statute.

On April 4, 2011, The United States Department of Education sent a "Dear Colleagues Letter" to institutions of higher learning, shifting the focus from college athletics to educational environment, specifically naming sexual violence as prohibited by Title IX. The letter defines sexual violence as "physical sexual acts perpetrated against a person's will or where a person is incapable of giving consent due to the victim's use of drugs or alcohol," including "sexual assault, sexual battery, and sexual coercion," and makes colleges and universities responsible "to take immediate and effective steps to end sexual harassment and sexual violence."

Much of the recent attention paid to sexual assault as a Title IX violation is the result of a lawsuit filed against The University of North Carolina in 2013 by Annie Clark and Andrea Pino, two undergraduates raped during their first weeks on campus. Both reported the attacks to the university, but they claim their statements were ignored or belittled. These two courageous women have made headlines for their anti-rape activism after they founded EROC (*End Rape on Campus*) to help other women file Title IX lawsuits against universities across the country. Their use of Title IX has changed the terms of discussions over sexual assault on campus. This strategy has forced even those who insist, "rapists cause rape" to rethink isolating perpetrators from the culture that protects them.

There are at least two profound philosophical implications to be drawn from this approach to sexual violence, signaling a major shift in how we view responsibility. First, educational institutions are held responsible for creating the environment allowing, if not fostering, sexual violence; or, conversely, and more to the point, they are held responsible for creating an ethos fostering women's education, which is not possible when one out of four college women is sexually assaulted and gender-based violence is a constant threat. The new use of Title IX marks a dramatic change in the attribution of responsibility for sexual assault and rape. Rape survivors across the country are filing Title IX lawsuits against their colleges and universities for allowing serial rapists to remain on campus, making the environment unsafe for female students. This strategy targets the educational institutions that harbor rapists rather than the rapists themselves and therefore holds schools responsible for sexual assault on campus. Rather than excuse the problem with the argument that a few bad apples spoil the whole bunch, this approach looks to systematic policies of disavowal and denial, to a dearth of attention to the problem, and a lack of consequences for perpetrators, along with the ways in which fraternities and sports culture perpetuate rape myths that women want to be raped or that blame the victims. In a society that values individual over institutional responsibility, this is a turning point. How successful it will be is another matter. But, conceptually, it forces us to think about the culture that spawns serial rapists on campus, and protects perpetrators instead of survivors.

Second, the use of Title IX in cases of sexual assault on campus switches the focus away from individual victims to gender-based violence. Rather than single out women as random targets of assault, or, as it happens too often, blame them for their own attacks through suggestions that they were asking for it by wearing provocative clothes, behaving in certain ways, or drinking, the focus shifts to the environment in which women are under a constant threat of being sexually assaulted. Just as the shift away from individual perpetrators forces us to concentrate on the culture or ethos that produces sexual assault and serial rapists on campus, the shift away from individual victims makes us focus on gender-based violence and the culture that targets women for sexual assault.

Title IX as a strategy to address sexual violence against college women heralds a watershed in the way we view responsibility. Anti-rape activism is on the vanguard of transferring the blame and responsibility from individuals to social systems and institutions. If ours is a rape culture, then the solution must also address the culture of sexual violence that perpetuates sexual assault and gender-based violence.

The irony is that, while anti-rape activists and survivors are using Title IX to force colleges and universities to address the problem of sexual violence on campus, this same piece of legislation is also being used to shut down discussions of rape on campus, the very kinds of dialogue necessary to combat rape myths and rape culture. The risk is that educating about such violence itself becomes a "trigger" for past trauma as students demand safety not only from harmful deeds, but also from any talk of sexual assault. This makes Title IX a double-edged tool in addressing this issue. We could speculate that turning Title IX against those on campus who speak out against this serious problem is actually an attempt to combat this dramatic turn in thinking about responsibility and who—or what—is responsible for gender-based violence.

Title IX has gone from addressing funding and quantifiable differences between resources spent on men's and women's athletics and educational programs to dealing with the ethos of educational institutions in terms of whether or not they empower girls and women. This is a first step in moving from concerns with mere formal equality in education to social justice for women. At least, as long as we use Title IX to open up rather than shut down discussions of rape culture and the contributions of rape myths, sexism, and hostility towards women to the prevalence of sexual violence.

07.04.2016

D. Food Matters

Veganism without Animal Rights

GARY FRANCIONE AND ANNA CHARLTON

We are going to defend what may appear to be a controversial position: that our moral rejection of meat, dairy, eggs, and all other animal products as food is required according to our conventional morality concerning animals. That is, if you reject the idea that animals are things that have no moral value whatsoever, you are morally committed to adopting a vegan diet. And you don't even need to embrace a theory of animal rights.

Let's start with a hypothetical: You encounter Fred, who enjoys imposing pain and suffering on animals. Fred keeps a number of animals in his basement and goes down regularly and causes them to suffer physical pain, fear, and distress, and he then kills them. Fred is otherwise a lovely person; his penchant for killing animals does not affect his dealings with other humans in any way. When asked about why he does this, Fred explains that he derives pleasure and amusement from these actions.

Would anyone not regard what Fred was doing as morally objectionable and, indeed, as morally odious? Of course not. Would such a reaction assume that the objector accepted the equality of humans and non-humans? No. Even if we think that animals have a lesser moral value than humans do, we would still object to Fred's fetish, as long as we believe that animals have some moral value.

Most people believe that animals have some moral value but that it is not objectionable per se to use and kill animals for human purposes as long as we do not impose unnecessary suffering on them. And necessity must exclude suffering imposed for the reason of pleasure, amusement, or convenience. If imposing pain for pleasure, amusement, or convenience may be considered as necessary, then there is nothing that can be considered as unnecessary. If pleasure, amusement, or convenience can be considered as "necessary," then the conventional wisdom about animals is that we can use animals as long as we don't impose unnecessary suffering, or gratuitous suffering. So in Fred's case, conventional wisdom would say that Fred should not impose more harm than is necessary for him to derive the pleasure and amusement he seeks. But no one would regard that as a plausible understanding of "necessity."

This is precisely why most people object to blood sports such as fox hunting and bull fighting: they involve imposing suffering and death on animals for the purposes of pleasure and amusement.

So the question becomes: on what basis can we justifiably kill almost 60 billion animals a year worldwide (not counting fish)? Under the best—the most "humane" of circumstances—the amount of suffering we impose on animals in the process of using them for food is staggering. If we believe that unnecessary suffering is wrong, how can we justify that level of suffering? Indeed, even if we made animal agriculture much more "humane" than it presently is, there will still be suffering, fear, distress, and death. And there is no morally coherent distinction between meat and other animal products, such as dairy and eggs. They all involve suffering, distress, and death.

Given that we have criticized Fred, what do we have to say in our defense if Fred points to his critics as hypocrites who consume animal products? Until recently, most people have believed that it was necessary to consume animal foods and that, without those foods, humans would shrivel up and die. Many people still believe that today.

This belief is not justifiable. We've known for centuries that humans can live without consuming any animal protein. To the extent that anyone holds that belief today, it is a testament to the combined power of advertising and a corporate-controlled media reinforcing our desire for eating what we are used to and what tastes good to us in light of our past experience.

The view that we need animal foods for human nutrition is clearly and unequivocally false. It is now acknowledged by just about every respected professional organization, including the American Heart Association and the Mayo Clinic, as well as by governmental agencies all over the world, that a diet consisting only of plant foods can not only be perfectly healthy, but is almost certainly more healthy than a diet heavy in meat, dairy, and eggs. But whether a vegan diet is more healthy, it is certainly not less healthy and animal foods cannot be considered necessary for human health. There is also broad consensus that animal agriculture is an ecological disaster.

So, in the end, what's the best justification that we have for imposing suffering and death on many billions of animals?

Animal foods taste good.

We enjoy the taste of animal flesh and animal products.

We find eating animal foods to be convenient. It's a habit.

How, then, is our consumption of animal products any different from Fred's situation? It's not. Palate pleasure is no different morally from any other sort of pleasure.

The usual response at this point is to say that there is a moral difference between Fred and someone who goes to the store and buys animal products. There may be a psychological difference but there is no moral one—any more than there is a difference between someone who commits a murder and someone who pays to have the murder committed. And there is no difference—psychological or moral—between Fred and a hunter.

So if we object to what Fred does, we are acting inconsistently if we don't stop eating animal foods and go vegan at least in those cases where we are not starving to death on the proverbial desert island or lifeboat. In those situations, different considerations obtain. Indeed, there have been instances where humans have eaten other humans in those situations and we have regarded that conduct as immoral (and illegal) but as excusable under the circumstances.

Some argue that our consumption of animal foods is traditional and that many animal foods are culturally significant. If something is morally wrong, the fact that it is a tradition or culturally significant cannot rescue it. There is no more enduring a tradition than sexism and misogyny, aspects of which are accorded considerable social significance.

What about plants? This is the very first question that every vegan gets at a dinner party. Plants are alive; they are not sentient. They do not have the subjective experiences that the animals we consume as food do. They react to stimulation; they do not respond. They do not have interests; there is nothing that they want, desire, or prefer. And even if plants were sentient, veganism would still be a moral imperative given that it takes many pounds of plants to produce one pound of flesh.

Please note that we have showed you that, unless you embrace the idea that animals are merely things that are outside the moral community, you are committed to veganism. And we never even mentioned animal rights. That is because we don't need that concept unless we are talking about situations in which there is a plausible claim of necessity and we need a rights analysis to understand and resolve the conflict. But 99% of our uses of animals, including our numerically most significant use of them for food, do not involve any sort of necessity or any real conflict between human and nonhuman interests. If animals matter morally at all, then, even without accepting a theory of animal rights, those uses of animals cannot be morally justified.

06.13.2015

Hunger

Claire Colebrook

One way we might think about the present is by way of an all too natural epidemic of hunger confusion. Here is what we are so often told by those experts who explain a series of disorders ranging from hunger in its literal sense, to broader problems of consumption (of information and resources, for instance): "we" evolved as hunter-gatherers with metabolic and psychic systems that favored short-term high consumption that would serve us well should times get tough. The very brain that will later give us the right to say "we" and to consume other animals by way of industrial technology is what required and allowed us to develop an energy-rich diet. In order for "us" to evolve with big technology-creating brains, "we" had to develop a taste for fat.

Sadly, those same brains that have discerned this evolutionary genealogy are not so quick to adjust to the high availability of energy-rich foods. In short, we are suffering from an obesity epidemic precisely because the most natural thing in the world—hunger—is confused. One might say that this confusion is not accidental but essential: we developed undue hunger to feed our brains, with our brains then able to detect high-energy foods, and then able to develop technologies to produce those high-energy foods. It is not only our bodies that are weighed down by the fat we consume and carry. Cognitive performance becomes sluggish when a high-fat diet is combined with the sedentariness that our big-brained techno-science made available: what does not kill us makes us weaker.

It is perhaps no wonder that a "paleo" diet has such a lure: if our brains cannot speed up and notice that they have altered the world and the speed of consumption, then we should act and eat as if we were still subjected to a world of simple scarcity. If our hunger is constitutively confused—oriented to high-consumption in a world overburdened with consumables—then let's create a private paleo world where we eat as if there were only the scarcest and simplest of foods. (And hasn't the same thing happened to liberal ecological morality: whatever the complexities of the globe, act privately as if our world were otherwise—eat organic, recycle, drive a smaller car…).

The confusion of hunger is also, again according to those who know our species' history better than we supposedly know ourselves, altering our relation to information. In a world of scarce resources, competitiveness and fear, it made sense that we would develop a capacity to consume multiple sources of information quickly.

But, then, with a long (colonizing) history of enabled leisure we allowed ourselves, as Katherine Hayles put it, the luxury of "deep attention" rather than "hyper-attention". Because of all that hunting and gathering that generated the big brain and, hence, generated technology, we could sit down and read Jane Austen, and start to think deeply about profound moral questions and the history of "man." Our moral theory could liberate itself from mere survival and the minimal moralism of being decent only to those with whom we were adjacent; we could—as Henri Bergson argued—develop from a morality of mutual cooperation towards a spiritual religion concerned with a completely virtual and futural humanity.

We might say that our spiritual hunger is constitutively and felicitously confused: we act towards others not only with a sense of self-interest, but with a broader concern for humanity to come. Unfortunately, as with the hunger for food that developed to the point of gluttony, the hunger for information and cognition has—as Bernard Stiegler tells us in *States of Shock*—developed to the point of stupidity. We are now falling back into the hyper-attention from which deep cognition evolved. This may help us with video games and day trading, but it is perhaps the worst skill of all if we are to think the complex temporalities of climate change.

And so, before we even consider the temporal complexity of the problem of climate change, we might note this: what we have come to think of and esteem as "the human"—man as a political animal with a sense of himself as a being oriented towards the care of others—is already under the pressure of its own constitutive hunger. The "original" desire for complexity and technology has positively been folded back into desire and allowed the human organism to over-consume the world's resources and then over-consume the resources of those it does not deem to be sufficiently human.

"Man" is an effect of hunger confusion; when "he" finds that the planet he so successfully mastered and rendered consumable is starving, his thought is not of rethinking the dialectic of hunger but of going on a diet. If we manage consumption now, we might develop a little more, and then live a little longer—sustain, survive, adapt, mitigate, but do not rethink the trajectory of this thinking animal.

Rather, then, than argue that we should de-confuse hunger—have us all return to a simpler, frugal, paleo or eco-friendly appetite—I would suggest that we embrace hyper-confusion. Rather than say that "we" evolved but that our hunter-gatherer and simple narrative brains cannot cope with the moral and resource-complex worlds that "we" generated, we might think of refusing that simple confusion of economy. Rather than say that we have been too clever for our own good and that we have developed techno-science without thinking enough about what it took from the planet and stole from most humans other than those who think of themselves as the "we" of humanity—let us shift that confusion of hunger out of the temporal narrative.

It is not the case that there was ever a "we" that embarked upon a journey of complexity, riven by a time lag (between a body that is over-fed and a brain that is stuck in a too simple past). That split is always among some who think of themselves as the "we" (the "we" who unfortunately destroyed the planet and who now declare "us" to be anthropocene humans) and some who have no hunger for any future "we."

Let us imagine this at its simplest: there are those whom the "we" consume—not only animals, but future and present humans not blessed with the burden of cognizing the wonder and blessedness of the species. Do we think the various species on the red list have even the simplest hunger for the future? Or are most modes of life living on with the most confused of hungers, a hunger that is constantly thwarted and not even granted the luxurious temporality of thinking of a future that is tragically bereft of life as we know it. Perhaps, then, the "we" who are so hungry for a future—the "we" that dreams of geo-engineering, colonizing other planets, averting existential risks and enhancing the species—perhaps this "we" should thwart its hunger for the future and think of desires not tied to the rational self-interests of this wondrous history of brain-heavy man? That hunger might be radically con-fused: conjoined and fused with a life not its own, a life that does not appear as a personal surviving life of one of "us."

11.09.2015

Feeding Cars and Junking People

Robert Albritton

Today, we are experiencing a global food crisis. Close to one billion people have to cope with hunger, and many more have to deal not only with the malnutrition that stems from lack of food, but also from the one that derives from eating too much junk food. This latter form of malnutrition is promoted to a large extent by food corporations that have discovered the human love of sweets, a love that is close to an addiction for many people. As a result, now 2.1 billion people world-wide are overweight and according to *The Lancet*, a leading medical journal, this represents an "obesity time bomb" that endangers the future health of people around the globe, and also threatens to bankrupt most healthcare systems.

In *Let Them Eat Junk: How Capitalism Creates Hunger and Obesity*, I explore many dimensions of a set of global food problems that are reaching crisis proportions. For example, it is now common for commentators to refer to a "global obesity epidemic." While this awareness is a good thing, I wish more attention were paid to the "global hunger epidemic," even though many people take this as simply the way things have always been. But should we really accept that the underlying cause of one-third of all child deaths under five is malnutrition, and that, according to estimates by the World Food Program, 16,000 children around the world die each day from hunger-related conditions? Even in rich America over 45 million people live in poverty. Further, 20 percent of all American households are dependent on food stamps, including 22 million children; yet Congress cut the food stamp program by 7 percent in 2014. It did this despite the shocking growth of poverty that caused US households dependent on food stamps to increase by 52 percent in the past 5 years.

Hunger and obesity on a global scale are very large problems to analyze within a short article. Hence, I will narrow it down to one topic: US corn production and distribution. The US produces 40 percent of the world's corn harvest, placing it far ahead of other countries, but it only exports about 15 percent (exports to Mexico of US subsidized corn have devastated Mexican corn farmers). Though corn can be a healthy food, in the US very little is consumed directly as a part of human nutrition, for over 40 percent is converted into ethanol in order to feed cars, while 36 percent is used as feed for livestock—it takes 425 gallons of water to produce 4 oz. of beef—which in turn becomes meat for human consumption, and much of the rest (other than exports) is converted into high fructose corn syrup (HFCS), the main sweetener of most junk food and a major contributor to ill health: diabetes, heart attacks, obesity, fatty liver disease, etc. On average American children get 20 percent of their calories from HFCS.

HFCS is the sweetener of choice in most junk foods, and this results in its being the number one source of calories in the American diet. It is cheaper than sugar derived from sugar cane or sugar beets, largely because the US government subsidizes corn (starting in 2015 farmers must choose between price protection or quantity protection) and has placed import duties on other sources of sugar. The average American consumes 41.5 lbs of HFCS per year. Dr. Lobstein of The World Obesity Federation has argued that the food industry has particularly targeted children, because eating habits are established early and continue throughout life. Children now eat more than they did three decades ago, "translating to roughly $20 billion in additional business for the food industry."

Having discovered long ago that most humans have a "sweet tooth," the food industry now adds HFCS to most processed foods (74 percent of packaged foods). Research published over a year ago in the journal *JAMA Internal Medicine* argues that people who consume 25 percent or more of their daily calories from added sugar nearly triple their likelihood of dying from heart disease. Further, it has been known for years that the high intake of added sugar can be a causal factor in cancer, diabetes, fatty liver disease and many other chronic diseases. On the one hand, the US government gives large subsidies to the corn industry, while, on the other, the USDA (US Department of Agriculture) claims that healthier diets would save $75 billion a year in medical expenses, which now include 16 million Americans with heart disease, 25.8 million with diabetes, and 31 percent with fatty liver disease.

The production of HFCS typically uses about 5 percent of the total US corn crop, and, as already pointed out, 40 percent goes to ethanol. 90 percent of the corn crop is genetically modified to be immune to herbicides, the active ingredient of which is "glyphosate." This is highly problematic given that even the conservative WHO (World Health Organization) has stated that it is probably a carcinogen. Furthermore, weeds have in time built a resistance to glyphosate, so that more and more has to be used to kill what are becoming superweeds. Finally, as more people get exposed to more glyphosate, they manifest a variety of diseases. For example, in Argentina, in places where glyphosate is widely used, birth defects have gone up fourfold. A recent study by an MIT scientist claims that in combination with other chemicals, glyphosate is a causal factor in autism spectrum disease, and that at current rates 50 percent of Americans will be autistic by 2030.

According to existing legislation, the US is planning a four-fold increase in corn biofuel by 2022, and all of this corn will be GM. US subsidies for food and farming over the next ten years come to nearly $1 trillion. In 2012, 283 million lbs of glyphosate (mostly produced by Monsanto as "Round Up") were dumped on American corn fields, and this will steadily increase with the greater acreage of biofuel corn and with the growing resistance of weeds to this herbicide. Further, as more and more acreage is converted to highly subsidized corn destined to be biofuel, the prices of other crops and hence of food in general will increase as their supply decreases and the supply of corn for biofuel increases. At the same time as more corn is grown for biofuel and less for food, the prices of foods based on corn will increase. It has already been estimated that this was the main cause of an increase in the price of food in recent years. For example, corn prices increased by 21 percent in 2009 as a result of the use of corn for biofuels.

The short-term profit orientation of most capitalist practices is radically inadequate for dealing with long-term social and environmental costs. It gets us into trouble by ignoring the most important variables when it comes to the future quality of the environment and of life, which are, of course, thoroughly intertwined. One way forward would be to collect all the profits generated by capitalism and then redistribute them in accord with criteria that advance long-term human and environmental flourishing while reducing social and environmental costs. This would require a transparent economy and new democratic institutions that would include expertise, practical experience, and people most impacted by the particular economic arrangements.

Food could increasingly be supplied by ecologically friendly means informed by advanced studies in ecology, as well as by practical knowledge gained at local levels. Farms could mostly be run by cooperatives, families, or communal forms of organization. Last but not least, it could increasingly be understood how much health depends on a healthy diet, how much all human flourishing is integrated with environmental flourishing, and how much the food system needs to be part of this integration.

06.22.2015

Part III

Interventions

A. Of God and Gods

Divine Violence in Ferguson

Slavoj Žižek

In August 2014, violent protests exploded in Ferguson, a suburb of St. Louis, after a policeman shot to death an unarmed black teenager suspected of robbery: for days, police tried to disperse mostly black protesters. Although the details of the accident are murky, the poor black majority of the town took it as yet another proof of the systematic police violence against them. In U.S. slums and ghettos, police effectively function more and more as a force of occupation, something akin to Israeli patrols entering the Palestinian territories on the West Bank; media were surprised to discover that even their guns are more and more U.S. Army arms. Even when police units try just to impose peace, distribute humanitarian help, or organize medical measures, their *modus operandi* is that of controlling a foreign population. *The Rolling Stone* magazine recently drew the conclusion that imposes itself after the Ferguson incident:

> Nobody's willing to say it yet. But after Ferguson, and especially after the Eric Garner case that exploded in New York after yet another non-indictment following a minority death-in-custody, the police suddenly have a legitimacy problem in this country. Law-enforcement resources are now distributed so unevenly, and justice is being administered with such brazen inconsistency, that people everywhere are going to start questioning the basic political authority of law enforcement.[1]

In such a situation, when police are no longer perceived as the agent of law, of the legal order, but as just another violent social agent, protests against the predominant social order also tend to take a different turn: that of exploding "abstract negativity"—in short, raw, aimless violence. When, in his *Group Psychology*, Freud described the "negativity" of untying social ties (*Thanatos* as opposed to *Eros*, the force of the social link), he all too easily dismissed the manifestations of this untying as the fanaticism of the "spontaneous" crowd (as opposed to artificial crowds: the Church and the Army). Against Freud, we should retain the ambiguity of this movement of untying: it is a zero level that opens up the space for political intervention. In other words, this untying is the pre-political condition of politics, and, with regard to it, every political intervention proper already goes "one step too far," committing itself to a new project (or *Master-Signifier*).

Today, this apparently abstract topic is relevant once again: the "untying" energy is largely monopolized by the New Right (the Tea Party movement in the U.S., where the Republican Party is increasingly split between Order and its Untying). However, here also, every fascism is a sign of failed revolution, and the only way to combat this Rightist untying will be for the Left to engage in its own untying—and there are already signs of it (the large demonstrations all around Europe in 2010, from Greece to France and the UK, where the student demonstrations against university fees unexpectedly turned violent). In asserting the threat of "abstract negativity" to the existing order as a permanent feature which can never be *aufgehoben*, Hegel is here more materialist than Marx: in his theory of war (and of madness), he is aware of the repetitive return of the "abstract negativity" which violently unbinds social links. Marx re-binds violence into the process out of which a New Order arises (violence as the "midwife" of a new society), while in Hegel, the unbinding remains non-sublated.

Are such "irrational" violent demonstrations with no concrete programmatic demands, sustained by just a vague call for justice, not today's exemplary cases of what Walter Benjamin called "divine violence" (as opposed to "mythic violence," i.e. the law-founding state violence)? They are, as Benjamin put it, means without ends, not part of a long-term strategy. The immediate counter-argument here is: but are such violent demonstrations not often unjust, do they not hit the innocent?

If we are to avoid the overstretched Politically Correct explanations according to which the victims of divine violence should humbly not resist it on account of their generic historical responsibility, the only solution is to simply accept the fact that divine violence is brutally unjust: it is often something terrifying, not a sublime intervention of divine goodness and justice. A left-liberal friend from the University of Chicago told me of his sad experience: when his son reached high-school age, he enrolled him in a high school north of the campus, close to a black ghetto, with a majority of black kids, but his son was then returning home almost regularly with bruises or broken teeth—so what should he have done? Put his son into another school with a white majority or let him stay? The point is that this dilemma is wrong: The dilemma cannot be solved at this level since the very gap between private interest (safety of my son) and global justice bears witness to a situation which has to be overcome in its entirety.

03.09.2015

Notes

1.   http://www.rollingstone.com/politics/news/
the-police-in-america-are-becoming-illegitimate-20141205.

God, Charlie, No One

JEAN-LUC NANCY

Translated by Patrícia Vieira & Michael Marder

"Blessed be Thou, No One": this verse of Paul Celan appears in his poem "Psalm". This formula, like much of the poem, imitates a phrase in the Psalms of David ("Blessed be Thou," or "Praise be unto Thee, Lord"). As various commentators have emphasized, and as is clear to anyone with some understanding of the spirit of "monotheism," far from being blasphemous or "atheist," this formula enunciates a deeper truth shared by the three great Abrahamic religions (and, in a completely different register, also shared by Buddhism). Namely, that "God is not 'someone.'"

When one says, "I am X" (for example, "Charlie"), one identifies with a name that refers to a specific person. Many may have the same name but each makes it more specific through one or more other names (family name, sometimes that of the region, of a profession...). "Someone," a person, is a concrete existence, recognizable in the world even if one cannot be reduced to any kind of pure and simple "identity." There are religions in which the gods have proper names because there are several of them (at times, a great number) and each has a particular mode of presence, with specific functions. Each can, therefore, have its own figuration that distinguishes it. These are not persons; they are figured presences that derive their life from the persons who pray to them and perform their rites.

The name "God" is not the name of such a figure. For this reason, the unique "god" of monotheism, in all its instantiations, cannot be represented. The images of God are not, in the first place, forbidden; they are, above all else, impossible. Even there where they are not formally prohibited, the faithful know full well that these images are not God (this is true even when the images are attributed a sacred value, as is the case of the icons in so-called "Orthodox" Christianity). "God" is nothing but a common name—god, a god—used to signal, rather than to define, that which escapes every name, that which is unnameable.

Each version of monotheism indicates, in its own way, this unnameability. For the Jews, God has a name that cannot be uttered. For the Christians, he has a kind of name by default, a defective proper name, that is the common name "god" ("deus" in Latin: the light of the sky, the day). In Islam, God has multiple names that refer to his qualities, and an oft-quoted tradition attributes 99 names to him, while the 100th remains unknown. The name *Allah*, which is a modification of an older denomination, denotes the infinite distance from the true name.

A common and very profound characteristic of monotheisms is that the affirmation of the one god is much more symbolic than arithmetical. The one god is a god whose uniqueness escapes every kind of recognition, determination, and identification. As the Quran affirms, he is "the Impenetrable" and "no one is equal to him" (Surah 112). If no one is equal to him, he himself is not equal to "one" according to any value we could attribute to unity and to uniqueness. To limit myself to an example, saying that he is "alone" has no more sense than saying that he is with everyone.

It is, therefore, impossible either to understand or to identify in some way this god that cannot be compared to any other god. It is only possible to worship him, if one wishes, in a way that would be deemed the least imperfect. We can further think that the division of monotheism into several big branches—at least three, but each also divided in its turn— is nothing but a distribution of possibilities or of chances created by the opening up of a relationship. This distribution according to historical moments, places, and languages, is always renewing the forms of worship.

This does not mean either adulation or enslavement to idolatry, but, rather, the exact opposite. One of the distinguishing features of monotheisms is the rejection of "idols," that is to say, in ancient Greek, of images in the sense of appearances, visions, or phantoms. It is simply unthinkable to imagine that which has no relation with any kind of presence or representation. At most, we can, in the words of Montaigne, "imagine the unimaginable" (*Essays*, II, 12)—which means to make the effort to abandon every identification with and every fixation on our subject, even at the level of language. "Do not burden your heart with an idea that pertains to Him; you risk assimilating Him to what He is not" (Bistami, *Shatahat*, 203).

The tradition linked to the refusal of idolatry is the prophetic one. Prophets are not those who announce the future; they are those who speak "for," in the Greek sense of the word. Moses, Jesus, Mohammed—the three great prophets do not exclude the others—speak for the one who does not speak because he is not a person. They speak for No One. They convey "a speech that comes out of fire without any image," as Moses put it in Deuteronomy 4:12, or they receive the task of reading or spreading the word ("Read!," *Surah* 96). Insofar as they are prophets, they are admirable, prodigious men we could call saints, but they remain men, whose lives are well known. The texts that they write are entrusted to our understanding and our reflection. These writings come from far away in our history and they have been, and continue to be, read and reread, recited, commented upon and interpreted. The word of No One is not set in stone, since no word is: the meaning of words is revived and played out again and again, indefinitely.

This is why one says that the "signs of God are obvious in the hearts of those to whom the Science has been given" (*Surah* 29, 49). The Science in question is the knowledge acquired through meditation on the impossibility of giving only one meaning in our languages to the word of No One. That word tells us, above all, not to freeze any meaning of any word in any language. If there are many languages and many possibilities of meaning in each of them, it's because language points to something beyond it, towards an infinity of meaning and towards a truth that exceeds all signification and all naming.

That infinity of meaning, which is simultaneously obvious and obscure, is the true experience of our Jewish, Christian, Muslim *and* philosophical traditions. Philosophy reflects the infinity of meaning but steers clear of the possibility of naming anything as a supreme name, including the name "No One."

Philosophy is embroiled in all this history of the Mediterranean, Greek, Jewish, Arab, Roman, and European worlds (I am leaving aside here the parallels and the differences that link it to Hinduism, Buddhism, Taoism, etc.). In Greek philosophy, the name "god" no longer refers merely to the different kinds of gods, all with their own proper names, but to a category without a name, i.e. the divine. The latter does not indicate a kind of person or of existence but the fact that meaning is infinite and that the truth exceeds all attempts to pinpoint it. Philosophy rejects the possibility of attributing an immutable meaning to words, which entails rejecting the possibility of saying "Blessed be Thou" to some "one" or even to love the whisper of a name.

Even so, anyone can have very good reasons to name No One. No criticism can be opposed to this gesture. The demand of both monotheism and philosophy is simply that the name should not become an idol. It should not become the representation of a "being" or of a "person." And those who have faith should know that they utter this name, or this misnomer, beyond all possibilities of naming.

The faithful should also know that the one God, or No One, prescribes neither a fixed law nor a determined social, political, or economic regime, even if he does establish a certain number of precepts for his adoration through this or that prophet. Because if all is prescribed, fixed, and unchangeable, divine infinity is denied. God/No One becomes a fetish, that is to say, a false god or an idol. This false god can become an instrument for all sorts of desires for power and domination.

Since all figurations and all names of "god," can be utilized in this way, it is legitimate and even advisable to criticize all instances of its use. This does not harm in any way the faith of those who trust in what lies beyond all names and figurations. On the contrary, it would honor a faith that does not lend itself to being usurped by interests of power and domination. The Christian faith was tainted by the colonizers and the conquerors; this should not happen again.

The true God, or the truth of "god," lies not in fetishism, that is to say, in the superstition of names, of figuration, and of various representations such as money, arms, verity, purity, salvation, and so on. It truly lies beyond these, in infinity, which is in another world but which opens itself here and now, each time, in the world where we live.

Infinity is neither enormous nor unattainable. It is simply this: not to get attached to something determinate, fixed, identified, named with a supposedly proper name.

03.02.2015

The Muslim 'No'

Michael Marder

Each of the three monotheistic religions, commonly referred to as "Abrahamic," has its own affirmation of faith, a single statement held to be fundamental by its adherents.

In Judaism, such a proclamation is *Shema* (*Listen*), drawn from Deuteronomy 6:4. It reads: "Listen, O Israel: The Lord is our God, the Lord is One!" Observant Jews must recite *Shema* daily—for instance, before falling asleep—and it is supposed to be the last thing they utter before dying. Even in the most private nocturnal moments and on the deathbed, *Shema* announces monotheistic creed, in the imperative, to the religious community, united around "our God" who is "One."

Christianity, too, has its dogma going back to the Apostles' Creed, dating to the year 150. Still read during the baptismal ritual, the statement of faith begins with the Latin word *Credo*, "I believe" and continues "…in the all-powerful God the Father, Creator of heavens and earth, and in Jesus Christ, His only Son, our Lord, conceived by the Holy Spirit, born of the Virgin Mary…" *Credo* individualizes the believer; not only does it start with a verb in the first person singular, but it also crafts her or his identity through this very affirmation. While the Judaic *Shema* forges a community through a direct appeal to others, the Christian profession of faith self-referentially produces the individual subject of that faith.

The declaration of Islamic creed is called *Shahada*, "Testimony." In contrast to its other monotheistic counterparts, however, it commences with a negation. Its first word is "no," *lā*: "There is no god [*lā ilāha*] but Allah, and Muhammad is his messenger." Formulated in the early part of the eighth century, it plays an integral part in the conversion process and is the first of the Five Pillars of Islam. The first part of the "Testimony" is a confession of *tawhid*, or the oneness of God. Its rigorous monotheism hinges on repudiating the existence of any other gods, which, itself, borders on atheism. (The four opening words in the English translation of *Shahada*, "there is no god," may be easily conflated with an atheist conviction).

Generally speaking, it is highly significant that the Islamic affirmation of faith is a negation of other deities and religions. Some will, no doubt, take this as evidence of the intolerance lodged at the very heart of Islam. For my part, I do not think things are that straightforward. After all, the Córdoba Caliphate (929-1031) was respectful of ethnic and religious diversity under Muslim rule. In the medieval Islamic world, astronomy, mathematics, and medicine were thriving. Arabic translations of and commentaries on Aristotle proved indispensable to the transmission of the Greek classics they helped reintroduce in Europe. So, the question is: how can the same principle of *Shahada* stand behind these developments and the current rise of the Islamic State?

I suggest that the negation, with which the Testimony begins, is the common element motivating the great achievements of Islamic science and philosophy, on the one hand, and the fundamentalist purges of non-believers, on the other. The negative form of *Shahada* broaches the indeterminate space of freedom, untethered from a specific ethnic community as much as from the subjective identity of the believer. Sweeping the ground clean of all idols, fetishes, and gods, the most recent of the three monotheisms endows its followers with the possibility either to create something new in this clearing or to carry the destructive drive through to its conclusion, destroying and negating itself. There is nothing inherent in Islam as such that could influence the choice one way or another. What proves to be decisive here is the historical conjuncture at any given moment, as well as the capacity to endure and sustain the heavy burden of freedom.

Amidst the crumbling traditional values of the West, with its own "death of God" announced by Friedrich Nietzsche, the religious "no" waxes more destructive than ever. Its response to the passive secular nihilism resulting in apathy, relativism, and the loss of meaning is the active nihilism of fanatical fervor, intolerance, and insistence on the absolute truth... of nothing in the form of the negation. Although it appears that the fundamentalist option is the exact opposite of the liberal West, the two nihilisms resonate with and reinforce each other logically, ideologically, and militarily. Disenfranchised and disenchanted young people from Europe who, having converted to Islam, join the ranks of the Islamic State fail to realize this secret complicity. Adrift and in search for meaning, they fall into the trap of yet another, more deadly, nihilism, which they mistake for a certain and secure foundation lacking in the milieu they are familiar with.

All this is not to say that basic religious pronouncements in the affirmative, like the Judaic *Shema* or the Christian *Credo*, are in any way superior to the basic negation in *Shahada*. Quite the contrary: the inaugural "no" holds a greater potential for freedom than they do. Nor do I claim that every Muslim person and community responds to the provocation of negativity in the same manner. Indeed, many in the past and in the present have embarked on a more difficult path of radical enlightenment and creativity, indebted to the dismantling power of the negation. But as the battle for hegemony in the Muslim world rages, it is crucial to understand what is at stake in the most recent incarnation of the fundamentalist destructive fury, where it is situated on the global theologico-ideological map, and which alternatives are available to the thoughtless dismissals (or endorsements) of Islam so prevalent today.

05.25.2015

B. Disasters, Natural and Cultural

The Tenth Anniversary of Hurricane Katrina

Warren Montag

Allegory, particularly in the form of personification, was one of the most important forms through which late Medieval society attempted to understand itself. And few literary texts display the ways in which allegory served to capture and bind together the abstract and the concrete, the temporal and the eternal as William Langland's *Piers Ploughman*, a work composed in the late fourteenth century. At the conclusion of the text, the narrator, Will, awakens from a dream vision. What has been revealed to him, however, does not pertain to the spirit, but to the flesh. He is starving, and the soul can no longer ignore the demands of the body. Frightened, and without any prospect of a meal, Will encounters the allegorical figure of Need. Need offers him a kind of salvation, but it is a salvation of the flesh: he may take what is necessary for his survival without regard to conscience or doctrine, for "Need has no law and shall never fall in debt for the things he takes his life for to save." Just as he needs no one's permission to drink water from a ditch, Need tells Will, he may appropriate the food or clothing he requires not to perish from hunger or exposure, even if they are the property of another.

Langland here invokes the principle, by his time established in canon law, of *"necessitas non habet legem,"* reminding us that *necessitas* was typically understood not as "necessity" (defined in opposition to freedom or chance), but as physical need, above all, the need for food to sustain human life: need has no law, that is, laws determining ownership and use of goods do not apply to cases in which an individual, lacking food, clothing or shelter, faces the risk of death. Moreover, this principle indemnified those who stole to supply a third party with necessities, as well as those who did not steal food or clothing, but objects that could be sold in order to purchase what was necessary to existence. To be sure, the great Medieval thinkers, from Thomas Aquinas to William of Ockham, disputed the fine points of this principle: whether urgency required a suspension of property right (*jus*) or simply restored the original community of goods granted by God to all humankind; whether the act constituted the crime of theft from which the thief, after the fact and more or less automatically, would be immunized, or whether the act was performed outside the law's jurisdiction, in a pre-legal state in which property as such did not exist. The principle itself, however, was never really in dispute: the allegorical figure of Need was this principle brought to life and given voice.

Today, we have little taste for allegory even in its historical incarnations. There appears little hope that Need will come alive and speak to us as he did to Langland's Will, and even less that he would deliver, or we would hear, a lesson in what might be called the non-illegality of theft in cases of starvation or exposure. To understand how completely this doctrine has been forgotten and the extent to which its forgetting is the necessary condition of political and economic thought from Locke and Adam Smith to the present, we might turn to what in fact is an allegorical figure we do not recognize as such, the personification not simply of a powerful hurricane, but of both the state of need and the state of exception: Katrina. The occasion of the tenth anniversary of Hurricane Katrina allows, or compels, us to acknowledge the extent to which the principle "need has no law" appears unthinkable, as if it were nothing more than a superstitious remnant of the "dark ages," without any connection to the economic realities of our time.

Although within a few days of the hurricane, nearly a thousand people had died in New Orleans itself, many directly or indirectly from exposure, or the lack of water, food and medicine, few observers thought to question the enormous mobilization of resources to combat "looting," a term that designates precisely the acts that Langland's Need tells us cannot justly be prevented or punished. Even the public declaration by the Governor of Louisiana that national guard troops had been given the order to "shoot and kill" looters, despite the fact that the residents had had by that point no "legal" access to drinking water for three days (during which the average temperature was 35 degrees Celsius) and no significant measures had yet been taken to provide them with food, water and medicine, did not seem particularly noteworthy, let alone deserving of condemnation.

Perhaps Katrina spoke, and speaks, to us, as if she were Need's own child, in incomprehensible words of wind and rain and water. Like Shakespeare's Tempest, the storm embodied and represented in its violence the violence of the neo-liberal order itself, as if Katrina's fury were a dim allegory of a far more extensive destruction. This destruction operates according to the double strategy displayed so vividly in New Orleans ten years ago. On the one hand, the state acts by refraining from action, by exposing populations to total destitution, at the same time that it appropriates and offers up for sale vital resources which, once appropriated as property, confer on the proprietor immunity not only to the claims, but to the needs, of others. On the other, the rights and privileges granted to property owners are regarded as so absolute that those who violate these rights, irrespective of the circumstances that lead them to do so, can be killed with impunity (and not only by agents of the state but increasingly by private individuals).

Can we imagine what Need would say to us now, at a time when states have been ordered by their creditors to liquidate emergency food supplies and to allow the private appropriation of water, when climate change makes exposure to the elements a matter of life and death, that is, when the age-old right to subsistence, and finally existence, has been revoked in order to secure the world for capital investment? But Need, coextensive with our physical existence, is already among us, urging us to revoke the revocation of the right to go on living, to submit property right and market providentialism to the demands of life, and above all to resist the necro-economy that recognizes no limit but the power of those who refuse its inhuman order.

08.31.2015

Chernobyl as an Event: Thirty Years After

MICHAEL MARDER

There are those exceptional instances, in which a date or a place stands for a particular event that happened then and there. "9/11" and "Chernobyl" symbolize in a recognizable shorthand two traumatic occurrences, two catastrophes that have since become watersheds not only for the American and European consciousness but also for world history and politics. Why the tendency to represent these events in such shorthand? Do we lack the time or the space to elaborate upon them in more than a word and a couple of numbers? Or is something else, something more profound, masking itself behind this marked brevity?

Perhaps to symbolize an occurrence by means of a date or a place is a way to speak about the unspeakable. In so referring to traumatic events, we scarcely indicate them, keep them encrypted, or let them barely peer from the crypt of the unrepresentable. Perhaps, then, we cordon off, circumscribe, and condense them to a numeric or geographical inscription in order to tuck them into a far corner of the mind and not deal with them in all their excruciating, intolerable details. Psychoanalysts have a word for this mental operation, namely disavowal.

One thing is certain—there is always a price to pay for the tricks of our psychic economies. Supplanting the event (only one event, no matter how traumatic), the date and the place become exclusive and exclusionary. Or, even, egoistic. "9/11" names one event and, with this, erases multiple others, not the least of them the one now known as "the other 9/11," the day in 1973 when General Augusto Pinochet carried out a bloody *coup d'état* in Chile. "Chernobyl" not only designates the explosion of Reactor 4 at a Ukrainian nuclear power plant on April 26, 1986 but also expunges from collective memory the repeated massacres of its Jewish residents during the Russian Civil War and by the Nazi occupying forces during the Second World War. The shorthand goes hand-in-hand with a pretentious supposition that nothing else of what has ever happened or will ever happen on that day or in that place really matters. The event prohibits all other events, including those that have already come to pass. It is like a black hole that sucks into itself the past and the future, along with vast stretches of space and language itself.

I have noted how events designated by a date or a place mark a day in a calendar or a geographical locale with their exclusive and exclusionary associations. Chernobyl is, in this sense, the most eventful of all the terrible events; it brands not only our conception of a given place but that very place itself, making it unfit for human habitation, extending a sizable "zone of exclusion," from which we are barred, around it. This place that lends its name to an event loses every feature of place-ness, to the extent that it no longer admits anyone into its midst, unless you are willing to risk your life by staying there (as some older residents of Chernobyl, who have refused to be evacuated in the aftermath of the disaster or who have clandestinely returned to their abandoned homes, have chosen to do).

There is yet another price to be paid: when the conditions of possibility for any experience, among which Immanuel Kant counts space and time, blend with whatever is conditioned by them, they flip into the impossible. Chernobyl is this conditioned conditioning, an atopos where nothing can happen, at least for humans who have been permanently expelled from that non-place. It is the event of no event, the event that singularly negates the future, crushing it under the weight of nuclear eternity. Chernobyl, or that which now goes by that name, does not fill out the schema of experience because the radiation, which continues to emanate all around it, is not accessible to our senses. But despite—thanks to?—its elusiveness, the event of Chernobyl also overwhelms our finite sensibility and nullifies the experiential schema itself. The conditioned conditioning turns out to be totally unconditioned and deadly in its absolute excess.

Nothing can happen in Chernobyl anymore and a lot is happening there, just not for us. In this post-apocalyptic workshop, the specimens of *Homo sapiens* have receded to the background, while "wild" flora and fauna have made their comeback. The choice between reality in-itself, including its animal and vegetal instantiations, and reality for-us proves to be a false alternative; the post-Chernobyl world—a place now acquiring temporal, chronological connotations—is a reality for the plants and animals that live and die and, in some cases, adapt to an environment laced with high levels of radioactive elements. Still, however vigorously we dehumanize the event, the shadow of *the future of no future* hangs over all living beings, and even the earth, in Chernobyl's exclusion zone. If reports are true that the plants harmed by extreme radiation are not decaying as they should, then the current vegetal and animal growth in the "radioactive reserve park" is unsustainable and might be short-lived, seeing that the soil will not be enriched through the normal decomposition of organic matter. A place arrogates to itself the title of an event to the detriment of its placeness and of eventhood as such.

As we begin working through the "event" of "Chernobyl," it is not advisable to dissolve the former in the latter, for instance at the level of everyday discourse: "Chernobyl happened." A series of tough considerations await us. What have our technologies done to a place exemplary of human-induced devastation but certainly not alone in suffering our impact? What has that place, converted into a vessel for the event, done to us? Where does the "event" of "Chernobyl" leave the consciousness rendered impotent by its effects? How does it influence human and other-than-human bodies? A lonely word, which is moreover a geographical locution, cannot cope with the thinking of the event. Taken in isolation, it prompts us to act out, rather than work through, the nuclear trauma. In place of a designation for place, we sorely need both something less and something more than a word: a *logos* no longer confined to human discourse and capable of bearing witness to the unbearable.

04.25.2016

A State of Foreclosure: The Guantánamo Prison

Jill H. Casid

One month has passed since U.S. President Barack Obama held a press conference on February 23, 2016 to announce the plan for the "once and for all" closure of the Guantánamo Bay prison as a means of "closing a chapter in our history." That "Plan for Closing the Guantánamo Bay Detention Facility" was submitted to Congress by the Department of Defense seven years after President Obama signed the executive order (on January 22, 2009) that set the mandate "promptly to close detention facilities at Guantánamo." It is not just that this closure is behind schedule: the closure itself cannot come to a close.

Under the heading of "closing," the plan lays out neither an end to indefinite detention nor a check on growing mass incarceration but, rather, a technique of transfer for the remaining 91 detainees. That closure cannot come to a close but must take the shape of transfer is not exceptional; it is integral to the state of exception that is the ongoing war on terror. Transfer, far from a problem with this particular closure plan, is a tactic of the broader closure problem that is the carceral state. To transfer is to extend the temporal illogics of indefinite detention across an undefined and spreading global geography. It is to produce state power by a transferential expansion that is precisely without end in a death-world driven by a psychosocial economy of violent foreclosure.

Whether Guantánamo closes or not in this extension of endless war, we inhabit a terror-zone in which the making of the death-worlds of the living dead ostensibly "over there" (in the occupied territories and extra-legal limbo zones of the "black sites" referring to unseen incarceration) are also "right here" as the limits not just on right but also on the sensible. What electrifies, what makes palpable the disavowed filaments of connection between the death-worlds ostensibly far away, in the floating

Guantánamo that cannot come to a close and those of mass incarceration right where we are?

Consider U.S. artist Laurie Anderson's installation *Habeas Corpus* (October 2-4, 2015) that cast a projection of former detainee Mohammed el Gharani from an undisclosed location in West Africa into the interior of the Park Avenue Armory in New York City.[1] It cast his live-feed image onto a colossal white plaster rendering of a seated figure in an uncanny and virtual reversal of the Lincoln Memorial, in which the imprisoned takes the grand seat, white turns to black, and the history of slavery returns as the present condition of the carceral. The projection and magnification trick of the single and massive beamed-in figure converts the over-there into the unavoidably here. But the device of the story-telling projection also, at the same time, points to the limits of the monumental and sovereign figure of the solitary and surviving witness against the weight of the foreclosure of loss and vulnerability.

Reckoning with the death-worlds in which we lose ourselves demands a recognition of the contaminated mixtures of affect and the development of a capacity for an improper geometry, one committed to drawing lines that connect the non-reciprocal and the incommensurable. That closure must be held out as a promise, endlessly deferred in time and ceaselessly extended spatially, is fundamental to the fantasy logics of detainment that extend the prison as if it were the psychic space of fortified resolution. The expanding prison of indefinite detention does not close the wounds of injury and loss by incarcerating those who are made to figure their infliction. Rather, indefinite and expanding detention functions as a technology of violent foreclosure— a means of expelling even the possibility of the mortal facts of vulnerability by the violent transfer of the inevitable wounds and losses to come onto those detainees who are made to flesh them out for us. The closure that continues to enclose without ever closing is the fossil fuel that powers what is condensed by the promise of the carceral state of foreclosure that is our current condition: that the infinitely extensible detention camp-prison could once and for all close on the materialization of a fantasy of security as an impossible invulnerability. This closure that cannot close but, rather, resorts to transfers as a means of deferral and extension produces death-worlds in which vulnerability and loss cannot be acknowledged or even registered as such because they have been foreclosed in the push to get over and get past.

Latin for "you shall have the body," *habeas corpus* promises recourse against unlawful imprisonment by the action of a writ that is to deliver a chance for appearance before the law. In a letter from June 12, 1863, then president Abraham Lincoln defended the executive action to suspend *habeas corpus* with a biopolitical diagram of the state as a body that must be treated by extreme measures to restore it to the norm of presumptive health: "Nor am I able to appreciate the danger … that the American people will … lose the right of public discussion, the liberty of speech and the Press, the law of evidence, trial by jury, and *habeas corpus* … any more than I am able to believe that a man could contract so strong an appetite for emetics during temporary illness as to persist in feeding upon them during the remainder of his healthful life."

This Civil War past of a slavery that is not at all over returns in this moment of police killings and mass incarceration as the crisis ordinary of chronic war where an "appetite for emetics" fuels the addictive security fantasy of the state as a delimited body from which indefinite dangers to public safety can be vomited out. Gut fear and insatiable appetite for emetics—from water-board flushings and forced feedings to the interminable terminal of the inside-out of the vomitoria of forced confinement—can never be completely expelled as that fear and appetite are also ours. The transverse action of gnawing terror does not just return but also grows with and by the force of the viscous vulnerability recast as threat from the outside-in that it attempts to expurgate. The state of foreclosure puts us in a situation of living death without end. It is a situation of death-in-life that demands a modality of not transversal grief but of transversal vulnerability as an uneasy practice of care for what cannot be foreclosed.

03.21.2016

Notes

1.   For views of Laurie Anderson's *Habeas Corpus* at the Park Avenue Armory, see http://armoryonpark.org/photo_gallery/slideshow/laurie_anderson

Redemption Rodeo

Jacob Kiernan

The price of admission is $20, but my mouse hovers over the Check Out button with a tinge of trepidation. My reluctance? To give money to an institution that forces hard labor at 2-20 cents an hour, houses its residents in 6 by 9 foot cells, and murders with the authority of the state. A timer on the page counts down and at, :23, I finalize the order. Tickets to the Angola Prison Rodeo are sent to my email.

In *Discipline and Punish*, Michel Foucault traces the 17th century turn from draconian displays of torture, public stoning and the guillotine towards modes of imprisonment with the hope of "reform." In opposition to displays of brute monarchical force, this reformative prerogative became the foundation of the modern prison system. For us, the lingering question raised by Foucault's work is: where has this reformative agenda gone today?

The Angola Prison Rodeo seems a brute and blatant return to this performative mode of "justice." The prison website lists the Rodeo events: Bull Riding, where untrained inmates attempt to stay on angry bulls, Wild Horse Race, where three-man teams try to rope a horse for long enough for a team member to mount it (a latent parody of escape), Convict Poker, where four inmates sit at a card table in the middle of the arena playing poker, when "suddenly, a wild bull is released with the sole purpose of unseating the poker players" and, the finale, Guts and Glory, where an inmate attempts to remove a poker chip fastened to "the meanest, toughest Brahma bull available." The contests are explicitly violent and obviously gladiatorial.

In 1998, a documentary about Angola Prison was released called *The Farm*. It provides a moving insight into one of the largest prisons in the United States. Angola, once rated the bloodiest prison in America, is

18,000 acres—larger than Manhattan—and is surrounded on three sides by the Mississippi river. 70% of prisoners are sentenced to life without parole; the majority of the rest have sentences so long they will die within the prison walls. Angola also houses and executes death row prisoners. And, twice a year, for one month, it hosts a rodeo where prisoners perform for a packed stadium of entertainment-seekers and fellow prisoners.

The documentary is a tragic and necessary introduction to the bi-yearly festival. It follows six prisoners, including a 22-year-old newly sentenced to life without parole and inmates who have been inside for 20 and 25 years. Clips abound of angry German shepherds (bred on the facility for law enforcement), men (primarily black) being marched into the fields to grow cash crops like cotton, corn, and soybeans for four cents an hour (a clear evocation of the plantation that the prison was built on), and a slick-talking, unselfconscious warden explaining the economics and management of the institution.

Prisoners repeatedly talk about hope: hope of parole, hope of redemption, hope of escape—in dreams or in a coffin—as the warden smugly recites statistics about the miniscule number of prisoners granted clemency. Questions about the constitutionality of the death penalty are barely mentioned. And, those who give up hope, as one man who has served 25 of his 75 year sentence explains, fall into the darkest chasms of prison life.

In *The New Jim Crow*, Michelle Alexander argues that mass incarceration of urban blacks and Latinos in the 1970s was "a stunningly comprehensive and well-designed system of racialized social control." She contends that Ronald Reagan's War on Drugs was a racially coded backlash against the Civil Rights Movement. Prisons were used to "warehouse" inner-city youth, denying them proper employment, education and social mobility, while ingraining a deeply rooted sense of shame in them and, by extension, their race.

While most inmates at Angola are charged with violent crimes, the warehousing of primarily black men, who make up three-quarters of the prison population, seems undeniable. Perpetrated through the mechanisms of a radically biased court system, racist parole boards, and a hyper-conservative governor's office, lock-up in Angola is for life. In part, prisoners generate the means to sustain the institution that imprisons them, ranging from work in the fields and cattle farms to senior inmates working as counselors. Despite decades of education and community service, parole is almost categorically denied: reform is not Angola's agenda.

When I arrive at Angola, thousands of predominantly white Louisianans waddle towards a stadium surrounded by tall, barbed wire fences. A monolithic rock-climbing wall peaks over the top of the gates, as if poking fun at the dream of escape. The events draw around 70,000 spectators on Saturdays and Sundays. Inside, inmates are ramparted between pinched fences, hocking hand-carved rocking chairs, beds and trinkets (and at what a low price!); the craftwork entices hungry consumers, though the marketability of such a skill seems dubious outside the prison walls and within a global-industrial economy.

The stadium is packed: children gleefully run about, adults chat and cheer, popcorn and cotton candy is sold in the stands. Inmates, sitting stoically, are barricaded in their own sections of the arena. A few ranch hands lay hula-hoops in the center of the sandy stadium and half a dozen prisoners take their position within them. Suddenly, an irate bull is loosed, tossing the men in the air and goring them with uncovered horns. The last man standing, a stout white inmate, is the victor.

Inmates try to ride raging bulls—not one gets more than a meter out of the gate. Convict Poker is probably the most stomach-wrenching event. Four inmates uneasily sit at the table in anticipation. When the furious bull is released, it tears the table to shreds, tossing them aside, impaling their flimsy protective gear. Prisoners limp back to their enclosure; from the stands, it's impossible to tell whether with a sense of pride or just a tear in their gut.

As a spectator, the most frightening part of the Rodeo is that it is, in fact, entertaining. As the smell of fresh cracklins wafts through the stands, it's too easy to get lost in the clapping, shouts and excitement. But it is a racist prison system with its own political agenda that has hoisted these men on the horns. Incarceration has sown and grown such a maddening sense of boredom that inmates volunteer to be the objects of this violent voyeurism. Their self-objectification and the risks they endure yield a few bucks and, at best, a bump in their social standing within the prison walls.

In a Foucauldian sense, this brute display of violence is a manifestation of an antiquated form of judicial power: it latently threatens potential offenders in an age when disciplinary modes of power are at work well before any sentence has been handed down. The lives and suffering of these prisoners has become pure spectacle, not limited to the offended and their families (as with the prison's executions), but available to anyone with twenty bucks. Imprisoned by a biased system, inmates' lives, time and bodies have become a commodity that funds the institution that imprisons them.

Narratives of rehabilitation, upon which the modern prison system was formed, do not function within an institution where 90% of the inmates will never leave. There is no point in reforming for a society that you will never rejoin. In the context of a potent Christian philosophy, reformative narratives are reshaped into stories of religious redemption. The warden and prison pastors alike spread tales of redemption, which are internalized by prisoners force-fed false hope.

The Angola Prison Rodeo functions as self-flagellation for inmates within a racist and self-perpetuating prison system. Narratives of Christian guilt are used to exploit prisoners and paying spectators take pleasure in the violence inflicted upon the "guilty." Profits from the Rodeo are routed back into the prison, which then warehouses more young black men. Louisiana, which has the highest incarceration rate in the world, keeps 1 in 55 adults behind bars. However, incarceration is big business throughout the United States, and the Angola Prison Rodeo is a loud and unapologetic display of how profitable those incarcerated are, and a revelation of a population unfazed by the brutalization of "irredeemable" bodies.

11.21.2016

C. Democracy Woes

Blackmailing the Greeks: The End of Democratic Europe

PATRÍCIA VIEIRA AND MICHAEL MARDER

The opposition of the Eurogroup to the Greek government's plans to hold a referendum on July 5 on the proposals of its creditors reveals, beyond a shadow of a doubt, that the European Union is not a democracy. It is a heavily bureaucratic order that rules by decree and imposes its authority onto smaller, weaker member states. Many of the policies it undersigns emanate from non-elected financial institutions that do not represent the will of the Europeans. In other words, it is moving ever farther away from the democratic aspirations that energized the European project and beckoned with a promise of freedom and prosperity for its citizens.

Particularly disheartening was the statement by the German Finance Minister, Wolfgang Schäuble, that, by holding a referendum, Greece was tacitly putting an end to negotiations. The very framing of a popular vote on the bailout terms as a "nuclear option," which could explode the entire edifice of European collaboration on financial matters, is indicative of the establishment's allergy to true democratic procedures with their oft-times uncertain outcomes. For what could be more democratic than a popular vote, where the people as a whole can determine what they consider to be their best interest? Why should the Greeks be prevented from deciding upon their future, if not out of the Eurogroup's desire to dictate the country's destiny and seal its fate as a destitute nation, mired in growing levels of debt, in order to continue filling the creditors' pockets with euros?

Throughout the lengthy process of negotiations, the Greek government and, by extension, the Greek people have been infantilized, cast in the role of capricious children, who do not wish to follow the rules of the rational parental authority of the Troika. For instance, the symbolic refusal of male ministers—including the Prime Minister—to wear ties was interpreted as a sign of their frivolity by the likes of the President of the European Commission, Jean-Claude Junker, rather than a political statement that rejects the "business as usual" technocratic management prevalent in Brussels.

Along with other Southern European countries, Greece is persistently depicted as a society in an immature condition, its members unable to realize what is good for them in the long run. Syriza's initiative to change the disastrous pattern of European policies vis-à-vis its country is seen as a teenage rebellion, too idealistic to take into account the demands of "the real world" that are presumably identical to the Troika's decrees. The exclusion of the Greek finance minister Yanis Varoufakis from the Eurozone finance ministers' meeting on Saturday afternoon smacks of a punishment meted out to an undisciplined child who refused to comply with the norms established by its wiser parents. It is as though the Greeks, among other citizens of indebted EU states, are unready to govern themselves and make sovereign decisions that will impact their lives and livelihoods.

The concrete economic proposals for raising funds, drafted by Alexis Tsipras' government, have been rejected not because they are unrealistic, but because they do not conform to the hegemonic vision of his European "partners" regarding who should be shouldering the price for the crisis. While the authorities of Greece wish to spare its people more hardship and suffering, the institutions that comprise the Troika aim to impoverish the country still further by cutting the already meager pensions and raising the sales tax, which is the least progressive form of taxation, in that it is uniformly imposed on millionaires and unemployed workers alike. The outlines of the impasse are thus exceptionally vivid. On the one hand, there is an aspiration to build a Europe of and for its citizens, while, on the other hand, there is an ambition to maintain the Europe of business interests and to continue enriching the obscenely wealthy few.

This standoff has culminated in the concerted effort we have been witnessing over the past few days on the part of European Union authorities to blackmail Greece: either the country complies with the unsustainable requirements of its creditors, causing the lives of its citizens to deteriorate further as the country sinks deeper into debt, or it faces the collapse of its economy by being forced to default on its payments and leave the Eurozone. Between the devil and the deep blue sea, as it were, the government's answer was to restitute sovereignty back to the Greeks and ask them to express their collective opinion. That course of action was construed as a cardinal sin in the eyes of a Europe leaning ever closer to a totalitarian organization of political life.

The refusal of the Greek government to comply with the decrees of the Eurogroup, which it has rightly characterized as humiliating, is far from an adolescent revolt. Its intention to hold a referendum is an attempt to restore the very democratic ideals that the EU espouses, at least nominally. The present clash between the Goliath of the Troika and the Greek David is, in the last instance, not over the details of a financial deal, nor even over a broader economic plan for an isolated member state, but over the precise seat of sovereignty and the choice of a de facto political model in the EU for the years and decades to come.

If Greece is removed from the Eurozone through unilateral political wrangling that refuses to listen to the voices of the Greeks themselves, the entire project of a democratic European Union comes tumbling down. At stake in the decisions to be made on the Greek situation are the future contours of Europe: whether we are going to have a union of bankers and financiers or a union of peoples. Greece and its government stand at the forefront of this battle for the heart and soul of Europe.

06.29.2015

Why Trump Is Still Here

Linda Martín Alcoff

Why has Trump, or Cruz, for that matter, made such a strong showing in the presidential election? This question has been debated for months, by journalists, by social scientists, all the way from Fox News to MSNBC. Beyond all the pundits' predictions of a quick nosedive, and an easy transition toward other candidates who represent what passes for Republican moderation these days, the race-baiting, carpet bomb-promising, avowedly Islamophobic extremists on the ticket had staying power, even rising to the top. Why?

Let me offer an explanation. White people.

The problem isn't the innate or unchangeable nature of white people, nor is it the economic interests of white people, who for the most part don't have a whole lot. Nor is the problem all white people. Nor is it even, sad to say, *just* white people. But still, with these caveats in mind, in all seriousness: the problem is white people.

The problem is what has come to be called "the epistemology of ignorance." This is the idea that an individual, or more likely, a group or community or society, can develop mechanisms to protect and maintain and pass down to the next generation their colossal ignorance. Ignorance about their own country's history, about their economic prospects, and about the environment in which they live, including both the social and the natural ones.

The idea here, which has been picked up by numerous philosophers working in epistemology (the theory of knowledge) in recent decades, goes beyond a lack of knowledge. It's not just that folks are not knowledgeable. It is that their lack of knowledge is the product of some concerted effort, a conscious choice or, in actuality, a series of choices. Certain news articles, or news sources, are avoided, certain college courses are kept away from, certain kinds of people are never asked for their opinion on the news of the day. The boundaries of the bubble of ignorance are monitored, protected, even nurtured as a positive good.

In other words, the resultant ignorance about the history of Islam, or the real effects of carpet bombing, or the high prevalence of rape in every society is not the product of a lack of effort, but of a sustained effort. And it is an effort that has become more rather than less difficult since the civil rights movement led to a greater integration of our public institutions, media, universities, and workplaces. Yet, it is an effort that continues to pay dividends.

In particular, ethnic studies programs have been under attack, banned in some states' secondary education, zero budgeted by colleges, kept off the lists of required curricula. Officials in Arizona went so far as to enter high school classrooms to confiscate textbooks. These are the very books and courses that might correct the ignorance. And white students who have the temerity to sign up anyway sometimes have their tuition paying parents asking, why are you wasting our money?

Of course, there is widespread ignorance among almost all of the populations in the United States. Comedians (many of them white) have continually enriched their careers from skits involving real people offering dismally uninformed answers to questions about global geography, the political institutions and histories of nations outside the U.S., and other matters. To some extent, the ignorance is nation-wide, not race-specific. But here is where the immigrants living amongst us have an advantage: they at least know something about the areas of the world from whence they came. African Americans have the "advantage" of painful family histories, not to mention painful family experiences in the present day. As do Native Americans, Asian Americans and Latinos. These groups don't live in bubbles in which racism and the legacies of slavery, genocide, and colonialism are only vaguely visible through light-filtering shades.

The real answer to Trump's staying power is the conscious perpetuation and protection of these layers of ignorance in white populations by individuals and too often by institutions and the mainstream media.

Political scientists are well aware of these trends, including those in the business of consulting on electoral politics to help people get elected or to help with tricky bond issues. How do you get a largely white electoral district to vote for non-white candidates? Or to support an increase in taxes for the purpose of improving urban schools or saving urban hospitals? An ingenious answer has been found that actually works: avoidance.

By carefully crafting candidates' profiles and the wording of proposals on municipal bonds in such a way that race will not come to mind, that voters will not view tax proposals as racial redistributions, voters can actually be led to vote their true preferences for the candidate they take to be the most qualified or the bond issue they believe is legitimately necessary. The bubble does not get burst, and those inside can stay safe and secure, yet their impact on those outside the bubble can be mitigated. This strategy has worked, and produced real results. It's brilliant.

However, it is a colossal mistake. White people have a right to their own opinions and judgments, but they do not have a right to their ignorance. We have got to stop playing the avoidance game, the practice of avoiding topics at the family gathering that might trigger an outburst from the bigoted Uncle. The result of this game is that Donald J. Trump is leading in the polls.

Bernie Sanders provides an instructive counterexample. When activists from Black Lives Matter presumptively attacked him from the floor of one of his stump speeches last summer, he let them speak. He invited them for further conversations. He hired them into his campaign, not just to knock on doors, but to help lead strategy and develop agenda. He sat down for a five hour videotaped interview with Killer Mike, the brilliant Hip Hop artist and cultural analyst, filmed in Mike's barbershop in Atlanta. In other words, Sanders admitted there were things he didn't know, and he sought knowledge from the people who did. This is a true political revolution.

02.08.2016

The Con Artistry of the Deal: Trump, the Reality-TV President

MICHAEL MARDER

Four days prior to the US presidential elections, I read Trump's *The Art of the Deal*—a manual for con artists and, as it turned out, an updated version of Machiavelli's *The Prince* for the media age. Having dismissed the Trump candidacy early on in the primaries season as a marketing gimmick intended to promote his overall brand, I wanted to avoid making the same mistake at the very final stages of the campaign. The same cannot, unfortunately, be said of Clinton's team, which clearly did not do its homework. Were her advisors at least to skim through *The Art of the Deal*, they would have promptly realized that no amount of negative publicity could damage the Republican candidate, for whom there is no such thing as "bad" advertisement. Whatever the context, to be mentioned 24/7 on Cable news is, for Trump, a goal in itself, making him larger than life and, therefore, an ideal in which common folk can espy their own unattainable dreams and desires of grandeur.

Perhaps the most emblematic passage from the con artist's manual, and the one most relevant to Trump's political strategy, is the following:

> The final key to the way I promote is bravado. I play to people's fantasies. People may not always think big themselves, but they can still get very excited by those who do. That's why a little hyperbole never hurts. People want to believe that something is the biggest and the greatest and the most spectacular. I call it truthful hyperbole. It's an innocent form of exaggeration—and a very effective form of promotion.[1]

Isn't this precisely what Trump did throughout the presidential campaign? Did he not play to people's fantasies, be they about the revival of the country's industrial might or, on the darker side, about the possibility of achieving social purity by excluding every kind of threatening Other? Far from "innocent," the exaggerations in question helped Trump close the deal with the American public at the price of unleashing a whole range of sexist, racist, nationalist, and homophobic fantasies. It bears mentioning, however, that these fantasies were not created by Trump but merely driven out of hiding in the deep recesses of the unconscious, where they had been taking refuge from the superficial dictates of political correctness. Positively buttressed by projective identification with the "greatest and the most spectacular" business mogul, such phantasmatic construction of "America's greatness" put the self-professed artist of deals in the Oval Office.

The US already had its actor president in Ronald Reagan. And it is about to get its Reality TV president in Donald Trump. What this means is that not only the last dividing lines between fantasy and reality are being erased but fantasy itself, however ominous and disturbing, comes to dictate reality. To paraphrase Plato, Trump is going to be the sophist-king, a master puppeteer of appearances who knows how to manipulate them and to manipulate their very manipulation (e.g., by lambasting the mass media that have literally made him what he is today). As I mentioned in my analysis penned in March of this year for *The Philosophical Salon,* the manipulation of public opinion is nothing new; rather, what distinguishes president-elect from his rivals, including Hillary Clinton, is that "he fully assumes the bankruptcy of metaphysical ideals such as authenticity, essentiality, or firm principles, and acts accordingly... [T]he bygone values are supplanted by nothing—the nothing, to which everything has been reduced. Whereas Ted Cruz & Co. stand for the consciousness of this nothingness, Trump represents its self-consciousness, and this gives him an unmistakable edge."[2]

Instead of giving in to despair in the face of the current political success of con artistry (after all, a strong tradition exists in philosophy, according to which politics is con artistry; Plato uses this conclusion to denounce the political realm of appearances as a whole, while Machiavelli builds upon it to enunciate the guidelines for successful politicians), I'd like to highlight two of its inherent limitations and one unexpected positive implication.

First. Note that, in the case of Trump's political ascent, the medium is not the message. The form he resorts to is decidedly postmodern: the mediatic construction of reality, recently theorized in William Egginton and David Castillo's fascinating book *Medialogies*. But the content is hypermodern, embracing exclusionary nationalism and industrialism. Inevitably, that contradiction, the power of which Trump has harnessed and which he has been riding thus far, will be resolved in favor of one or the other extreme, contributing to the process of post-electoral normalization. What will happen when @RealDonaldTrump (we can't overlook the irony of "Real" in the Twitter handle) switches to @POTUS? When the so-called political movement that brought Trump to power culminates in the static and homogeneous—all-male, all-white—Politburo-like structure of governance? When the new administration becomes one of the least transparent, most secretive in US history?

Second. All the self-contradictory promises the Trump campaign has made will have to give way to actual policy decisions, starting with the choice of Cabinet, which doesn't at all look like it will be comprised of political outsiders. As Hegel reminds us in *Phenomenology of Spirit*, possibilities, capacities, talents, inclinations, etc. are abstract and, because not yet realized, admit everything into their ambit. With their realization, however, certain possibilities fall by the wayside insofar as they are not acted upon or insofar as they stand diametrically opposed to those actualized. As a result, another crucial "Trump card," namely his resistance to being pinned down to one concrete position, will be lost. The author of *The Art of the Deal* is aware of this mode of taming the otherwise unrestrained fantasy: "You can't con people, at least not for long. You can create excitement, you can do wonderful promotion and get all kinds of press, and you can throw in a little hyperbole. But if you don't deliver the goods, people will eventually catch on." The point is that, given the self-contradictions he has been cultivating, Trump will have no other choice but to fail in "delivering the goods," even if he tries to do so. The very strategy that got him elected will backfire in the period of his presidency; it is one thing to break definite election promises, but it is quite another to break promises in fulfilling them.

The *positive implication* of the Trump presidency resonates with Slavoj Žižek's recent analysis of its prospects. Commentators are up in arms that Trump's stint at the helm of the US will spell out "disaster for the planet" and an assured defeat in the battle against climate change, disaster for the most vulnerable and the poor, disaster for race relations... They forget that the Paris climate agreement is too little, too late to keep the world livable, or that wages have not increased and that race relations have hit a new low under the Obama presidency. What the election of Trump signals is that the ideological screens concealing these and other unmitigated catastrophes have fallen and that we can no longer congratulate ourselves on symbolic victories while moving at full speed toward environmental and social collapse. That is how fiction realized makes disavowed reality itself real.

11.11.2016

Notes

1.   Donald Trump, *The Art of the Deal*, New York: Random House, 1987, p. 58.

Brexit: The Importance of Being Able to Leave

DANIEL INNERARITY

Everything that preceded the announcement of a referendum on whether the United Kingdom should remain in the European Union was a political absurdity—demagoguery, irresponsibility, shameful concessions—with one exception: it has politicized an issue that was placidly resting on unquestionable mechanisms. We do not hear a lot of good news out of Europe, which is why I am taking the opportunity to point out one piece of positive news, even if it may be only an unintended consequence of a bad decision: from now on, there will be less excuses to shelter European policies within the limbo that has protected them from the decisions of Europeans. Politics is returning to the European Union, not because of the dynamism of its institutions, but prompted by the pressures of populism.

The Monnet method of bureaucratic integration has been mechanical and furtive, dominated by necessity. This is revealed by the language of integration: benign despotism, integration by stealth, spill over, irresistible enlargement, irreversibility.... The principal drivers of integration, on the right and on the left, have been governed by a crude determinism presupposing that the desired institutional improvements would inevitably follow economic development. The principal strategy of integration consisted of conceding primacy to processes over results and accepting as a given that success was guaranteed. That led to the idea of irreversibility, the lack of contingency plans and the absence of any reflection about a possible failure, of "exit options" in case things did not go well, something particularly obvious in the case of the single currency, which was agreed upon as an irrevocable commitment.

It is still a paradox that, while the Treaty of Lisbon admitted for the first time the possibility that a member state could leave the Union, membership in the Eurozone continues to be irreversible. No appropriate instruments have been designed for the management of crises, sometimes increasing the risk of future crises in favor of immediate short-term advantages, or leaving a large number of technical and institutional problems unresolved. When there has been a crisis, European leaders have not known how to do anything but convince their electorate that there was no choice; their rhetorical strategy consisted of replacing their habitual absolute optimism with catastrophic visions of what would happen if integration or the monetary union were to fail. This is the conceptual framework in which the so-called "bicycle theory" of European integration was formulated, which posits that integration should not stop, especially in times of crisis. (Although, as Ralf Dahrendorf said, "I often cycle in Oxford, and if I stop pedaling I do not fall; I simply put my feet on the ground.")

All of this had a certain logic, and I am not going to discuss its historical appropriateness or the advantages of its results at this time; I will limit my attention instead to questions about its future utility. What is central to the limitations of this method is the fact that a system designed to minimize decisions cannot make them entirely superfluous, among other things because there are always implicit decisions, in the same way that technical decisions always mask some political motivation. In the 1960s and 70s, in the age of "permissive consensus," when its main policies were distanced from people's daily concerns, the European project did not seem to need the explicit favor of the public. In the current context, which is very different, the type of discourse that is apparently most mobilizing (appealing to the need with which processes lead to established ends, completing what was put into motion, insisting that there is no other possibility…) is, precisely, what ends up irritating citizens the most.

Conflicts like the one related to the Brexit are taking the European project back to a space of free decision making. Integration is a free option, not the inevitable consequence of a process that escapes our control.

I do not have a magic formula for achieving the full democratization of Europe, but I would like to make a modest proposal of democratization centered on the type of discourse we must maintain. Let us begin by abandoning a functionalist language, the language of irresistible and pressing needs, while barely making use of expressions that appeal to our freedom of choice toward the future. The practices of the European Union, which are consensual and gradual, through procedural adjustments, also constitute a system that favors dissimulated or hidden decisions, decisions that are democratically unauthorized, sometimes in the form of non-decisions or submissiveness to technological objectivities. Even if the dictum "federate or perish" by Alterio Spinelli is true, it still speaks the language of coercion. All our vocabulary is one of pure necessity; none of it speaks to a free decision of the citizens. This is incendiary material in the hands of populists, who seek motives to denounce a conspiracy of the elite.

In the face of this type of surrender before a supposed historic necessity, the only democratically acceptable imperative is that Europe must be politicized. From this point of view, the existence of conflicts, questioning and tensions should not be considered a symptom that politics is not working properly, but an opportunity for politicization. The fact that decisions are not easily adopted or accepted is what makes them, strictly speaking, political decisions, beyond unquestionable technological motives.

We may need to thank the British one day for their contribution to politicizing the European Union. We will recognize it more if they stay than if they leave and will more fully appreciate a decision to stay, knowing that they could have left.

03.28.2016

Brexit: Why Referenda Are Not the Ultimate Democratic Tests

MIHAIL EVANS

Western societies understand themselves to be democracies, yet we rarely discuss what this means. Presumably, politics has to do with the people's choices, and the act of voting is taken to be the ultimate democratic test of their adequate expression. Those societies, such as Switzerland, where referenda are commonly used to decide on how the country should act on a given issue, are often seen to be particularly refined forms of democracy. It thus seems natural that the only possible way to resolve the question of whether the United Kingdom should remain a member of the EU is to "put it to the people." I want to argue that this is a mistaken view, which misunderstands the nature of our democracy. I will do so by drawing on the work of a somewhat neglected Dutch political thinker, Frank Ankersmit.

Often, when we speak about our societies as democracies we imagine them as descendants of the ancient Greek political system. But there is a danger of overlooking important historical differences. The *polis* practiced direct democracy, in which every (male, non-slave) citizen had a direct say in the running of the city-state. Ours are representative democracies where we elect particular individuals to engage in the process of decision-making for us. It is often assumed that this change was necessitated by states becoming larger and more populous, the face-to-face decision-making process being no longer possible.

One political theorist, Frank Ankersmit, argues that the modern representative system is superior to direct democracy for our contemporary situation. He does so by looking at what is going on at the level of political representation. In order to understand this, he draws on what art theorists say about how artistic representation works. There are two main theories offered by the discipline of aesthetics. The first suggests that resemblance is central to representation. But this conception is not very satisfying because no acceptable criteria have ever been put forward for what a successful resemblance might be. Paintings, as art historians will tell us, might resemble each other much more than they resemble the objects in the world that they depict. If we adhere to the resemblance theory in politics we will find that every difference between the electorate and its representatives is a case of political misrepresentation. From this point of view, what matters above all is how much the representatives in the parliament appear to look like the population at large.

Ankersmit is much more convinced by the substitution theory, advanced by Burke, Gombrich and Danto, among others. For them, representation is a making-present again of what is currently absent. These aesthetic theorists stress that something original is going on in the process of artistic creation. Looked at from this perspective, without representation, there is no represented. That is, politically, without legislative bodies, there would be no nation as such. The very existence of representative institutions brings into being a political society, which would not exist otherwise. This theory further suggests that what is most important is the interaction between the represented and the representative, and in particular, that representatives should be in a position to transform the situation of which they are a part. Ankersmit argues that a politician must possess an "essentially aesthetic talent of representing political reality in new and original ways." Politicians then, contrary to received wisdom on the issue, need to have a certain distance from citizens in order to be most effective. Conflicts that appear hopelessly irreconcilable at the level of the population (the represented) are often resolvable at the level of representation (political institutions). A great example in our time was the peace settlement in Northern Ireland. Direct democracy viewed from this perspective risks undermining political artistry. Constantly consulting the electorate can be a way of passing the buck to the population, a way of "doing something" when nobody has the political inspiration needed to move forward. Arguably, this is the situation, in which we have found ourselves with the referendum on the British membership of the EU.

The role of political representatives is particularly important today, as many of the most important contemporary issues are ones about which people are conflicted. In the twentieth century, we had clear battles, such as capital versus labor. Today, many issues, such as environmental problems, are ones where most people suffer from the adverse effects they, themselves, cause. Ankersmit ultimately argues that what we need to do is make our political institutions more representative, that is, to widen the gap between the represented and the representatives so "that our legislative representatives be less responsive to the daily desires of their constituents and more attentive to the whole picture." The great challenges of our era are unlikely to be solved by constantly asking the populace what they want. If a political solution is ever found for climate change, it will be among relatively small groups of people who have been delegated the power to make radical change and who will produce a document as utterly surprising as was the Good Friday Agreement. Asking the population what they want through plebiscites, Ankersmit argues, works well for very defined problems that are not linked to wider contexts. What residents would like for a particular locality involves a fairly clear-cut and uncomplicated set of choices. For questions that are complex and interlinked with many other concerns, simplification will inevitably occur. Britain's membership in the European Union is an immensely complex and many-sided issue. Yet the recent campaign in the UK became a referendum on immigration (despite the fact that non-EU immigration has been as high or higher than that originating from the EU in recent years) and an outlet for an associated general feeling that politicians are not addressing the situation of those in low paid and precarious jobs.

There was an almost perverse reaction among the electorate to the fact that many of the opinion-makers in society were in favor of remaining. So much so that we could say there was a rejection of politics as such. Indeed, the accusations of democratic failure, brought to bear on the European Union, could equally well be leveled at the British political scene. I would suggest that what is profoundly wrong at the moment with Western democracies is that the art of politics has been replaced by the technique of politics. For some time now, democratic struggles between divergent points of view in the national and international areas have been replaced by a coalescence around an agreed-upon set of ideas. Politics becomes a wrangling about implementation rather than a competition among fundamentally different ideas. We are now asked to vote for the best managerial team to achieve a set of goals that, with minor variations, both political sides pretty much agreed on. Both in the EU and in the UK, there is a dearth of new ideas and a complete lack of political creativity. By default, the population was asked to decide on the future, but the vote and the debate that surrounded the referendum have still left much in the dark. The public has had its say and now, more than ever, we are in need of political artistry to find a way forward.

06.27.2016

D. On Refugees

Freedom and the Refugees

PATRÍCIA VIEIRA

Liberty is arguably the bedrock of modern, Western-style democracies. From the French Revolution's trinity "Liberty, Equality, Fraternity," the last term echoes nowadays as a quaint, out-of-the-grandma's-closet reverie. Equality fares a bit better. But while we firmly believe that everyone is equal before the law, things get more complicated when it comes to economics. Should everyone (and every nation) have the same amount of money? The rising inequality both within and between countries reveals that, good intentions and the Millennium Development Goals notwithstanding, reducing the differences between haves and have-nots is not high on the agenda. Liberty, however, seems to have held its ground. True, there are plenty of unfree societies, but Europe and the United States are persuaded of the urgency to improve this situation. Many a war has been and is still being fought today with the goal of "exporting" freedom and democracy to those countries that keep resisting them.

A key component of liberty is freedom of movement. People should be allowed to circulate within the borders of their own country and, ideally, also between nations. We are so enamored with freedom of movement that we have granted it even to non-human, more abstract entities such as companies and capital. Free trade relies precisely on the flow of money and goods across boundaries and borders, a circulation accelerated by economic globalization. The Schengen area that now encompasses 26 European nations—22 EU and 4 non-EU members—is part of this generalized push towards freedom of circulation.

In a globalized world of constant movement, refugees appear as grains of sand in a well-oiled machinery. The onslaught of economic migrants and refugees arriving by the thousands to the coastal areas of Greece, Italy and Spain, fleeing civil war in Syria and Iraq, violence in Afghanistan and

Pakistan, and economic hardship throughout sub-Saharan Africa in the hope of reaching what they conceive of as social and economic havens is testing faith in the advantages of freedom of circulation throughout Europe. Walls and fences have sprouted in the migrants' path, from Hungary to Calais, in the North of France, in an attempt to protect the European fortress from the waves of outsiders trying to get in. How do we square freedom of movement with the migrations of refugees? Or, better yet, what does the refugee crisis tell us not only about free circulation, but also about liberty itself?

We have been witnessing for quite some time a mutation in the concept of freedom, a transformation that the successive crisis of migrants and refugees—on the Mexico/US border, in Africa, in Southern Europe—have only made more apparent. The notion of freedom was originally applied only to people, who should be free from violence, danger, etc., and free to engage in the pursuit of happiness in whichever way they saw fit, as the US Declaration of Independence would have it. These two streams of freedom roughly correspond to the negative and positive liberty theory developed by Isaiah Berlin in the mid-twentieth century.

With the development of economic modernity, however, human freedom became increasingly associated to economic liberty, to the point where the former runs the risk of being eclipsed by the latter. Writing at the dawn of capitalism, Immanuel Kant already tied freedom of movement to that of commerce in his famous essay "Perpetual Peace: A Philosophical Sketch." On the one hand, each person has the right to be treated hospitably when they enter into someone else's territory, a precondition for peaceful coexistence that has fed into today's legislation on the Status of Refugees. On the other hand, the "spirit of commerce" that leads human beings to freely establish relationships with one another would also promote peace. For Kant, then, hospitality and commerce were two paths towards the common goal of a free and peaceful world.

From the 18th century onwards, freedom has increasingly become an economic value that displaced a more person-centered conception of the term. Human freedom has been reduced to an appendix of economic liberty, useful only insofar as it bolsters economic growth. Arguably, the Schengen Agreement was not about freedom of movement for European citizens but about the economic integration of European markets.

Nowhere is the contrast between human and economic-based free-dom clearer than in current discourses about the refugee crisis. While the migration of highly skilled professionals and other workers needed to fill gaps in the labor markets of advanced economies is generally welcome, refugees tend to be looked down upon as a burden to a nation. Even when they try to justify receiving large numbers of refugees in their coun-tries, European politicians are forced to resort to economic rhetoric by pointing out the benefits of rejuvenating the ageing European workforce with youthful migrants.

Freedom of movement for people, for the sake of their being-people, is on the wane. Beneath the veneer of humanitarianism, the economy rules supreme. The current refugee crisis unfolding on the borders and at the heart of the European Union reveals that liberty is only for those who promote economic growth. The freedom of circulation for commodities, capital, and a few select people will continue to hinge upon the shackles of the many refugees trying to reach European shores.

12.21.2015

Rescuing the Enlightenment from the Europeans

Nikita Dhawan

In his 1795 treatise *Perpetual Peace: A Philosophical Sketch*, the German philosopher Immanuel Kant argued that all "world citizens" should have a right to free movement, a right which he grounded in humankind's common ownership of the earth. One can hardly imagine a right that has been so extensively violated as the right to mobility. In this sense, the migrant is the bearer of Kant's message for the cosmopolitan right to move fearlessly and freely across borders, even as the humanitarian disaster unfolding at Europe's doorstep signals the European betrayal of Enlightenment principles.

Kant proposes cosmopolitism as a guiding principle to protect people from war and wishes to morally ground cosmopolitan right in the notion of universal hospitality. Promoting sociality and humanity, cosmopolitanism symbolizes a transcultural competence of negotiating cultural difference, a move beyond narrowly territorial understandings of identity and belonging. Irrespective of national, religious, ethnic, and gender differences, people appear as belonging to a single global community based on their shared pasts and entangled futures. According to Kant, a world citizen acts from the pluralistic standpoint of humanity as a collective actor, and not as an egoistic individual. Cosmopolitanism, based on the normative espousal of an expansive global consciousness, opposes narrow and limited territorial loyalties. We, as citizens of liberal democracies, are expected to take on responsibilities beyond the limits of our narrow self-interest, particularly in the face of growing global interdependence. Thus the Enlightenment notion of cosmopolitanism has as its normative ideal the pursuit of the perfect civil union of humankind.

The recent boat tragedies at the shores of Europe signal a failure of Enlightenment commitment to humanity and humanitarianism. We are once again witnessing a crisis of European claims to being upholders of global justice, human rights and democracy. The disenchantment with Europe in the aftermath of colonialism and the holocaust looms large anew. Current EU border politics amounts to letting migrants die in the name of securing European territory.

In his deconstructive reading of Kantian cosmopolitan ethics, the French philosopher Jacques Derrida discusses how Kantian hospitality is temporary in nature and hinges on the entrant not causing any trouble. Derrida traces elements of hostility intrinsic in Kantian reflections on hospitality and speaks of the "hostipitality" (namely, hostile hospitality) inherent in Kant's "conditional hospitality." According to Derrida, a truly cosmopolitan ethics would entail absolute hospitality, which is unconditional and is not qualified upon the guest fulfilling certain criteria or duties to receive it.

The vulnerability of those at the mercy of the sea is testimony to the fact that the progressive goals of the Enlightenment are at risk in Europe, the purported place of its birth. To counteract the pervasive disenchantment with the lofty principles of the Enlightenment necessitates rescuing norms of cosmopolitanism and humanitarianism from the cynical approach of EU migration policy. The recent Mediterranean boat disasters are a grim reminder that not only the migrants but also Enlightenment ideals are endangered in postcolonial Europe.

04.27.2015

By Sea and by Land: European Migration Routes

Claudia Baracchi

The situation is fluid and rapidly changing, information is not easily available through official news agencies (which, in and of itself, is remarkable), but it appears that the formidable migratory movement towards Europe, from east and south, is far from abating. The phenomenon is not recent, but in recent times has acquired genuinely biblical proportions. It is as if enormous masses of nameless human beings were moving according to the laws of physics, rather than the unpredictability quintessentially defining human individuals. By sea and by land, their movement resembles that of shoals, or flocks, and is similarly ominous, unstoppable. It is as if nothing would stay in its own place any longer, available as an inert resource, a disposable reserve, an obedient work force. A world order is being radically destabilized.

They have been arriving for months, years, crossing the Mediterranean from south and east on improbably overcrowded boats, striving to reach the northern shores. They often find death at sea and are buried there—on occasion a few corpses (but more frequently only the remains of a shipwreck) reach a Sicilian beach, less than 100 miles across from Tunisia. Or they travel by land, from East to West, mostly aiming to get to Germany. Some European countries have expressed the intention of controlling their borders, effectively suspending the Schengen agreement granting free circulation within the Union. The decision of Austria to erect a metallic barrier at the Austro-Italian border, following the example of others (Bulgaria, Hungary, Croatia), has caused some clamor—but indignation seems to be short-lived these days, and unable to translate into political action.

I am writing in early April 2016, shortly after the implementation of the agreement between the European Union and Turkey. Migrants reaching the shores of the islands of the Dodecanese (it is not clear that the migratory influx is decreasing, as authorities claim) are immediately arrested and confined in detention centers. They have no access to legal assistance or basic information about their situation. Médecins Sans Frontières and UNHCR (the United Nations High Commission for Refugees) refuse to take part in these operations because living conditions in the camps are deemed "inhuman." The camps in mainland Greece likewise present grave inadequacies: electricity, running water, and sanitation infrastructure are lacking or insufficient, which heightens the risk of infections—not to mention the often scarce supply of food, clothing, covers. The Greek-Macedonian border is closed and the Balkan route is no longer practicable. The Republic of Macedonia has pushed back incoming migrants with vigorous methods, occasionally resorting to torture. The refugee camp of Gevgelija, in Macedonian territory, is empty. At the Greek camp of Idomeni, just South of the border, there have been tensions among different ethnicities, clashes with police, and cases of suicide.

Whether by metallic fences or psychological walls, Europe is pursuing the illusion (pernicious as all illusions are) of impassable frontiers. As if the human swarm could be halted. In the last year we grew accustomed to see images on TV of entire families, adults and children alike, undeterred, dig their way under the fences (or barbed wire) to the other side, crawling in the mud. We have watched young people attaching themselves to the bottom of trucks at Calais, trying to cross the Channel and reach England. We have watched endless rows of people walking silently, eyes to the ground, across indeterminate distances, to very uncertain destinations. We have seen them at sea, hanging on to the floating remains of shattered dinghies.

Who are "they"? They come from impoverished Eastern Europe, from the Near and Middle East; from China, India, South-East Asia; from Northern Africa and the sub-Saharan regions. They come from countries ravaged by secular exploitation by foreign powers, economically impoverished to the point of utter dejection, politically unsettled under corrupt governments, murderous dictatorships, or raving fanaticism. They seek refuge. They come to survive—and possibly, even just marginally, to flourish. However dimly lit, as fragile as an idea, this is what sustains them in their quest.

And who are "we"? Where are we from, and to what end? Our own roots have become opaque to us. And it is far from clear whether or not there is life in them still—whether or not what goes under the name of "Europe" may yet vitally contribute to human becoming. This is a way of asking whether or not Europe has a future—for cultures, just like plants and anything living, are not immortal.

05.16.2016

Contributors

Robert Albritton is professor emeritus in the Department of Political Science at York University, Toronto, Canada. He is the author of various books, such as, most recently, *Economics Transformed: Discovering the Brilliance of Marx* (2007) and *Let Them Eat Junk: How Capitalism Creates Hunger and Obesity* (2009).

Linda Martín Alcoff is professor of Philosophy at the City University of New York, and author of, among other books, *The Future of Whiteness* (2015), where these and related matters are more thoroughly discussed. For more info, go to: www.alcoff.com.

Claudia Baracchi is professor of Moral Philosophy at the Università di Milano-Bicocca. Among her publications: *Aristotle's Ethics as First Philosophy* (2008), *Of Myth, Life, and War in Plato's Republic* (2002), *Bloomsbury Companion to Aristotle* (editor, 2014), *L'architettura dell'umano. Aristotele e l'etica come filosofia prima* (2014), *Il cosmo della Bildung* (with R. Rizzi and S. Pisciella, 2016) as well as various articles on Greek philosophy, the philosophy of history, psychoanalysis and the philosophy of art. She is a practicing analyst (with a philosophical orientation) in Milano.

Jay M. Bernstein is university distinguished professor of Philosophy at the New School for Social Research. His research has focused on critical theory, aesthetics, and ethics. Among his books are: *Adorno: Disenchantment and Ethics* (2002); *Against Voluptuous Bodies: Late Modernism and the Meaning of Painting* (2006); and, recently published, *Torture and Dignity: An Essay on Moral Injury* (2015).

Geoffrey Bennington teaches French and Comparative Literature at Emory University. He is the author of 15 books and many articles on modern French literature and thought, and has translated several books by Jacques Derrida. His book *Scatter I: The Politics of Politics in Foucault, Heidegger and Derrida* was published in 2016.

Costica Bradatan is associate professor of Humanities at Texas Tech University and honorary research associate professor of Philosophy at University of Queensland, Australia. He has authored or edited ten books, including *Dying for Ideas: The Dangerous Lives of the Philosophers* (2015), and written for *The New York Times, Times Literary Supplement, The Boston Review, Christian Science Monitor*, and other publications. He is Religion/ Comparative Studies Editor for *The Los Angeles Review of Books*.

Jill H. Casid is professor of Visual Studies at the University of Wisconsin-Madison. Her most recent book is *Scenes of Projection: Recasting the Enlightenment Subject* (2015).

David R. Castillo teaches on Cervantes and early modern culture, theory and criticism, and the cultural history of horror at SUNY Buffalo, where he served as Chair of Romance Languages and Literatures between 2009 and 2015.

Antonio Cerella is lecturer in International Relations at the University of Central Lancashire in the UK and convenor of the British International Studies Association (BISA) working group "Contemporary Research on International Political Theory" (CRIPT). His research lies at the crossroads of international political theory, continental philosophy, and political theology.

Anna Charlton is adjunct professor at Rutgers University School of Law. She served as Co-Director of the Rutgers Animal Rights Law Center from 1990-2000. She is co-author (with Gary Francione) of *Eat Like You Care: An Examination of the Morality of Eating Animals* and *Animal Rights: The Abolitionist Approach*, as well as various essays and articles on animal rights and veganism.

Claire Colebrook is Edwin Erle Sparks professor of English at Penn State University. She has written books and articles on literary theory, literary history, feminist theory, the philosophy of Gilles Deleuze, queer theory, visual culture and, most recently, two volumes on extinction: *Death of the Posthuman* and *Sex After Life* (2014).

Sarah Conly is the author of *One Child: Do We Have a Right to More?* (2016) and *Against Autonomy: Justifying Coercive Paternalism* (2013) and has published in *The New York Times* and *The Boston Globe*. She teaches philosophy at Bowdoin College.

Nikita Dhawan is professor of Political Theory and Gender Studies at the Leopold-Franzens University in Innsbruck, Austria and Director of the "Frankfurt Research Center for Postcolonial Studies" cluster of excellence "The Formation of Normative Orders" at Goethe University in Frankfurt, Germany. Publications include *Decolonizing Enlightenment: Transnational Justice, Human Rights* and *Democracy in a Postcolonial World* (ed., 2014).

William Egginton is the Andrew W. Mellon professor in the Humanities at the John Hopkins University. His most recent book, *The Man Who Invented Fiction: How Cervantes Ushered in the Modern World*, was published in 2016.

Roberto Esposito is professor of Theoretical Philosophy at the Scuola Normale Superiore in Italy. Until 2013, he was Vice-Director of the Istituto Italiano di Scienze Umane, full professor of Theoretical Philosophy, and the coordinator of the doctoral program in philosophy. For five years, he was the only Italian member of the International Council of Scholars of the Collège International de Philosophie in Paris. He is the author of many books including, most recently, *Living Thought: The Origins and Actuality of Italian Philosophy* (2012) and *Two: The Machine of Political Theology and the Place of Thought* (2015).

Mihail Evans is International Research Fellow at the New Europe College, Institute for Advanced Studies in Bucharest. He is a graduate of the Universities of Wales, Oxford, Nottingham and UWE, Bristol. His monograph, *The Singular Politics of Derrida and Baudrillard*, was published in 2014.

Gary L. Francione is Board of Governors distinguished professor of Law and Nicholas de B. Katzenbach Scholar of Law and Philosophy at Rutgers University School of Law. He co-authored (with Anna Charlton) *Eat Like You Care: An Examination of the Morality of Eating Animals*.

Luis Garagalza is professor of Philosophy at the University of the Basque Country. His work focuses on the relations between philosophical hermeneutics, language, and cultural symbolism. Among his books are *The Interpretation of Symbols, Introduction to Contemporary Hermeneutics*, and, most recently, *The Sense of Hermeneutics*.

Michael Allen Gillespie is professor of Political Science and Philosophy at Duke University. He is the author of *Hegel, Heidegger and the Ground of History, Nihilism before Nietzsche*, and *The Theological Origins of Modernity*. He is completing a new book, *Nietzsche's Final Teaching*. He is the Director of the Gerst Program in Political, Economic, and Humanistic Studies, the AB Duke Scholars Program, and the Visions of Freedom Focus Program.

Michael Hauskeller is an associate professor and head of the Department of Sociology, Philosophy and Anthropology at the University of Exeter, UK. He has published more than a dozen philosophical books including *Biotechnology and the Integrity of Life* (2007) and *Better Humans? Understanding the Enhancement Project* (2013), and more than 80 research papers.

Ágnes Heller is a Hungarian philosopher and Hannah Arendt Visiting professor at the New School for Social Research in New York. An author of two dozen books, she is one of the most prominent members of the "Budapest School." Her work explores, among other things, aesthetic theory, the nature of modernity, and the ethics of responsibility.

Daniel Innerarity is professor of Social and Political Philosophy at the University of the Basque Country, research professor at the Basque Foundation for Science (IKERBASQUE) and Director of the Institute for Democratic Governance (Globernance).

Jacob Kiernan is a graduate of the University of Chicago (Philosophy) and New York University (Comparative Literature). He currently works as an editor and freelance writer based in New Orleans.

Julia Kristeva is a literary theorist, psychoanalyst, author and philosopher. Since 1965, she has lived and worked in Paris, where she has held a professorship at Paris Diderot University since 1973. Kristeva is an enthusiastic European. Her early work was influential to the development of gender studies theory, though she rejects the primacy of collective identity, and with it the "feminist" label.

Daniel Kunitz is the author of *LIFT: Fitness Culture from Naked Greeks and Amazons to Jazzercise and Ninja Warriors* (2016). He writes about the body, the culture of fitness, as well as art and other topics for such publications as *Harper's* and *The Wall Street Journal*.

Susanna Lindberg is a specialist of German Idealism and contemporary continental philosophy. Having worked as a professor of Philosophy at the University of Tampere, Finland, she is presently an associated researcher at the Université Paris Ouest Nanterre La Défense. She is the author of several books, the most recent of which, *Le monde défait. L'être au monde aujourd'hui*, was published in 2016. She has also published many articles especially on the philosophy of nature, animality, and technique, as well as translations of Jean-Luc Nancy, Jacques Derrida and Maurice Blanchot into Finnish.

Jeff Love is professor of German and Russian at Clemson University. He has published two books on Tolstoy, *The Overcoming of History in War and Peace* and *Tolstoy: A Guide for the Perplexed*. He is also co-translator of *Schelling's Philosophical Investigations into the Essence of Human Freedom* and has recently completed a book on the thought of Alexandre Kojève.

Michael Marder is IKERBASQUE research professor at the University of the Basque Country, Vitoria-Gasteiz, Spain, and professor-at-large at the Humanities Institute, Diego Portales University (UDP), Chile. His most recent books include *Pyropolitics: When the World Is Ablaze* (2015); *Dust* (2016); with Anaïs Tondeur, *The Chernobyl Herbarium* (2016); and, with Luce Irigaray, *Through Vegetal Being* (2016).

Todd May is Class of 1941 memorial professor of the Humanities at Clemson University. He is the author of fourteen books of philosophy, including *A Fragile Life: Accepting Our Vulnerability* (2016).

Michael Meng is an associate professor of History at Clemson University. He is writing a book on death, history and salvation in European thought.

John Milbank is research professor of Religion, Politics and Ethics at the University of Nottingham, director of the Centre of Theology and Philosophy and chairman of the Respublica Think-tank. His most recent book is *Beyond Secular Order: The Representation of Being and the Representation of the People*.

Warren Montag is Brown Family professor in English Literature. Montag teaches 18th-century British and European literature with particular reference to political philosophy; he also teaches 20th-century European critical theory.

T. M. Murray is author of *Thinking Straight About Being Gay: Why It Matters If We're Born That Way*. Murray has taught philosophy and film studies in secondary and adult education for over ten years. She read philosophy at Oxford Brookes University, where she earned her PhD in 2012. She currently works at Hampstead College of Fine Arts & Humanities in London, UK, where she is a Director of Studies.

Jean-Luc Nancy is distinguished professor of Philosophy at the Université Marc Bloch, Strasbourg. Among the most recent of his many books published in English are *Corpus*; *Dis-Enclosure: The Deconstruction of Christianity*; *Noli me tangere: On the Raising of the Body*; *The Truth of Democracy*; and *Adoration: The Destruction of Christianity II*.

Kelly Oliver is W. Alton Jones professor of Philosophy at Vanderbilt University. She is the author of over one hundred articles and twenty books, including *Hunting Girls*; *Earth and World: Philosophy After the Apollo Missions*; and *Technologies of Life and Death: From Cloning to Capital Punishment*.

Adrian Pabst is senior lecturer in Politics at the University of Kent and visiting professor at the Institut d'Etudes Politiques de Lille. He is the author of *Metaphysics: The Creation of Hierarchy* (2012), and co-editor of *Blue Labour: Forging a New Politics* (2015). He has recently published (together with John Milbank) *The Politics of Virtue: Post-liberalism and the Human Future* (2016).

Martha H. Patterson is the author of *Beyond the Gibson Girl: Reimagining the American New Woman, 1895-1915* (2005) and editor of *The American New Woman Revisited: A Reader* (2008).

Richard Polt is the author of *The Typewriter Revolution: A Typist's Companion for the 21st Century* and has published on the philosophy of Martin Heidegger. He teaches philosophy at Xavier University in Cincinnati.

Gabriel Rockhill is a French-American philosopher and cultural critic. He is associate professor of Philosophy at Villanova University and founding director of the Atelier de Théorie Critique at the Sorbonne in Paris, France. His books include *Counter-History of the Present: Untimely Interrogations into Globalization, Technology, Democracy* (forthcoming in 2017), *Interventions in Contemporary Thought: History, Politics, Aesthetics* (2016), *Radical History & the Politics of Art* (2014) and *Logique de l'histoire* (2010).

Hasana Sharp is associate professor of Philosophy at McGill University. She is author of *Spinoza and the Politics of Renaturalization* as well as several articles on Spinoza, feminist theory, and, most recently, climate change. She has just published *Feminist Philosophies of Life*, co-edited with Chloë Taylor.

Doris Sommer, director of the Cultural Agents Initiative at Harvard University, is Ira and Jewell Williams professor of Romance Languages and Literatures and African and African American Studies. Her academic and outreach work promotes development through arts and humanities, specifically through "Pre-Texts" in Boston Public Schools, throughout Latin America and beyond. Pre-Texts is an arts-based training program for teachers of literacy, critical thinking, and citizenship.

Gayatri Chakravorty Spivak is a literary theorist and cultural critic. She is a professor at Columbia University, where she cofounded the Institute for Comparative Literature and Society. Her areas of focus include 19th- and 20th-century literature, the politics of culture, feminism, Marxism, and globalization. She has published numerous academic and literary books.

Kara Thompson is an assistant professor of English and American Studies at the College of William and Mary. Her book *Blanket* is forthcoming in 2017. She is currently finishing a book about time and settler colonialism.

Patrícia Vieira is associate professor of Spanish and Portuguese, Comparative Literature, and Film and Media Studies and associate research professor at the Center for Social Studies (CES) of the University of Coimbra. She is the author of *Seeing Politics Otherwise: Vision in Latin American and Iberian Fiction*; *Portuguese Film 1930-1960: The Staging of the New State Regime*; and co-editor of *Existential Utopia: New Perspectives on Utopian Thought*, among other publications.

Slavoj Žižek is a Slovenian Marxist philosopher, cultural critic, and one of the most distinguished thinkers of our time. Žižek achieved international recognition as a social theorist after the 1989 publication of his first book in English, *The Sublime Object of Ideology*. He is a regular contributor to newspapers like *The Guardian, Die Zeit* and *The New York Times*. He has been labeled by some the "Elvis of cultural theory" and is the subject of numerous documentaries and books.

Lightning Source UK Ltd.
Milton Keynes UK
UKOW04f0620150817
307328UK00001B/223/P